THE FINEST GOLD

Brad Cooper (born 19 July 1954) is an Australian former
freestyle and backstroke swimmer of the 1970s.

THE FINEST GOLD

The Making of an Olympic Swimmer

BRAD COOPER

SCRIBE

Melbourne • London

Scribe Publications
18–20 Edward St, Brunswick, Victoria 3056, Australia
2 John Street, Clerkenwell, London, WC1N 2ES, United Kingdom
3754 Pleasant Ave, Suite 100, Minneapolis, Minnesota 55409, USA

First published by Scribe 2018

Typeset in Fairfield LH by the publishers
Printed and bound in Australia by Griffin Press

Scribe Publications is committed to the sustainable use of natural resources and the use of paper products made responsibly from those resources.

9781925322699 (Australian edition)
9781947534735 (US edition)
9781925693232 (e-book)

A CiP record for this title is available from the National Library of Australia.

scribepublications.com.au
scribepublications.com
scribepublications.co.uk

CONTENTS

The successful coach places his finest china in a sturdy bag which he then slams repeatedly into a brick wall. If he finds a piece intact, that's his swimmer.

— OLD COACHING PROVERB

SPEED

The 20th Olympic Games,
Munich, West Germany, September 1972

'*Obviously you can't accept the gold under those circumstances,*'
insists the Sydney *Sun*'s Ernie Christensen from the edge of my
dorm bed; I'm still off balance from finding his baggy-suited form in
my room after dropping by to collect gear for tonight's 1500-metre
final. Hunched keenly at the foot of my bed with notebook at the
ready, his hack reporter cliche lacks only a fedora with a press pass
in the band. 'The gold' is the medal which might soon replace my
day-old silver for the 400-metre freestyle, on reports that its first
owner returned a doping positive.

My first news of Rick DeMont's pending disqualification had
come an hour ago at the briefest of briefings with our team sub-
manager, Stuart Alldritt. 'Keep mum about it or we're both in strife,'
he'd winked roguishly, leaving me to suspect it was not yet a done
deal. His only attempt at elaboration had been to mutter 'ephedrine
positive'. My reaction — I was still shell-shocked with a sense of
injustice at my 1/100th-second loss — had been a messy thrill of
shock, elation, and redress. Alldritt's news flipped my world from
Olympic heartbreak to a farce of firsts: the first electronic timing
to make you lose by inhuman margins, the first swim doping
disqualification, and then, *presto!* — my first gold. Except that I was
suddenly the one getting a fraction ahead of myself: Alldritt had
raised only the likelihood of a medal reallocation.

And now the brashness of Christensen's twin presumptions —

that I must reject a gold medal already mine — plunges me back into confusion. 'Can't accept?' I silently fret. *'Obviously?'* Is this a new sporting etiquette known to all but me? At barely eighteen, after a decade of waterlogged obedience, I need to add 'silver-tongued QC' to my CV to succeed; ditto the still-sixteen DeMont. My old craving to be both glorious and agreeable is suddenly a pathetic conceit. Pressed for the reply, I remind myself that Christensen's a tabloid journo fishing for a headline, and the jerk who'd just baited me with the line, 'The poor kid was DQ'd for taking his asthma medicine.'

'Of course I won't,' I scoff, 'until I get the full story,' relieved to have defused his dodgy ploy for now. After he springs for the door with a parting tap on my shoulder, I stay on the bedside chair to let the interview sink in; his neat impression's still on the bedclothes, but I'm left in turmoil. Why couldn't I have tartly answered, 'I don't make the rules, I just swim under them.' I'd been interviewed by scores of journalists in the past and had never felt steamrolled like this; even when the odd paraphrasing appeared in the stories, I hadn't minded, because I knew it simplified longwinded answers.

I dig for other slights too. Had he chosen his time knowing teammates and officials had already left for the finals? How had he known I'd be dropping in? Who'd given him permission to wait alone here, and pointed out my bed? *And what was that about an asthma medication?*

Soon I'm trying to forget him as I hurry off with my gear to the warm-up for my 1500-metre final, thankful only that I never use its full time allocation. And I needn't concern myself about a frosty reception from my coach, Don Talbot. We've been on near-mute terms for weeks anyway, from the day I impulsively jerked my arm free of his trademark custodial wrist clasp in a poolside pep talk. (I'm not sure who got the bigger shock, but he was spectacularly speechless for ten seconds.) I'm also over the 'novelty' of his chest-poking rebukes. It's strongly rumoured he'll be based in Canada after the Games, so those presumptuous handcuffs and savage pokes will soon be out of my life forever.

Yet Christensen isn't entirely to blame for my lateness. He kept a promise that he'd only be five minutes, but earlier in the Olympic Village I'd been unable to resist a chance introduction to Betty Cuthbert. I was immediately shocked and saddened to find running's former Golden Girl in a wheelchair with MS, though her own impish charm and easy banter showed not a trace of self-pity. Because just one Olympics separated the end of her career from mine, I'd anticipated the same vital figure of legendary press photos — lunging at tapes with neck thrust, mouth ecstatically open, short curls flying. Soon finding her as inspiring in adversity as in health, and relaxing in her humbling aura, I chatted longer than I'd allowed for. Leaving her for the dorm, I soon recalled that people of my father's generation called MS 'the athlete's disease', and wondered if a similar spectre stalked swimmers' futures. (I'd long been primed for such torments by an old schoolmate's serial ribbing that all repetitive exercise 'fried motor neurons', but had never thought this more than a geeky taunt until now.) Was it possible that humans, with our highly symbolic drive for identity, could push our bodies harder than nature intended?

But I'm jerked back to a more immediate concern as I follow the colour-coded overhead guide rails to the pool: the 1500-metre final itself. In a couple of hours, I'll dive in with the world's best time after DeMont's, yet with my fitness suddenly in doubt after experiencing an all-too-familiar breathing tightness in the heats. I'm hoping there won't be a repeat of the respiratory arrhythmia that left me clinging breathlessly to lane ropes in January's NSW 1500-metre championship.

But even before it's underway, my 1500-metre final seems caught up in a new Olympic controversy. There's a ruckus while we're still in the call-up room: DeMont won't be swimming! Cursing and gesturing in disbelief, the world record holder and pre-race favourite looks set to defy a flustered steward ushering him away, while two security guards approach as a precaution. Watching in near disbelief, I'm struck how little DeMont's hooded eyes have altered in expression, their usual whimsical detachment leaving his mouth to etch the limits of exasperation on his ashen face; how far he seems at this moment from any cliche of youthful athleticism.

Trying to get to grips with an odd sense of a kidnapping having taken place, I can only wonder if his removal is a late upshot from the 400-metre doping positive, the newly vacant seat beside me no help. A minute later, whatever remains of my full attention is glued to an in-house monitor screen showing my teammate Gail Neall's 400-metre medley final. There's no vision of the race itself, just columns where swimmers' lap times flash up when they touch for each 100-metre turn. But it's easy to see those column divisions as lane ropes, and when Gail's numbers take the opening butterfly leg, I suspect the excitement has gotten to her: some rate her lucky to be in the final. But when her times keep 'turning' first through the backstroke then breaststroke legs, with only freestyle left, a thrill of anticipation gooses through me: a former Carlile swimmer, Gail's trained all this season in the toughest distance freestyle lanes in the world under Talbot, so her freestyle has to be bombproof. In the still-confused pall of the call-up room, my involuntary half-leap from my chair when Gail's time 'touches' first could pass for rowdiness: it's one of the most exhilarating sporting triumphs I've seen. *Not* seen. I'd once winced to hear a commentator describe 'a calm Elizabethan adroitness' in Gail's appearance, but in that five minutes or so she reigned with a mastery of race and career timing.

In my own final, I stay with the early leaders, Australia's Graham Windeatt and the American Mike Burton, until I capitulate to a staccato tugging in my diaphragm at halfway. Though spared the humiliation of another stoppage, I free-fall through the field, sucking half-breaths instead of full ones, to finish a lap behind. After the race, I rediscover top gear to slip anonymously through the change rooms, avoiding Talbot and the press, except for one muffled call on the pool deck, to which I reply, 'Worst swim ever.' In the stands, I soon learn from teammates that Windeatt, after surging to a handy midpoint lead in what amounted to the race of his life, faded badly to finish ten metres behind Burton for the silver, though still recording a massive personal best to nearly beat my Olympic Trials time. Battling inexplicably poor form all year, he'd been mostly forgotten as a medal contender after almost a decade of being dubbed the world's most promising junior distance swimmer. Today's outcome has been both more, and less, than expected of him, and I'm in awe at his timely turnaround.

I soon learn from our manager, Roger Pegram, that DeMont was pulled from the 1500-metre for his own safety, over health concerns raised by the margin of his 400-metre doping positive. He tells me central-nervous-system stimulants like ephedrine boost aggression and pain tolerance: taken in large quantities, they can be harmful when athletes ignore their bodies' distress signals.

But for now, the glory is all Burton's. On top of his two golds from Mexico, he's also the first to defend an Olympic 1500-metre title, smashing his Mexico winning time by twenty seconds and squeaking under DeMont's recent world record. Ancient for a swimmer at twenty-five, and short at five foot nine, he's now touted beyond measure for toughness. The childhood sporting all-rounder was famously run over by a truck at twelve, and poured his heart into swimming only after surgeons told him his contact-sport days were over.

Yet I'm also finding the truck mishap a confusing motif for his achievements. Its usual dredging by eulogists hints he should have achieved far more, while others who say the accident was 'the making of him' seem to imply the opposite. *Which is it?* I wonder. Viewed from the serendipitous angle, his adversity could be a competitive edge rivalling doping. *Could there one day be testing for perverse advantage?* I muse facetiously, knowing I and others might have been similarly 'privileged'.

Next morning I'm keen to see what Christensen made of our interview. Passing a news kiosk, my eyes fix with horror on the syndicated heading — I'm too livid to read the rest — blazing 'Cooper Doesn't Want Gold'.

'As if!' I scoff in embarrassment to puzzled teammates, though privately heartened by the now publishable assumption the gold's headed my way, in the continued absence of official word. Yet my heart sinks again at the perception created by that headline. *Creep,* I hiss at the memory of Christensen and every other journalist.

On another newsstand, I find pundits already blaming hair for my minuscule losing margin. 'The long-haired Cooper,' one paper lectures. Even our normally helpful assistant coach Ursula Carlile, wife of coaching legend Forbes Carlile, has publicly weighed in, adamant my barely-over-the-ear wisps made all the difference. But I'm betting her husband's bristly crew cut or Talbot's buzz cut would have caused more resistance. *Where are the double-blind trials showing the disadvantage?* For someone with an exercise-science background, Mrs Carlile's preferred personal workout suddenly seems to include a lot of jumping … on the bandwagon.

At lunch in the food hall, the full circumstances of the disqualification are revealed — minus the spin. I'm told by officials that DeMont's an asthmatic who was taking the ephedrine-based Marax, despite pre-Games warnings about prescription-doping risks. In our 400-metre final, he'd far exceeded the therapeutic exemption level (itself based on prescription norms), but the bigger surprise to me is that the rules allow doping tolerances at all, even on medical grounds.

PART ONE

~~~~~~~~

GILLS

(1961–1972)

FROM ABOVE

We boys skip-walk-skip down busy Denham Street to keep up with Mum's bouncing polka-dot skirt. It's 1961, I'm seven with a brother two years either side, and I'm thinking what a bright and blowy Saturday morning it is when I'm suddenly pinned to the footpath beneath a crushing length of something fallen from above. 'Get it off, please-please get it off,' I croak with the last breath I might ever take. Adults turn to stare but none rush to help; some smile. Now my brothers crouch over me to lift either end of the object, which, with mighty groans and stagger-steps, they lower to the footpath. When I spring to my feet, Mum swats each of us over the head and snaps, 'No more Capricorn jokes!' She's right, of course: we've been in Rockhampton far too long to still be getting flattened by rogue Tropic of Capricorn dashes dropping from the sky. Especially when they're just pretend ones on a map.

Later, when Dad comes out of his manager's office at the Wintergarden Cinema, where we've met for morning tea, he finds us boys gawking at the big wall photo of downtown Rocky, taken from the sky. 'Just like an Asian shantytown from above, boys,' he booms in his white sports coat and bow tie. 'Block after bloody block of rusty tin roofs!' And he'd know, because before Rocky we were in Singapore. That's where we boys were born, not that I remember much except for smells, tastes, and words like *ah-ma* and the one we still use for a pee, *si-si*. That's for a boy pee, at least. And one of my only picture memories is of splashing around in our water-ski enclosure, Mum helping us boys take turns to swim underwater through her legs by reaching down with a shove. Then I was eating an apple in the shallows and saying it tasted salty but okay, and that was my picture-thinking finished till Rocky.

Today, instead of the usual weekend matinee at the Wintergarden, there's a charity fashion show, with Mum as top model. That was her old job in her Sydney catwalk days with a lady called June Dally-Watkins. Dad's on the mic to *spruik* the models, whatever that means. And soon he'll say his favourite line that makes people laugh for some reason: 'There, but for the god of grace, go I!' Whenever the models take a break behind the curtains, we boys do a few quick laps of the stage in sailors' suits or the latest smart corduroy overalls, or even the lemon satin pyjamas with monogrammed pockets we wear to bed.

'Were Daddy's Singapore bosses famous runners?' is a question my mother says — *for the love of Michael!* — she is *sick and tired* of hearing.

'No, darling, I've already told you, their names only made them sound like runners,' she tells my younger brother from the stove. 'Maybe they got those silly names so they'd never be called Rick.' Run Run Shaw and Runme Shaw were Chinese squillionaire brothers who started Asia's biggest cinema chain, Shaw Brothers, and it was Dad's job as marketing director to get people to their Hollywood movies. It's also why our lounge-room walls are covered in framed photos of my parents lounging and dancing with Elizabeth Taylor, John Wayne, and Ava Gardner; famous actors were always flying in to help Dad do his job. He picked them up at the airport in our Borgward cabriolet, made sure they turned up on time and not too drunk for the galas he organised, and a few days later returned them to the airport.

When visitors ask *how on earth* my five-foot-ten dad and the six-foot-three John Wayne posed level with arms on each other's shoulders in those photos, my mother sniggers, 'He stood on a box, that's how!' to make them laugh. That's when Dad's hands go up like he's under arrest and he protests, 'Don't look at me: the duke said it'd make a better photo if we were level, so he left the room and came back with that crate. *Champion fella!*'

Why we left film-star Singapore for shantytown Rocky can start fights. 'We'd still be there if you hadn't called their bluff on that last pay rise,' is how Mum explains it to Dad. And he says back that he was promised an even better job in Sydney, but by the time we arrived, those Sydney bosses only had Rocky left. 'There's your burned bridges for you,' is usually her last word. But to our Friday party regulars tonight, between the jokes, savouries, and drinks, Mum doesn't even mention the pay-rise business. She tells them instead that we left because of the world-famous race riots when Singapore wanted to become its own country. 'Terrible times,' she tut-tuts. 'Cars on fire, the odd crazy man running around with a machete; we didn't know if we'd be alive next week, and the boys were terrified.' Now she reminds her friends why we're still in Rocky: 'At least country people don't pretend to be something they're not!' before using a handy silence to return to the story about her film-star girlfriend whose photo she's pulled from the wall. 'As … *I was saying*, this one was definitely your *pillow* of society,' when suddenly everyone's doing that body-snapping cough-laugh that party people do.

Dad's name is Ashley, but he's been Gary from the day he became Australia's youngest cinema manager at nineteen, because he's supposed to look like the actor Gary Cooper. 'Sure, from the hairline up,' Mum always snaps, 'though I think he's more William Holden around the eyes and Adolf around the chops.' And Mum herself is meant to be the spitting image of Virginia McKenna, which is why she's showing off a framed contract to double for

Virginia in *A Town like Alice*. 'This piece of paper's made me a household name in our kitchen, at least,' she sighs. More laughs.

Tonight's party is a Latin Night, and there's been lots of terrible music. Arriving men had to dip their fingers in a can labelled 'axle grease' and run them through their hair, though it's really just a mix of Vaseline and Californian Poppy. You won't hear Elvis Presley or Johnnie Ray on Latin Night, just this other stuff of ladies whisper-singing and running their words together fast, which Mum calls bossa nova. When I go over and tap her elbow to ask what language they're singing in, she says, 'Foreign, darling,' before Dad butts in with, 'Quadruple Dutch,' the chuckling man next to him, 'All Greek to me,' another, 'The port-you-grease,' until almost everyone has a turn, the haw-haws louder with each guess. Now *West Side Story* is playing, and the volume's turned up when Mum disappears before shuffle-stepping back in a side-split skirt, shaking maracas above her head and swinging her hips with sharp half-steps for tassels to jump everywhere. She's singing along, 'I like to leeeve in Amer-ica,' and repeats it a few times, her final effort keeping America's last 'a' going so long it squeals, followed by yips of 'oi, oi'. Now a man shuffles across to follow her, grabbing her hips. A lady latches on to him likewise, my father behind her, and soon the whole room's weaving around with those maracas waving high up front like centipede antennas, everyone still shuffling, hip-swinging, and oi-oi-ing, until we boys are told by Mum when she passes, 'If you can't stop gawking, go to bed.'

We Coopers are down from the great Lord Shaftesbury who freed all the kids from the coal mines in olden-days England, and Dad would have been the latest Lord if not for some family skulduggery. I'm told all this has nothing to do with us boys being called 'Little Lord Fauntleroy' when we're fussy with dinner, or *makan*, as we still call it; and that's after we've been called to the table by Mum shrieking, *'Mari sini bunya.'* (Whenever Dad's finished eating, he leans back, rubs his tummy, and groans, *'Sudah habis.'*)

•

My silver medal in the Central Queensland under-eight freestyle championship proves I'm the second best for my age in this part of Australia.

We joined the swimming club last season because we water ski on weekends and need to be strong swimmers. On our first club night, Dad let us shake hands with the captains, Peter Hunt and Marilyn Stock, and then their bodies were left floating around inside my head forever because they seemed so perfect. As we waited for our first races behind the blocks, floodlights sent pointy shadows between our legs onto the concrete, and you could grow them long and skinny or short and fat by how far your legs were apart. Or you could keep them going between fat-pointy and long-pointy by bouncing on the spot.

Whenever my father changes into his cossies, which he can't call anything but 'trunks', he reaches down their front to make sure his tossle is pointing to the ground. As his hand dives in for the double tuck, his knees bend in sharp concertina movements, and for a second or two he's one of those little corkscrew men you pop wine corks with. When he swims before club, he never goes far or fast but you can tell he's supposed to be good by the tilt of his head and the bend of his elbows, and when he breathes he'll wink at you. Other times he'll dive to the bottom of the deep end with one of us on his back, which is scary but fun because we know he'll run out of air before we do.

Our two ski boats wait all week on trailers under the house

like varnished upside-down eagle beaks. Both have 100-horsepower Evinrudes clamped to their transoms, and their own names of Ski-Daddle and Ski-Malaya stencilled on the bow. I'm still on two skis, but my older brother has moved on to one, which is much harder; I tried my very first single last weekend and lasted five seconds. The best skiers launch through the air from floating ramps in the middle of the Fitzroy River, or go barefoot.

I'm glad we'll be skiing at Yeppoon on the coast soon, because I hate missing our landing pontoon to end up lost in reeds on the downstream banks. And last week I circled so wide that I hit the shore and tumbled into somebody's picnic, bruising my chest on a tent peg. People say the Fitzroy's full of crocs and sharks because of the meatworks upriver, but Dad says you don't get sharks in rivers. That only leaves crocs. And you always see bloated cow guts snagged on low branches overhanging the mystery swirls at the far bank, where boat drivers make a wide pass to scare you into falling off. When you come off your skis in the middle of the river, you spear down into the brown can't-see-a-thing below, and when you surface you see one of your skis drifting ten yards to the right, and the other, ten to the left. This is suddenly the world's biggest problem when you don't know which to swim for first, since you just might choose the one where your hand brushes something solid below. Luckily I've swum for the correct one every time, quickly pulling it beneath for a guard while I paddle to the other. Then I put both skis back on lightning quick and hunch over to make them into a special shield while I wait for the boat to circle back, the tow rope dragging behind with its wooden bar skidding and flipping along the surface like some maniac fin. When the driver slows right down for you to grab that passing bar, you never miss, because you know you'd die of just waiting for another slow circle.

Rivers and pools are different. Unlike the mud-flavoured river, pool water looks and tastes of nothing much, but Dad says it's up to your swimming arms to turn it into something by pulling deep and hard. In a pool, you're the total boss of your body, but in the river you're just this dumb lump of struggling meat watched from below.

Our first weekend at Yeppoon is spent not skiing, but helping to finish the new ski clubhouse and pouring concrete for our own shack's downstairs toilet and shower, or 'ab-*looo*-shuns' as Dad yodels it. After lunch upstairs, he drops onto the lounge and groans, 'Wake me in an hour, boys.'

'How long's an hour, Dad?'

'Forty winks!' is how long an hour is.

We can't find Mum, so to use up winks we wander the Causeway Park shore, discover a dinghy, and row it onto the bay. We're wondering how many winks are left when it starts to rain and we turn back. But as we circle, my oar's jerked from my hands when the blade catches on chop, and by the time I'm back on my seat it's slipped out of its bracket and is drifting out to sea. We try rowing with one oar; my older brother and I stroke and stroke until the boat completes a part circle, when we place it on the other side to pull hard there, repeating this for a while in increasing drizzle. Now we've lost sight of the shore because it's suddenly raining cats and dogs and a wind's come up. As my brother wonders out loud what's the point in rowing when we might be heading out to sea a half-circle at a time, we hear one of the ski-club boats roar close by in the rain, and somehow they've seen us, because they've turned back to pull alongside. After we're helped aboard, the men attach a rope to the dinghy, and we're the happiest boys ever to be speeding for shore.

'You're lucky I don't spiflicate you all,' Mum shrieks, running down from our shack as the boat pulls in. I've never seen her so cross, but she won't spiflicate us or even slap legs in front of our rescuers, and we follow her back. 'You can count your lucky stars your father's not here, is all I can say,' is all she can say when we're back inside, so I'm glad all this has taken much longer than forty winks and that it's such a big day for lucky stars.

•

A few Sundays later, we've had to stop skiing while the boats give joy rides to underprivileged kids for the Capricorn Festival, where the town's main streets are clogged with floats, streamers, and banners. It's been fun to sit with the squealing kids as they grip the inside rails of what they call *the speedboat* and squint fierce X-rays into the spray. Dad's also set up a stage near shore for the odd singer to sing and a DJ to play records, and where the mayor and a priest are climbing up to speak. After the priest steps down, Dad says it's nothing but a complete coincidence that the very next song the DJ plays is 'Ring of Fire' by Johnny Cash. 'Down, down, down, and the flames get higher,' Dad belts out into a pretend microphone, as if he's the one up on stage.

Later, Mum tells us boys to watch the causeway bridge for her brother Uncle Martyn, who himself is almost a priest, and who's driven all the way from Sydney in his new red Mini. He's on his way further north, but will stay an hour to say hello. We're already sick of watching after three cars go past and still no red Mini with an almost-priest at the wheel, and decide to play marbles on the ground instead. Soon we're looking up and being introduced to this Uncle Martyn, before getting stuck straight back into our game. But he stays and sits on an old drum to watch us fire off our shots, chuckling whenever we call the odd marble *thissy* and *thatty*. 'Where did you get those wonderful words, boys?' he asks. I like it that Uncle Martyn thinks *thissy* and *thatty* so funny, but we can't tell him where they came from until my younger brother says, 'Maybe from the marbles themselves.'

'For goodness sake,' he roars, 'from the very marbles themselves!' before we boys look at each other and can't help laughing along too. Seconds later, the only grown-up to have ever noticed our *thissies* and *thatties* is gone.

Heading home in the dark, we've just taken a high bend when the car gets a jolt from nowhere, and suddenly we're being chased by a sparkler where the boat trailer's right wheel used to be. Cursing those underprivileged, but now 'smart-arse', joy-ride kids as if they're to blame, Dad hits the brakes, and the missing wheel bounds past before dropping over the black hillside. Fifteen minutes later, all of us still searching with only cigarette lighters and the moon to see with, there's a round gleam in a gully and that's our wheel. Dad rolls it back up to the trailer, but the missing axle pin which let the wheel come off still needs replacing, and he asks, 'Is a man supposed to go around with a spare pin in his trunks all day?' When he eventually finds a loose nail in the boot, he hammers it with a rock as far as it can go into an axle hole too small for it. 'Touch wood, boys,' he says, driving off slowly. Waking up later in the back seat, we boys cheer to see the boat's made it home.

•

Next day at school, we've started our first class upstairs after playing tag downstairs right till the bell, when the teacher growls something I don't understand, about me — *Cooper* to him — looking like 'a dog's breakfast'. I wonder why he'd say this, because our wire-haired Foxie at home never has breakfast. But when I'm snapped at again, this time to tuck my shirt in, I suddenly get that I'm a mess from all that running around. We're soon reciting the usual *am-are-*

is-was-were, when the headmaster suddenly speaks over our teacher from the old grey box on the wall above his head. Again, it's my name I'm hearing, the only eight-year-old name to have made the school swim team, now being told to take itself immediately to the headmaster's office to learn more about next week's carnival, and suddenly a Cooper has gone from dog food to being famous enough to walk out of class.

•

Waiting to leave for the next ski day, we're playing with our neighbours the Cox boys in their front yard when the oldest, Jim, asks which Cooper wants to be lassoed; the Coxes will lasso anything for fun because they're always roping cows in the cattle trucks their dad drives. I instantly yell 'ME', and shoot across their lawn for our yard. Next thing, I'm trying to breathe through nostrils full of our rose-garden soil, with my brothers shaking me and shouting, 'Wake up, wake up, he got you clean around the ankles.'

A few seconds later, Dad pulls up outside in our new Holden with boat and trailer in tow, and we're soon heading for Yeppoon, my parents discussing last night's ski-club meeting, when it's 'by-laws' *this* and 'minutes' *that*, 'the Department of Harbours and Marine' and 'permission blah blah', with Mum getting off so many blah blahs between her cigarette puffs that the car feels set to explode. Maybe I'm still not right from being knocked out, and when I say I feel sick from the blah blahs and smoke, Dad orders all windows down. This blows Mum's hot cigarette ash over the back, before she flicks what's left of her Craven 'A' Cork-Tip out the window with an angry 'Thanks very much, everyone.' And I'm everyone.

When the fresh air has me feeling better, I tell Dad he should have asked last night's club meeting to buy beautiful, coal-black outboards like the Mercuries on the other club's boats to replace our plain white Evinrudes, and he promises we'll be using them over his dead body. 'They're full of rust' is all he seems to know about Mercuries.

•

A bunny's the shape we see in a bright full moon heading for Yeppoon at dawn, but it's also the front name of our swimming coach, Bunny Williams, at the warm Memorial Pool, with its two life-sized toy cannons outside aimed over the heads of invading customers. His family skis with us for free, in a swap for free swimming coaching, though Mum says we Coopers come out ahead because Bunny keeps tossing the odd shilling into my younger brother's lessons to help him go the extra yard.

And last weekend, even my older brother's schoolteacher Miss Spengler came skiing. Dad said we 'abso-*loot*-ely insisted' on giving her free lessons to return the favour of her taking my brother to church. Which was odd, since Dad usually can't stand god-botherers. (It was the first time any of us boys had been to Sunday school.) Miss Spengler had told my parents that every child deserved at least one day of their lives in church, and last week it deserved my brother. When she didn't turn up for school on Monday following the skiing lessons, Dad said she was clearly suffering a bad case of the rooster-rushes: all first-time skiers get the rushes because they can't balance without crouching right down on their haunches, where a rooster tail of spray shoots up between their skis all day, resulting in diarrhoea. 'Let's pray for her speedy recovery,' he kept saying.

The only other god-botherers we know are the McFarlys, our neighbours in Lane Street before we moved to North Rocky, and

Mum and us boys still visit them. They're a special type of god-botherer Dad calls *harmless crackpots*. One day I was playing in their front yard when a tiny white box containing a silver medallion tumbled from the sky, stopping right at my feet. The McFarly girls recognised it instantly as a gift straight down from God and said I was blessed to have been chosen. '*I'll say*,' I said; to be the only one chosen for a God medal had to beat winning a medal just for swimming. When I told everyone over dinner, Dad said it was an old trick of the McFarlys to toss those boxes from their front window near unsuspecting kids. Then he asked, 'I don't suppose you still have God's medal on you now?' and I suddenly realised I'd lost track of it after the oldest McFarly girl opened the box to show me. 'I rest my case,' he said. Mum told me to ignore him: 'You're lucky God's always in the McFarly neighbourhood looking for deserving children.'

She said it didn't matter anyway, since we boys were now proper Catholics. 'When we took our long holiday at Nanna's in Sydney last year without your father, Uncle Martyn had you all confirmed.' Martyn was in the seminary then, and he reminded her it would be her sin if we boys were never allowed into heaven. I don't remember the confirmation, only the great toys Nanna gave us; my favourite was a black plastic gun holster, but I'm a sucker for black and shiny.

The only other bit of that Sydney visit still in my head — besides waking early most mornings to the smell of toast, and the sight of Nanna in the kitchen in her bottle-thick glasses, dressing gown, and bandaid-coloured horseshoe of a hearing aid and on her second pot of tea or sucking ice — is being in a Kogarah phone box one dark afternoon with Mum. When I asked who she was ringing, she covered the mouthpiece and shout-whispered down, 'I'm calling about a job.' Then I asked how much jobs cost and couldn't believe it when she hissed back, 'Jobs don't cost money, *they give it.*' Obviously I didn't know much about jobs, money, or owning things back then, because when I pocketed a stone from the roadside, I wondered if that meant I owned it. But I threw it back anyway when I saw how many more I could take or own any time I liked; I could come back with a wheelbarrow. And now I remember one more good thing about our special Kogarah holiday: the shop on the hill, smelling of a hundred years of lollies, biscuits, and spotlessness.

Mum says my God medal changed me, since I keep telling people that what we see is not always what it seems. Take the clouds: sitting on our front step yesterday after the Cox boys chopped their chooks' heads off to eat their bodies for lunch (that is, once those flapping fountains stopped crashing around the yard, maybe watched by heads still on the stump) when there seemed nothing left to do but stare at the sky with my younger brother, I told him that even though clouds drift so slowly, you might find they were speeding if you were actually up there. He didn't answer, but maybe his head was still full of chooks' heads seeing their bodies run off. And with us boys dressed in whites and being driven to the YMCA today, we're passing an ugly old house in a gully, covered in vines and flaking paint. 'That old shack might be nice on the inside,' I announce. *No reply.* But after a pause, a much older boy we've given a lift to says, 'Shush, so your father can concentrate on driving.'

'There's no two ways about that,' Dad calls back.

GILLS

'Open the gills. *Someone please open those gills!*' my mother calls from her bedroom this morning, one of the rare Sundays we're not skiing. She says gills for windows because that's what they look like: tall, all-in-a-row, swing-out-sideways windows down every side of the house. And also because the humidity makes her feel like she's breathing underwater. The gills are open day and night all summer except for storms, so when she carries on like this she must think we've gone around closing them.

Mum loves turning things into simple pictures. When we wanted to know how our stomachs work, she answered, 'Just like little non-stop sewing machines.' If we ask why the radio always has the news, it's 'So we'll know if we're invaded.' And when the windshield of our old Triumph Mayflower smashed on the way to skiing last year, she shook the glass off her pleats and said one day windscreens would be made of see-through steel.

She's forever telling me I'm Dad's favourite, by far. 'In fact, I'd go so far as to say you persecute your eldest and ignore your youngest,' she told him in the car after skiing last week.

'Persecute?' I asked from the back seat.

'Yes, always criticising.'

Maybe she's right, I think, after we boys beg for turns to push the mower, when Dad tells my older brother he's not pushing it nearly as fast as I did, '*And he's half your age.*' (I'm not half his age, of course — more like three quarters.) And this could also be why, instead of going to the dentist to remove a molar after I 'put on a

24

show', Dad let me be operated on. But I'll never, ever, do that again, because the chloroform gave me evil nightmares of being crushed by some hot, buzzing, chainmesh blanket.

Sometimes I think my father just likes criticising and playing jokes on anyone at random, not just on my older brother. When we went fishing for the first time, he stopped at a bait shop to buy us some gear. 'Who wants a rod and who wants a reel?' he asked. 'And be snappy.' I'd never heard of either, but surely a longer word bought more gear, so I chose 'reel'. But my brothers, who'd yelled 'rod', were soon unbuttoning long shiny packets to pull out beautiful segmented black rods to screw together, while I was left nursing what looked like a miniature plastic wheel rim with a few strands of nylon around it. Not only this, but their rods actually included a reel.

And it's Dad my older brother suddenly runs upstairs to this afternoon after I call him the world's worst swear word in a backyard fight. Watching them jog back down, I know I'm in for it. When they pull up, my brother stands with legs wide apart and arms folded, and Dad says, 'Now, let's get both sides of this story.'

Both sides? I wonder. *Surely there's just one: I swore, and now I'm in trouble.* But amazingly my tongue's already worked out this both-sides business when it answers, 'I, I thought it was the same as those other *unt* words you call us when you're angry — runts and munts — because there's only a one-letter difference.' As soon as this is out, he turns and heads for the house, my brother left standing with only his mouth wide open now, though I must have taken a clip under the ear, because a slight sting's started up.

Barely a minute after my brother skulks back to the house, Mum's skipping down the stairs as fast as her loafers can carry her, calling, 'I hope you don't think you've gotten off that lightly.' Next thing, I'm being hauled inside by my left ear until we're at the bathroom sink, where she skids a cake of Cashmere Bouquet across the facecloth she's soon poking around inside my mouth to mop up what's left of the filthy swear word. 'Soap must taste fabulous,' she's saying for the whole house to hear, 'because it's only one letter different from soup,' when Dad calls back from the lounge, 'Good one, Betty.' Soap doesn't taste fabulous, of course. It just tastes spotless and slimy, and could never be mistaken for food, even if it is a cake.

Mum has even told me, and everyone else, that I was Dad's favourite *before* I was born. 'How could that be if I wasn't even alive?' I usually ask.

'Oh, you'll hear about it one day,' is all she ever says back.

•

Last week, the President of America was killed. When the news about President Kennedy being shot in the head started playing on the radio in our lounge room, my mother stopped sweeping to say 'shush', and all I remember now is that shush, a news flash, and floorboards being half-swept forever.

Tomorrow we leave for Sydney, where Dad has a new job running the Regent cinema in George Street. So today we're visiting the McFarlys for sandwiches and a last goodbye. After a while sitting around on their lawn, we move upstairs, where their house is the same as ever: louvres opened wide, the usual smell of that big grey Sunday chunk of meat boiling all day in its tall pot, dark varnished doorjambs hung with curtains not doors, all the McFarly girls skirt-whirling between Singer sewing machines in their black hair-curler hair and black framed glasses, and everyone talking low except Elvis Presley in the radio singing 'and I don't have a woo-den heart' and then Wayne Newton going on about his donkey Shane.

When we're leaving, Mrs McFarly brings out going-away gifts, including packets of plastic farm animals for us boys. Before climbing into our car for the second-last time in Rocky, I run back under their house for a final look at their brand-new green VW Beetle, and stroke the badge on its bonnet.

After an all-day drive the next day, Dad pulls over at a Brisbane corner store and comes back with a large bottle of Tristram's Lemonade. 'Tristram's is the best lemonade in the world,' he gasps after the world's longest swig, before passing what's left around. An hour later, we pull into the Nobby Beach caravan park on the Gold Coast for the night.

As we're called to bed, I'm crouched outside the toilet block, scratching a hole in the ground to bury the McFarlys' farm animals so I can come back and dig them up one day when they'll have turned to stone. At least that's what happened to an entire Siberian forest on the news the other night. A *petrified forest*, the news reader said. As my mother explained, 'Thousands of trees all fell over in the mud one day, and after a long time the minerals turned them to stone.'

'How many years again, Mum?' I asked.

'I don't know — squillions.'

PHENOMENAL

My brothers don't like swimming anymore. Never liked it in the first place. *Hate it, in fact; don't want to train, full stop!* This is what Dad's been getting from my mother in the hallway of our Maroubra duplex this Saturday morning. It's 1965; I'm going on eleven, my older brother's turning thirteen, the younger nine. 'Brad's the only one who wins and qualifies for the championships you drive him all over Sydney for, the only one who's always interested,' she says, 'so why don't you stop pestering the others.' *Fair enough*, I think to myself.

'I've made a note,' Dad says back, his *made* heavy as lead to lodge in her head. And now even he looks heavy, letting himself out the door into the front yard. This is how he cools off after arguments, though they're usually about money, when he'll throw his arms up and howl, 'We'll all end up in the poorhouse,' wherever that is. Other times if it's about Mum's housekeeping, he'll do something crazy like take a stiff broom to the hallway carpet and savage its entire length. Then he'll make us boys wet hundreds of sheets of newspaper and lay them along the hall as some kind of dust magnet, though he never says why the dust has to be rescued from its lost and found in the high rays. Sometimes Mum drags us boys into things by ordering, 'You'd better not treat *your* wives like this,' and I'd feel sorry enough to agree if I knew who was doing today's treating.

Whoever starts their rows, Mum usually has the last word by screeching, 'You'll end up a lonely old man somewhere.' To see where Dad ends up in our front yard, I follow him out, and he's bang in the middle, scanning the empty sky with hands on hips. 'What's up there?' I ask, looking up too.

'Nothing,' he says with a sharp lung-suck, 'I'm just taking in this salubrious Maroubra air.'

'What's *salubrious* mean?'

'Clean and bracing,' he says, heading for the kerb, where he strokes our new Holden's duco. 'They're definitely making cars more streamlined,' he tells the duco, and I decide not to interrupt about *streamlined*, because one new word a day will do. Anyway, he's acting weird, and I wonder if it's from last Saturday's car crash: it was only the two of us heading down Alison Road as the traffic slowed ahead, when I suddenly had to shout because his eyes seemed busy beaming us to something on the horizon. When he slammed the brakes on, I head-butted cars in the rear-vision mirror, smashing glass. (There were still mirror bits in my scalp when we got home, Mum spinning me and inviting everyone to come pick themselves out of my dome.) We clipped the car in front too, but its driver said not to worry, because his bumper only took a nick, while our indicator was totalled. Dad gave him a fiver anyway, and he shook Dad's hand, saying 'Good sport' over and over. We were already a pound down after buying second-hand footy boots in Randwick, from a family from 'the Old Dart'. The last time the boots had seen action was back in England too, and obviously on a muddy pitch. 'Thuss real Luncashire mod 'tween them stoods,' Mr Wilson from 'Luncashire' said, as if his old Pommy dirt should have cost extra.

'Should we phone quarantine?' Dad asked him.

'Please y'self, but yer parnd wornt be gorn to quarantine,' he laughed through half-brown horsey teeth, the wall half-moss behind him.

This is our second place in Sydney; our first six months were in a duplex in Wentworth Street, Randwick. 'How quaint,' Mum kept saying as we dragged our belongings in. 'P & O in white stucco.' It was only a block from Centennial Park, itself as big as Rocky and heavily defended by sandstone blocks and iron spikes that made me think of England and the Beatles. Rocky had no Beatles, but kids were singing 'All My Loving' across the quadrangle on my first day at Randwick Public, where Reg Gasnier was scribbled big on every footy and passed around as the greatest of all time. On my first morning there, cars screeched almost right into me when I followed boys across the road to buy a carton of strawberry milk. Then the shopkeeper came running out to explain that those other boys didn't almost go under a car themselves because they'd pressed the walk button, allowing them to cross. 'Walk button?' I asked.

Our only swimming training in Randwick was in an ocean pool with local boys the Bell twins, because it was too late in the season to join a proper squad. Almost nothing happened in that duplex if you don't count my older brother pistol-whipping me with the butt of a metal replica Luger, and using my head for archery practice on his birthday. The knock from the Luger had no effect, if you don't count blood and an inch-long scar across my temple. When he shot the arrow across the room and got me on the cheek, I was glad it still had its rubber stopper on, but not glad enough to resist charging at him: we both got at least ten punches in before he was even halfway out of his chair, and I only stopped when I thought there was too much blood. But then I found every drop of it was mine, from a gash where my knuckle had caught the chipped mantel glass above him. An hour later, I was returning from the doctor with eight stitches.

We were laying into each other again a few weeks later at Clovelly rock pool after he jumped from the edge directly onto my head to give me the shock of my life. And maybe my brother landing on me stunned my brain into action, because this was the day I made myself instantly twice as good at butterfly. All I had to do was pop my backside twice as high whenever my head and shoulders plunged down, making my kick deeper and more powerful without even thinking; and soon I was going up and down, up and down, like the big swimmers you see at carnivals. The only problem with doing butterfly properly was that it was suddenly as hard as running; with the other strokes, I still got to choose whether I ran or walked.

Ever since Dad tossed a book about the great Czech Olympic marathon runner Emil Zatopek onto my bed last weekend, I haven't stopped reading it. Emil was so dedicated, he invented all these crazy ways to train. Instead of wasting electricity by washing his laundry in a machine, he jogged on it for two hours in the bath. And to increase his lung capacity, he'd take a massive breath in some park to see how far he could sprint on it, eventually checking the mileage of that single tank by lifting his head to look for landmarks wherever he'd blacked out. When he married a promising javelin thrower, they tossed spears at each other in their yard each evening, snatching them mid-air until she ended up with an Olympic gold medal. When Emil's career ended, he scored a job as a Prague garbage man, and the Czechs loved him so much they waited at their doors to cheer and clap as he shouldered their bins to the lorry. Some even ran beside him for a block or two, patting him on the back. I bet he loved being cheered up and down those streets, and I wish I'd been there too.

Ten minutes after my parents' hallway spat about my brothers' swimming, I'm back on the lounge reading about Emil when Dad returns to announce he's taking my older brother for a try-out with the Botany Harriers running club (he's been asking to go running for ages). 'If that's what he wants, the Harriers is the place to start because it's the oldest running club in Australia,' Dad tells us all. This makes sense to me too, because Dad started his swimming with the oldest swimming club, Abbotsford, on the inner reaches of Sydney Harbour.

'We'll be back in a few hours,' he calls. I don't go with them, because I have no interest in running, despite my admiration for Emil; I run like a penguin anyway, with my short legs and long body. When they return at noon, they're cheerful enough, though Dad heads to the bedroom for a nap after complaining of tiredness. When he wakes, he asks who's coming to the beach and gets a loud triple-'me' from us boys.

On the sand at Maroubra, towels are dropped as we race in to swim out beyond the waves. There's a bit of seaweed today, snagging on my fingers as I pull through. Dad's out first; he loves charging across the shallows like a bull before leaping over the waves we boys get stuck on. Now, at last, we're all out the back, where I need to tread water but Dad can still stand. *Funny*, I'm thinking, he hasn't said anything yet: by now he's normally challenging us to catch a wave, but today he just keeps pushing his fingers through his greying temple hair and gazing around blankly. He blinks down Malabar way, tosses seaweed into the distance, spins, leans back, and peers towards Coogee, fingers raking his temples even more fiercely. Now he looks at us, just … looks, before asking, 'And who are you boys?' After a whole minute of explaining we're the kidnapped kids of the Gollombollock tribe and other silly rubbish, we suddenly see he's serious.

Even though he no longer knows us, we convince him to race us back to the beach, making him break all the rules he's taught us about never going with strangers. 'He's lost his memory, that's all,' says my older brother as we climb from the surf. *That's all?* I wonder, though I'm relieved someone has words for it. We lead our big new friend to the car park, and even though he can't remember his who, where, and why, his amnesia seems to have totally forgotten to include the *how* — of driving. Almost magically, his hands seek out the ignition and gear stick, his feet play the pedals, and we're backing out of the parking bay. Now we point-point-point him all the way up Moverly Road as he continues to operate the car effortlessly.

After navigating him into our driveway, we run inside to Mum, shouting, '*Dad's lost his memory.*' Soon we're all at a table on the front lawn, watching him sip his favourite pineapple juice as if sipping's a miracle. He hasn't spoken a word, but seems to know we're his family, and there's this goofy smile on his face sometimes. Now Mum goes inside and comes back with the transistor. 'Music might trigger your memory,' she chirps, now giggling for some reason: 'Maybe Acker Bilk's "Stranger on the Shore" will come on.' That's his current favourite.

The next morning, when my younger brother asks Mum why Dad was crying in the night, she changes the subject, but by day's end he's calling us by name, and after a week he's back at work. Simple as that. What a relief! But I guess our big move to Hawaii is off; he'd been tossing up for weeks about a job offer in Honolulu. Mum now puts his amnesia down to a delayed concussion from tackling a bag thief in the city recently. 'He's not young anymore,' she says, '*pushing sixty.*'

A month later, we're watching *The Mavis Bramston Show* on TV when the best swimmer for my age in the whole world, Graham Windeatt, is welcomed like a star and given a seat beside the adult panel guests. I can hardly believe this. When Mum puts her fork down hard on the table and says, 'Oh, *that* boy's absolutely phenomenal,' Dad and I look at each other, both probably thinking: *Phenomenal? — she hates swimming!* But I'd heard of this Windeatt even back in Rocky when he was supposed to be setting world records for nine-year-olds. He's meant to be our next John Konrads, and even trains under Konrads' old coach Don Talbot. Now the show's regular funny men are trying to make Windeatt say clever things about his coach or parents. 'And — *ah* — whose ghastly job is it to wake you for your five a.m. training?' Gordon Chater asks. 'I have my own alarm,' is the reply. Somehow I suspect they won't get a laugh out of Windeatt tonight, with his deep-in-thought eyes and cresting Menzies eyebrows, mouth set in this strange smile (but not really a smile, more a kind of 'I find this quite amusing' look). Still, it's great to see boys my age can be famous enough to be on a show like *Mavis Bramston*.

In bed, I wonder why I didn't ask Mum what *phenomenal* meant. But that's easy to work out now: any time I hear anyone say *phenomenal* from now on, I'll know they're talking about something or someone as rare as Graham Windeatt.

Within a week, I get to see Windeatt in person at the NSW championships, where he's sensationally beaten for gold in the eleven-years boys' 100-metre freestyle final by a tall boy nobody's ever heard of from Broken Hill, Lee Ravlich. One of my Maroubra club mates, Jim Findlay, gets the bronze and I take tin, as Dad calls fourth. I said a special prayer before the race, but I'm not sure if fourth proves it worked. At least *I* think it's pretty good, with a two-second drop in my best time, even if I was five seconds behind the winner and four behind Windeatt.

By now, Dad's been back to normal for a month, even remembering to do the same old angry backlashing of his left arm if our heads get in the way of reversing the car. Normal, except for his appearance: his eyelids are less even, their line kind of ropey, making him look really tired.

The season's last racing is the state primary-school titles at

North Sydney Pool in March. I'm halfway down the pool in my 50-metre freestyle final when I pull up breathless with the shock of the diving end's dark canyon-like depth suddenly below. I breaststroke a few yards to recapture my breath before another go at freestyle but must now flip on my back to keep the deep-end dizziness out of my head, and suck hard on the entire sky before limping into the wall with head-up freestyle after everyone's already left the water.

I'm still a bit teary and double-sucking after making my way back to the stands, where Jim Findlay says, 'Ah, come on, Brad, it's not that bad.' Sitting now, I try to remember exactly what took my breath away this time. Maybe it really was the surprise of that inky depth jumping up at me. Or was it the cooler water of the end of the season? (I'm sure the cold caused my previous two stops, one in an ocean pool at the start of the season, the next in freezing Canberra.) And those long, scary surnames on the race program didn't help either: fancy handles like De Greenlaw, van Hamburg, Blumenthal, Ravlich, and, of course, Windeatt. Then there was the absolute grand-daddy of scary names, Marcus Lincoln-Smith, the boy with the — according to my mother — *famously* webbed toes, though my relieved inspection before the race discovered only the barest of joins between the little toes. Anyway, because all those strange names read like a list of knights in some ancient jousting tourney, I was on edge well before the gun.

Dad doesn't get around to taking my brother running again, but in winter he enrols us in a weekend basketball comp in Randwick to get Mum off his back about swimming. And one gloomy Saturday soon after we move into a flat in Duncan Street opposite our new Maroubra Bay school, he returns from work and takes us to the school oval to kick a footy around, not even bothering to change from his suit trousers and Florsheims. After he puts up the three

towering punts we boys chase down and kick back, we head home.
What was the point of that? I wonder, though we don't ask why
we've left so soon: I'm sure Dad's left his amnesia behind, though
he's acting like he's left a bit of himself behind with it.

But then, I actually like living in Duncan Street and having to
walk up and down a three-level stairwell behind amber glass panels
giving our skin its daily case of play-hepatitis. And one day on the
way home from school, I have no idea why I've stopped walking to
gaze up and down the street, when every building seems suddenly
so still and toy-like. *Yep*, I decide, I wouldn't mind if I stayed turning
twelve forever.

Yet I also wonder why we've had so few visitors in Sydney,
the very city my parents grew up in. Where are the old Sydney
names they'd chuckle about in Rocky — Dad's eastern-suburbs
knockabouts like Bruck and Betty Wheeler; his best swimming
mate, Sep Prosser; and the lifeguards who swam marathon laps of
Botany Bay with him? Those laps must have been so much fun.
Then there was the rally driver 'Gelignite Jack' Murray from his
young water-ski days on Manly Dam. And what of June Dally-
Watkins and my mother's old modelling friends? In Rocky, there
was a party at our house almost every week, full of laughing
anybodies we'd only known a short time, and all those weekends
water-skiing with what seemed like half the town. The only night
that people have come around in Sydney, we boys waited outside
to guess which headlights would pull up at our flat, and there were
just two. But tonight, almost as if she's heard me thinking, Mum's
taken us to visit an old modelling friend, now single and caring for
a bedridden daughter with a muscle-wasting disease. Her flat's tiny,
with barely a light turned on, and once we've gone in to say hello
to the poor little girl on her bunk in the dark, I can't wait to leave.

In winter when there's more time to play in the neighbourhood,

I become good friends with the boy next door, Rick. I'd vaguely known him through backyard guerrilla wars, when gangs of boys chucked twopenny bungers over fences while hiding in bunkers of white-goods boxes; those skirmishes raged for a week after cracker night until most kids ran out of bungers. After an hour of timing each other to run circuits of his backyard this afternoon, and with neither parent home, Rick invites me inside for a drink. After he opens their fridge, I see more meat than I'd find on my plate in a year, and when I ask about it he lists a ton of different cuts, from run-of-the-mill cow meat like eye fillets and T-bones, to rabbit, tripe, trotters, tongue, and brains. 'Dad loves his tucker,' he says. I've seen his dad in their driveway, and he's huge and loud.

When I'm offered a glass of chilled water, it looks clear enough, but I'm sure I can taste all those species of animal blood in the first sip, and leave it gladly on the servery when Rick offers me a guided tour; he says there's something in his parents' bedroom I have to see. Above their king-size bed hangs a wooden relief sculpture, jam-packed with people in the nude. 'Have a closer gawk,' he chuckles, and now I find men bending over women from behind; below these, couples lying down or sitting on each other, more crouching, some entwined lengthwise. 'Christ,' I groan, then 'Christ' again, and *Double backflip quadruple* Christ,' and Rick can't stop laughing as he hurries me out in case we're sprung. When we walk to the beach, it's now my turn to show him something: a trick I invented, using guerrilla-war surplus bungers to blow up anemones in shallow rock pools. 'All you do is place the bunger in the anemone's mouth, and it straightaway clamps the bunger in place for you,' I tell him.

'And it still explodes, even if it's wet?' he asks, like he'll explode too.

'As long as half's still above water when you light it.'

For the next ten minutes, it's boom, boom, boom, until the

entire pool's decorated in white spots where anemones once clung to granite.

After the second round of inter-school footy fixtures, I'm dawdling home along the beaches when I strip to my togs for a surf at North Maroubra; my brothers are making their own way home from different fields. I've only just noticed it's stormy, the water's swirling, and no one's around. As I slowly wade to thigh depth, I'm wondering if it's still such a great idea when I find I've already taken the plunge, and from my first stroke there's a scratch of seaweed from face to foot. I'm also on a high-speed conveyor belt out through the surf, the waves themselves sucked pancake-flat by the rip, and I don't know whether to fight it and sprint for shore, or calmly stroke parallel to the beach until it weakens, as lifesavers advise. But I'm petrified of being dragged even an inch closer to New Zealand, and turn to flail for the beach for a whole minute of getting nowhere, some twenty yards out. Miraculously a wave lifts high enough for a spill to carry me halfway back, and when I stretch my toes down, there's the planet again. Now I'm doing the special dolphin dives Dad taught us, diving down to push up from the bottom for a snatched breath at the surface before heading back down again, though barely gaining half a yard on each thrust. I keep these up till another wave dumps me where it's shallow enough to wade again, the undertow still tearing at my hips. On the beach, I lie exhausted until I have the energy to climb back into my footy gear. By the time I'm lacing up my Luncashire stoods it's raining hard, but walking home soaked is better than drifting the Tasman wet and dead.

One Friday afternoon when we're all in the car after shopping, Dad pulls over to the pub where an old Pommy cinema friend wants to chew his ear about a business idea. *Chew his ear?* I ask Mum. 'Sometimes you have to chew ear to get to brain,' she says. We're still waiting half an hour later when Dad comes back stumbling and weaving along the footpath, copying a drunk for fun. Driving off, he tells Mum what a dreamer his friend is: 'Thinks he's invented some machine to make home recording of TV shows affordable,' he laughs. 'Wants me to buy in and help him find a backer, but it's all pie-in-the-sky stuff.'

A fortnight later, we're leaving for Brisbane, where Dad will be the boss of a brand-new drive-in theatre at a place called Keperra.

I'LL NEVER BE
A CHAMPION

When my parents split up after six months in Brisbane, Dad and I leave the rented Kenmore family home for a boarding house in Indooroopilly, closer to town. I decided to go with him after Mum said she wouldn't have time for my swimming. Not *decided*, actually, since nobody seriously thought it would be any other way. Then there was her other problem of never having learned to drive, putting carnivals out of the question too. This suited my brothers because they got to quit, while I wanted to keep at it. When we were all saying goodbye, Mum went from someone cheerfully waving in a doorway into this crazy lady yelling, 'You look after him,' which made me instantly the luckiest boy alive to be stepping through a car door I'd be slamming shut in a second neat. It was strictly windows-up waving as I floored my pretend pedal to leave that racket behind.

And I wouldn't have cried at school the next day had a teacher not wandered into the empty classroom where I'd decided to spend the lunch hour alone. 'You should be out playing; get outside now!' he barked, before I burst into tears and dropped my head to the desk. Lucky for both of us, he was gone when I looked up.

I don't know why my parents separated, but there was one bigger-than-normal stoush about Mum always being far too nice to the oldest son, a university student, of a family we knew from Rocky. We didn't even know they'd moved to Brisbane until they spotted Mum at the post office. I remembered them because they'd owned the only Porsche in town, Dad always saying *their* dad 'stood out like a sore thumb' for wearing pink blazers everywhere. (Another Rocky friend, the pie man Sid Sawyer, owned the only Citroen in town, and he was always pulling a crowd by making the springs rise and fall by touching something on the dash.)

This season was my best ever, with a win in last week's Queensland Primary Schools 50-metre backstroke championship. 'That showed Carew a thing or two,' Dad said when I showed him my medal in the famous Valley Pool stands. I'd left John Carew's squad at the Jindalee pool a fortnight earlier, after he and Dad had a blow-up at training; I watched the pair waving their arms at the far end of the pool as I talked to the manager's sons, the Lacey boys, at the entrance. When it was over, my father's walk along the pool didn't look normal: he was leaning forwards as if held up only by a headwind, his stride rounded and rolling, shoes stabbing up and in before striking the concrete hard. It must have been his 'I was *that* far from decking him' walk.

'You know, this Carew clown said you'll never be a champion,' Dad tells me on our first night in the boarding house, 'and then he says, "Take him away, he's too skinny."'

When I nod to agree, he asks, 'Can you believe the man?' — answering himself this time by repeating it without the question mark and giving 'believe' his heavy treatment, laughing finally. *As if I give a tinker's either way*, I think back, because I'm a state champion now. That's champion enough, surely, even if I was racing kids a year younger because of a mix-up in my last interstate grade transfer. Anyway, I wonder if Carew really said those things. Who remembers exactly what's said in a fight?

Our boarding house is at the top of Moggill Road opposite the rail overpass, on the bus routes to my Kenmore state school and Queensland University. It's sprawling and haunted looking, all gables and lattice, and our long, thin room at the very back feels set to topple down the slope below. In bed at night, I pretend I'm in one of those grand teak mansions teetering above the headwaters of the Ganges in *National Geographic* magazines. But I don't hear the Ganges' roar, of course, just the gurgle of a suburban trickle at the foot of the block, and an almost-whoosh after rain.

Dad says most of the young men boarding here are uni students down from the country. 'It'll do you good to be around them,' he tells me, as if their intelligence will be seeping through the walls. I love the Beatles' 'Strawberry Fields Forever', with its snaky rhythm and strange Indian sounds. Most of it's this sleepy-dreamy talk struggling for a tune, when it suddenly all spills into a kind of kids' chorus with 'Straw-berry fields for-ever'. It's on the radio most mornings while I'm dressing for school, but it's not the only fantastic song here. Others are 'Matthew and Son' by Cat Stevens and 'Pamela Pamela' by Wayne Fontana. Having music going feels like being in two rooms at once.

My father's looking for work. He gave me a Sydney-addressed envelope to post a fortnight ago, and now he's fretting he hasn't received a reply to a job application. 'Did you post that letter?' he asks.

'Of course,' I reply, despite having forgotten to post it on the day he gave it to me. *And the next.* When I finally remembered on the third day, I decided sending it so late was beyond all forgiveness and kept walking. *Not* sending it meant nothing could be proved; it might have been lost in the mail. Maybe I should have thrown it away then too, but it's stayed in my schoolbag all this time, getting mangled between books from one class to the next to make me sweat every time I see it. This afternoon, as I swing my bag onto my bed to pull out homework, the lid flies open and books spill everywhere, the battered envelope dropping like an old lettuce leaf onto the chenille. When Dad's eyes rivet onto it, I expect the worst, but he only says, 'So you didn't post it after all,' like he's reading a sign. My face is on fire for the next minute and it's almost impossible to breathe, let alone breathe a word of reply.

A fortnight later, he's saying some of the brilliant uni students are on drugs. 'So watch out,' he warns. *Watch out for what?* I wonder. He's also heard the manager, a former chef, is a crook: 'He did time for cooking the books at his last boarding house.' *Yuk, no wonder*, I think back. Sometimes I play with that crooked manager's son under the building. At eleven, he's a year younger than me and seems a bit sly, come to think of it, but also tack sharp. Today he's been carrying on about Russians he met in their last boarding house. 'Do *you* like Russians?' he finally asks. *How on earth would I know?* I wonder, while actually replying, 'No, but I respect them,' totally clueless why I say such shit. All this time, the Hollies' 'On a Carousel' has been playing on a tranny in the laundry.

Saturday morning I'm downstairs moping around the long dark galley kitchen, where everything's olive green. When I open up the fridge to enjoy its air conditioning and check who has the best food for the weekend, a tall blond student in a baby-blue skivvy strides in like he's returned famished from the ski slopes. I step aside quickly in case he needs something cold, but it seems he doesn't. Instead, he spins me around by the shoulders and squints hard into my eyes like he's lost a parrot in there. *His* eyes are bloodshot, very bloodshot; maybe from all that study. Holding me there at arm's length, gazing down without blinking, it seems he's setting me up to say something hilarious — a real jokester. But then he squeezes my shoulders with raptor strength, gives me a neck-snapping shake, and says, 'These are the best years of your life.' Another shake. 'Do you realise that?' he asks, his face now twice the size because it's within an inch of mine. 'Do you really understand — your best years!' (*As if I wouldn't*, I'm thinking, heart thudding, though I can see they're not *his* best.) With all my strength, I smash through this psycho's left arm and bolt upstairs to our room. When my father asks why I'm panting, I say I ran up the stairs for exercise. 'That's the way,' he says, and now I know what he meant by 'watch out'.

We've moved again, to a boarding house in New Farm; our sleep-out is one half of the front enclosed verandah of a street-level, tin-roofed fibro place. The exact address is 212 Harcourt Street, but it's even more exactly like nowhere via anywhere. From the waist up, we're encased in louvres of random colours, mostly ale brown, slime green, and rose red, several cracked ones barely held straight by wire gauze. Some are just ply. There are no students because it's too far from uni, and after an entire week I haven't seen another boarder, even with four other doors numbered 2, 3, 4, and 5. It's spooky — you never even see the owners. Luckily the run of great songs continues on the radio: 'Happy Together' by the Turtles, and 'Different Drum' from the Stone Poneys.

I hate Harcourt Street. Nobody ever strolls the footpath in front of all the sagging lattice-wrapped verandahs, or under the sprawling confetti-leaved trees nobody's quite sure whether to call 'poinsettia' or 'poinciana', or near the scrappy pawpaw trees with the odd amputee branch capped by a rusty can; *maybe humans only come out at night here.* And all the roads are patched with random crossword squares of bitumen along their pale, news-sheet base. Weekends are so dead that even Ashley (I've been calling Dad 'Ashley' and he doesn't mind) must be feeling it, because we've headed down to the Gold Coast a few times. It's okay there, but I'm a little over paddling a hire canoe to death around the same flagged Broadwater course outside the Grand Hotel, where Ashley never glances up from his form guide and beer.

It's *so* quiet, he even stumped up thirty bucks for some dumb camp at Tallebudgera, but it's beginning to turn out the best week ever. On a drama and talent night requiring each cabin to present an act, my classmate Leah stars in a play where some old codger is terrorised by phone calls threatening a visit from 'The Vipers'. When they're finally at his door, the dreaded Vipers are in overalls and carrying ladders and buckets, and Leah hisses to the petrified owner, 'Vee are ze Vipers and vee are here to vipe your vindows.' Everyone else loves it too, because after that punchline they laugh, clap, and cheer.

This Leah's eyes seem an even blue from a distance, but up close you find they're all these splintery spokes of every blue. (I once overheard my parents talk about *leg* men and *breast* men, so I guess I'm just a face boy.) I forgot about Leah's hair. It's perfectly brushed and parted, swooping in neatly under her jaw to cup her face. And it's the first brown hair I've seen as its own colour, not just shades of failure to be blonde.

For my cabin's drama-night performance, we boys form a choir to sing 'On Top of Old Smoky', with supposedly side-splitting lyric substitutes taken from *Mad* magazine. But we're hardly second-rate or ordinary: we seem to have dropped right off the appreciation scale into *objectionable*, because only two people pity us enough to clap. Adding injury to insult the next day is a tumble I take at tennis. When some of us boys are told to race three circuits of court one for a warm-up, I'm leading the front group but don't expect the net cable to be connected right through to the next court, and have to be helped to my feet after being body-slammed by that thin wire roadblock.

THE SEA

Back in Sydney for reasons only Ashley knows, we're in the cushy front bedroom of what he calls a Federation brick bungalow, as guests of a Greek couple and their grey-skinned little boy. Through the venetians is the sports field of South Sydney Boys' High, where I start my first-ever day of high school soon.

Because it's midwinter, I'm not in training, but Ashley suggests we 'go and check out' the off-season laps being done by my old Maroubra club mates in the new South Sydney Junior Leagues Club pool. 'Almost everyone in Sydney trains through winter now,' he lectures. My response, 'okay', is the least I can do to feed the idea, yet not enough to prevent the following evening's visit, when I'm daunted by the sight of scores of bodies stitching the length of every foggy lane in a vast, atrium-encircled indoor pool.

On Saturday, we visit Ashley's old swimming mate Sep Prosser at his new Woollahra indoor pool, where one of his offsiders, the great John Konrads, offers me some tips. I'm instructed to swim ten laps of backstroke keeping a scrap of rubber fixed between my chin and chest, apparently to keep my head still — and it's suddenly the weirdest sensation to be floating in this strange above-ground, concrete-walled pool. It's like I'm bobbing in an overfilled bath and I'll spill over the side if I go crooked and bump into a wall from all this focus on a silly bit of rubber. And I see not the usual waterline view of coaches' hairy legs walking by, but only upper torsos sliding up and back like tin ducks in a sideshow shooting gallery. Anyway, now that the coaches have turned their backs to chat, it looks like

I was just given this scrap of rubber to keep me busy and make my neck stiff so that old Sep could boast to Ashley how much I'll have improved on climbing out, *and could we now please kindly leave?*

At the education department in the middle of Sydney for my grade placement on Monday, I'm interviewed by a nice tall busy lady whose long floral skirt never stops whirling around her like a dance partner, while Ashley sits in the reception. Half an hour of written tests later, she returns me to Ashley where we're to wait for the placements officer, adding cheerfully, 'Well, he's smart enough,' and I wonder what sort of report says 'smart enough'. Soon, a man with a weightlifter's body, presumably the placements officer, sprawls to face us on the settee opposite, his arms gathering its whole length and his legs spread. His trousers are a size small, he's wearing a tweed jacket with leather elbow patches, and his hair cut is a fierce short-back-and-sides with the top raked back like a pelt of glistening echidna quills. When our Holden idles between tall city buildings ten minutes later, Ashley turns the radio down, leans across, and asks gravely, 'What on earth did he have in those trousers?' And we laugh our way out of town.

In my school enrolment interview on Friday, the vice-principal gets chatty and suggests I might be a descendant of the famous social reformer Lord Shaftesbury; the Lord's actual name was Anthony Ashley-Cooper, seventh earl of Shaftesbury. At first I'm thrilled he picked up on this, but soon wonder if he really is some sort of history buff or if Ashley tried to gloss the appearance of blow-ins from nowhere; it wouldn't be the first time. 'I'm not too sure,' I tell him. 'My father seems to think so.'

When I head down the hall for my first day of high school on Monday morning, the Greek mum waits in an excited hunch near the door. She's in a padded cream dressing gown buttoned to the neck, collar flipped high like an Elizabethan lady's, and smiling with a keen, glazed squint. When I pause at the door, she slaps up my blazer shoulders with a cranky frown, slips my tie knot to a near-choke, and plants a blockbuster kiss on my cheek.

After school, Ashley and I are shopping in Anzac Parade when he dives into a phone box, leaving his grocery parcel and me outside. 'Quick call about a job,' he says. I'm still at the half-open door when he starts dialling and hands me his handkerchief with instructions to fold it into a small square, and when I hand it back he stuffs it into the mouthpiece. I don't know whose ear he'll be chewing through that snot rag, but wonder how he expects to be heard clearly. When he finally talks into it, his voice is much higher and faster than usual, and then his hand snakes back to close the door on me.

Our visit to watch my old club mates train must have made an impression on Ashley, because on Saturday we've pulled up at the Coogee RSL indoor pool, where I'm supposed to do some easy laps for my own introduction to winter training. We're still parked outside, where I'm saying I don't feel like it; I want to wait until we settle somewhere or return to Brisbane. 'But we're already here,' he barks, 'so you're not backing out now.' After a bit more back and forth, I say, 'Shut up,' I'm slapped, and we're heading back to the Greeks.

When I leave for school on Monday, Ashley says he'll pick me up for lunch; apparently we'll drive to the beach somewhere. *This is odd*, I'm thinking; it's never happened before. On the lunch bell, I go straight to the school gate and soon we're heading down O'Sullivan Avenue and crossing Anzac Parade before winding along Fitzgerald to the beach. I notice he's brought something to eat, though it's just this miniature Tupperware tub on the seat between us, a faint impression of crackers under the lid. (I'd seen us buying lunch at a cafe.) But we don't stop at the beach. We climb Marine Parade instead and swing onto the headland where other lunch cars are parked. Suddenly it's dark and blowy, hovering gulls jerking on gusts like L-plate puppets above the first few cars. But we don't join these; we must be going further for privacy. Neither do we pull up at the middle pack, but cruise through a last scattering to within a pool width of the cliff — trust my father to want to outdo them all! And we keep on, not accelerating but at a steady roll. When *do* we stop? I wonder. Suddenly the only future I can see is sideways, and as I jump out the door Ashley throws himself across the seat to make a clutch, his hand brushing my leg, but I'm already on the gravel. *Yes, fantastic!* 'Get back in,' he barks, still stretched sidelong on the bench. *Not on your life!* I glare back, dusting myself off and jogging for the road, while he does a three-point turn and rolls the car back. To be on the safe side, I head twenty metres down Marine Parade to wait; across the road, the unshaven cafe owners watch from their flickering servery. Nothing's said heading back to school.

After school, Mrs Greek invites — orders — me to sit at her kitchen table, where I position my legs in front of the chair she pulls out; with gentle pressure on my shoulders she eases me towards the formica's white swirls. Today she's teaching me about her birthplace, and opens a waiting atlas to the western *Hellas* coast, and an island spelled *Lefkas*.

'Leff-kuss,' she proclaims. 'Now you say!'

'Leff-kuss,' I say back.

'No, Lefk-*garce*,' she corrects.

'Lefk-*garce*?'

'No-no, *Levvv-f*-garze!'

There must be tiny differences I'm not picking up, maybe because I wasn't raised among rocky outcrops and Thalassa like her. I know about this Thalassa because I glimpsed it on a travel brochure on this very kitchen table on my first day here. ('What's Thassala mean?' I'd asked Ashley afterwards. 'I think you mean Thalassa,' he explained, 'the sea.')

Of course, I'm never going to say Lefkas perfectly, like the Swiss teacher at school who can't help saying 'Chermans' for Germans and 'walley' for valley, and Indians who say 'garment' for government. I give it one last shot: 'Leff-vvv-guzzz?'

'*No-no-NO!*'

Suddenly I'm teary because I hate being wrong every time. My left hand has been resting on the atlas all along, and she's had hold of my wrist, squeezing and pushing sometimes like it's a tiller on the map's sea. Is this squeeze to hiss a longer s? This nudge to Turkey for a softer k?

'LEVFKGUZZ-UH,' she says one last time, a little growly. When I can't reply, she sighs loudly before abandoning the tiller and slapping both hands on the sides of her dressing gown to huff, '*You definitely not coming to Lefkas with us!*' and we're both laughing. I get a history lesson instead. She mentions the name Periander and tells me confusing facts about an isthmus. Is she saying Lefkas wasn't always an island: that some rich old king cut a canal through it for his olive ships to pass? And I'm in her little Sydney kitchen 2000 years later and care?

When her husband enters the lounge room on Saturday as I watch pop songs on TV from their mustard settee, he's all yacht, his big singlet-spinnaker-belly lifting him along. He breezes in, looks at me, the TV, then me again, disappears back to his wife in the kitchen, and returns (did I hear her shoo him back?). He stays this time, swings his belly my way, and then back to watch Ray Brown and the Whispers singing 'Wonderful World'. When Ray warbles, 'Don't know much about *his*-tor-y, don't know much ge-*ol*-ogy,' Mr Greek turns to me and mutters, 'This singer, he don't know much, don't he?' When I finally get it and reply, 'Yes … no … yes he don't — *doesn't*,' we're roaring like pirates.

BEST PRACTICE

After the Greeks, we score a bedroom in the brick walk-up penthouse of Yugoslavs on a nearby headland. Through their thin balcony's pot plants is a sweep of beaches, headlands, and a hazy city skyline. Their son's three years above me at school and three inches taller, but talks way lower. I keep accidentally calling him Janko, even though he's made it clear his parents let him legally become Peter 'because Janko was too woggy'. (I still can't believe he said 'too woggy'. I definitely couldn't have if I was a wog, though I'm sure it's why I like him so much.) And now I wonder if Peter should be told that wearing an oversized tan leather jacket, with its huge thirsty-dog-tongue collars and cave-skills needlework, is like wearing Janko on a billboard. But I wouldn't dream of it.

Ashley seems delighted with the provision of eiderdowns here. I've only ever slept under blankets before, and love the lightness and instant fluffy warmth of our new covers. 'Continentals have used eiderdowns for ages,' he declares, as if we are both now temporary Europeans who snore more glamorously beneath world's best practice. But I bet Europeans don't snore with a shiny new gun under the bed. That's where Ashley keeps the pistol — sitting snug in its own shoulder holster — that came with his new job as a security officer at some local refinery.

Janko's sister is my age, thirteen, and currently goes by the name of Candy. Big boned and curvy, she'd have been handy pitchforking hay around the farm Janko says his parents left behind. I'm betting she was a Dagmar or Drusilla before their visit to the names registry, but won't spoil things by asking: she seems the type for an angry denial. Anyway, I've decided I'm a fan of this family for their open-mindedness on Christian names, even though the parents are a little standoffish around the unit. In fact, I suspect they have an entirely separate living quarters behind some locked door because I rarely see them in the kitchen.

Lying in bed tonight, Ashley's chopping and changing stations on the Hitachi when I recognise the faintest slice of 'Harrigan', an old-time number we had to dance to at the Tallebudgera school camp. 'Can you get that station back please?' I gush. When he drags the song back in from the star-crackle, he quips, 'That's older than I am.'

Now there's a knock on the door. When I answer it and Peter's there inviting me to his room, I glance back at Ashley, who croaks, 'Sure.' I follow Peter up the hall to his room, where Candy leans against a wardrobe to my left. 'Hi,' cracks her hard palomino-tan face, the opening riff from 'Pictures of Matchstick Men' pinging from an unseen tranny. Just when I'm wondering what to say, Candy saves me the trouble by asking if I'd like her to take her shirt off.

Shirt's hardly the word for a tight Bonds crewneck more like a slap of undercoat than anything ever folded in a drawer; the only reason I don't break out in a rash of double-yeses is Janko. He's standing a metre along from her, leather-swamped arms folded on his chest, and eyeing me slyly. I know Candy's waiting for a reply, and she won't wait all night after an offer like that. 'It's okay,' chirps Janko, goofily dropping his arms and uncrossing his legs, apparently reading my mind. And because this is surely code for *I'll leave you two alone now*, I no longer feel rushed to give Candy her instructions. But when he's still there thirty seconds later, more relaxed than ever, I'm at a complete loss, and the word 'no' smothers all hope of seeing his sister's chest tonight. At this point, there can be only one utterance more disappointing, and it leaves my lips: 'I have to go because my dad's strict about bed time.' And soon I'm listening to Ashley saying, 'That wasn't long.'

'Their parents are a bit funny about bed time.'

THE OLD MONEY

Today's attempt at laps takes place in the Coffs Harbour Olympic pool, just a five-hour drive north of the Yugoslavs because we're halfway to the Stardust drive-in, near the outer limits of Brisbane, where Ashley starts his new job tomorrow. The water is cold because it's still winter though technically spring. A cold pool is a cold body, but it's the eyes that feel it most, and soon these cold eyes beading up and down the lane locate a black blob, which could just be a clump of leaves on the bottom of the deep end. Maybe it is and maybe it isn't, but what I'm finding is that on every approach my body does a little detour to avoid ever being directly above the blob. 'Why the crooked swimming?' Ashley asks when I stop at the shallow end after twenty laps. 'I keep getting a stitch up there,' I suggest, and he says, 'Come on, we might as well go,' and we go and go until we pull up at dusk in this town just big enough for its one public pool and one drive-in theatre for me and Ashley to slot right in.

We're renting the left half of an old Queenslander backing onto rail tracks at the bottom of a hill so steep I'm sure that's why our street was named Dark Street; at the top of our hill is not the top of a hill at all, but the flat land everyone else lives on. When the town pool opens 'for summer' a week later, I train with the local swim club until Ashley hires a separate lane there to coach me on my own; in the very next lane is another boy already coached solo by his dad, but they operate from the far end and we don't talk to them. Club swimmers call that boy Laphead for obvious reasons, and within days I'm overhearing *my* new nickname of Lanehead.

One warm October morning, with the Hitachi on the sink rattling cutlery and belting out the Monkees' fabulous 'Pleasant Valley Sunday', Ashley shares his plans to boost takings at what he calls 'this town's old dinosaur drive-in'. As I sip my daily eggflip, he's running promotional ideas by me, this first a letter-drop promising free LSD to patrons in November. 'But it's only a gimmick, a play on words,' he clarifies. 'LSD is actually the old notation for pounds, shillings, pence; it's the old money for the old money — *get it?*' I don't get it, but it seems he'll be shelling out random pennies and threepences as customers enter: 'It's a way of getting tongues wagging with a bit of harmless fun.'

The idea of promising movie-goers free drugs, only to short-change them with petty amounts of soon-to-expire currency at the pay booths, seems fine by me. What would I know compared to a father who was once marketing head of the world's biggest cinema chain? Trying to appear interested, I ask if his plan can get us into trouble. 'What if hundreds of tattooed people turn up and riot when they don't get their free drugs?'

'Great point,' he mutters, jotting a pretend note beside his list.

Near Christmas, after a neighbour tells Ashley a stranger's been lurking in our street at night while he's at the drive-in and I'm home asleep, he says I'll have to come to work with him for a few nights. '*Cat Ballou*'s playing,' he says, 'with big Lee Marvin, so at least you've something lively to watch.'

I'm happy to go see big Lee and his unshaven amigos fill the night with great dollops of technicolour, but oddly I've also developed a dread of tiny motionless grey things: after a moth refuses to give up its ceiling possie in the car on my first night of *Cat Ballou*, I sit out on the asphalt. When Ashley brings out a milkshake, he asks why I'm out here. 'It's too hot in the car,' I lie.

'Well, you'll have to get back in,' he says, 'a reversing car could skittle you.' So back in with the moth I go until Ashley leaves, when I'm out again. Luckily — and because I've made a point of leaving the windows down — the moth soon gets the hint and I'm back inside for good, windows up. Except that I can't understand why I'm suddenly so scared of the world's most harmless insect, a tiny life I could snuff out in the blink of an eye with barely a powdery smudge left on my fingertips. I can't be sure, but I suspect it's connected to the Coffs Harbour blob fear.

Moving interstate again means I'm back in primary school, where a boy in my new class, Mack, is also a swimmer. When I visit him on the weekend, I'm told his father, the tallest dad I've ever met, was a prisoner of war. He looks saggy and weak standing at the kitchen table where we've shaken hands, his eyes dreamy and gummy. He's started to ask me something when his wife butts in, 'Now, don't be askin' Brad about his family and where's he's from 'n' all. He's a swimmer just like *that one*,' she says, nodding at Mack through a half-scolding, half-joking singsong accent I faintly recognise.

'She's Irish, in case you hadn't noticed,' Mack says when we're outside.

When I ask if his dad has the flu, to look so hangdog, Mack says he's 'never really recovered from Changi'.

Mack and I like drawing, so when my father gives him a lift to a carnival today in Nambour, we spend the entire trip sketching our own series of Prince Valentine comic adventures. (Mack himself could be a cartoon character — freckles, button eyes, gaps between his teeth, wild cowlick for a fringe.) Mack's only a breaststroker, but I have to say the way he does it in his carnival race makes it look almost worthwhile. He has the longest kick and glide I've ever seen, and he draws his shoulders up ever so slowly as he begins his underwater pull, then those same shoulders do a big loose jump for this goanna tongue to flick out of his chest, and that's his hands.

With no carnivals the following weekend, Mack cycles to my place to play, and I want it to go well because he's our first guest since the divorce. When he tells me he's been in a wrestling program at the YMCA since he was seven, we spend an hour grappling in the backyard. Suddenly he remembers a new technique a visiting instructor showed him. 'It's not exactly wrestling,' he says, 'more like a karate move. Want to see it?'

'Who wouldn't?'

'You wait right there,' he orders from a strange oriental crouch. Without warning, two heels thump my chest and I'm flat on my back two metres away, completely winded, while he lands cat-like on all fours and bounces to his feet. Dusting myself off, I decide it's the official end of our friendship, except at school where it'll be business as usual because he can't be avoided.

Because Mack and I are the only ones in class who can render a decent likeness of anything beyond alphabet letters, our teacher Mr Grange tells us to sketch a three-metre-long mural — a frieze, he calls it — using only charcoal sticks on taped-together lengths of butcher's paper. The subject is ballerinas, and our finished piece will adorn the entire length of the blackboard this afternoon when parents arrive for end-of-primary-school celebrations. We sketch feverishly between flipping the pages of a coffee-table book on the Bolshoi Ballet supplied by Mr Grange; it's full of twirling, curtsying, and leaping dancers. If you close your eyes when Mr Grange speaks, he could be the *Homicide* series actor Leonard Teale, but when you open them again you find this slight man with a tiny waist, round shoulders, a large spongy nose, and no detective's hat in sight. He's also the only man I've ever heard call people *coves* ('When you boys leave, tell those coves in the corridor to report to me'). And he's an expert on opportunity. Knocking hard on the blackboard several times, he'll ask, 'Is that opportunity knocking?' and we'll answer,

'No, sir, because opportunity only knocks once.'

Mack and I are definitely being challenged by this new charcoal medium: if you stuff up a line you can't just rub it out like a pencil mistake. Yet it's been going well enough until we reach a certain area that in terms of draughtsmanship is one of the 'busiest' — the sudden tuck that marks the convergence of legs and body, with the odd fold and crease of leotard. I'm not at all sure we've been up to the job here, and when Mr Grange walks back in an hour later, his eyes nearly jump out of his head when he says, no longer in his charming Leonard Teale voice but in almost a shriek, to 'Get rid of those, those ... *private parts*' — with parents due in an hour.

We immediately tackle the stronger lines with some brisk smearing, but when this flattens the area into a shapeless mass, we add even more charcoal to rescue some form. It's only when we step back for a breather that we realise it's all become an indistinguishable smudge. 'Wow, Ballet de Bushes!' Mack yelps, annoyingly blind to our predicament.

As soon as Mr Grange returns a second time, he takes a sharp left towards us and I know exactly what's about to happen: he sweeps the entire mural off the floor with one sharp tug, his arms now flailing and tumbling the paper furiously without even glancing at us. Now he drives that messy ball deep into the wastepaper bin with an angry twisting of his foot so it can't pop out for a disgraceful encore in front of parents, but, when his shoe comes out, sticky tape has attached itself and the girls follow in a tangled conga line as Mr Grange hops and stumbles to regain his balance. When the dancers go back in a second time, under his hands now, he drops half a brick on them to be sure. _____

For Christmas, Ashley's bought me a bike with gears concealed in the rear hub instead of the usual mess of cables and cranks; it takes only the slightest back pressure on the pedal to change them.

'They're new in Australia, so yours might be the first in town,' he crows. The downside to being the local champion of cycling stealth is that mine has only three gears for hills, instead of the twenty-odd on my friends' obsolete derailleur set-ups. But I guess this is the price for Ashley's love of all things stylish and novel. Waiting beside the bike are some American-style Adidas running shoes he found in a Vinnies store, and a pair of ancient, rusty 20lb barbells to replace the sissy 5lb dumbbells I've used for years. Every morning now, I'll stand in the kitchen to contort my way through fifty butterfly strokes, feeling stronger every day. My gift to Ashley is the thickest book I could find on a bookstore bargain table, chock-full of famous quotes, from Socrates to Kennedy. When he picks it up, jiggles it up and down, and says, 'All this wisdom to get me safely across the road,' I wonder if he's gone totally bonkers to think a book so heavy and clever won't do more than save him getting skittled. We sit to a Christmas lunch of nuts and salad, the Executives' 'My Aim Is to Please You' on the radio, and I'm definitely tipping a big future for this fine Australian band.

In the new school year at Bream High, I soon find myself class captain. Although it's only a state school, they must think making us wear heavy-weave black shorts with a matching felt hat makes us look like toffs, but we're only hotter. Across the road in this pampas-flat end of town is the tiny bedsit we've found. Here Ashley sleeps with a thick oak nightstick by his bed, which is just as well, because he caught someone snooping outside his window last night. I didn't wake, but he says he reached through, grabbed a fistful of someone's hair, and whacked the back of his neck before the culprit broke free and fled.

Being voted captain in a show of classmates' hands was a surprise honour, but maybe it was only because they saw me pose for the local paper after I won a few minor medals at the state titles. (Following the photographer around the school grounds during lunch in only my speedos while we searched for dive props was almost as embarrassing as those occasional nude-on-the-school-bus dreams.) My first assignment as captain begins promisingly when our teacher leaves me in front of the class before darting off to the principal's office for a phone call. For the first minute, it's all heads down; I'm not exactly dizzy with power, but couldn't be prouder. And when I see the Turner boy lean his chair back to chat with Ducey behind, I seize the opportunity to act. Knowing I'm not here to be an ogre, I see humour as the middle ground and think up a ripper: in a mock teacher's voice, I boom, 'Turner, *turner* round,' not even sure if the pun will take. But within moments the class begins responding in a shower of appreciation, first with wads of compressed paper, followed disastrously by pencils and biros. Thankfully the teacher walks in before it's scaled up to chairs, though I quickly see he's speechless with disappointment, his wild-eyed and dismissive double arm sweep in my direction promising a review of my captaincy.

A fortnight later, Mr Grange's former pupils are invited back to share first impressions of high school. When he makes his grand entrance into the room that's been our holding pen for the past half-hour, I quickly see it for the brag-fest it is, each of us expected to charm him with reports of our successes, preferably in his favourites of maths, music, and drama. When it's my turn, I take care not to overwhelm him, by limiting my boasts to class captain. But he doesn't acknowledge me at all, his head swinging past like a boom of blinding pride to the next boy. *Christ*, I think, I'm still the Bolshoi-bushes boy.

It's the Olympic year 1968, and when our geography teacher mentions one of Germany's major cities, Munich, she singles me out to ask if I'll be competing at the Games there in four years' time. 'Who knows?' I say with a furnace face, knowing full well there are four Australian boys my own age who are faster, in addition to the several age groups above mine, each with its own contenders I'd have to beat when those Olympic Trials come round.

I know all this because *proper* swimmers (not the ones I hear coaches call their 'champion dreamers', who ask to be champions but train randomly and never in the holidays) always know our exact place in the scheme of things. We learn it in club-night gossip or from our results at the state championships — that's if we've made the qualifying times at weekend inter-club carnivals we attend all season. Or we devour the results in the newspaper sports pages when the Australian open titles are on, or 'The Juniors', which start at age fifteen. Then there's *The International Swimmer*, a magazine you buy with — but not *for* — its scholarly articles with accompanying photos of their balding authors, along with its three-month-old results and 'regularly updated' national rankings in every age, stroke, and distance. (No one knows why it's The *International* Swimmer, unless it was first published before Federation, when each state was its own overseas colony, since nothing beyond our shores gets a mention.)

And we're all steadily moving up that age-group elevator, the age immediately above yours always those few seconds faster — in everything — and the age above theirs likewise, and so on, until you're sixteen or seventeen, when everyone's nearly the same size and expected to be hitting their career peak. That's when your age-group days are supposed to crumble behind you like rusty trainer wheels, along with the almost weekly improvement you'll always have taken for granted — and suddenly you're out on the Serengeti alongside those big scary names you've idolised for years. Then there'll be nothing holding you back from the Olympics but times.

Because it's never about you against an adversary, like in boxing or tennis, where a tricky southpaw could have his jab in your face all day, or where you're chopped down by a fierce serve and volley your opponent has identified as your weakness. It's never personal, even when your times actually do race other times — with pool and swimmers attached. (Sometimes I try to imagine if they did make it a bit more mano a mano, where perhaps you could tumble and push off into the next lane for a few laps to draught on someone — as long as you were back in your own lane by the end of the race. Now that would be fun! Ashley says they actually had obstacle races in the first few Olympics, and wouldn't they have been something!)

When the town pool closes in April, Ashley suggests I extend the season a month by catching the train to Brisbane's heated Valley Pool three afternoons a week. 'In a few years, nobody will be talking about the swimming *season*,' he quips, 'it'll be year-round training for everyone.' Mack's parents are of the same mind, so I wait after school at his place for his mother to drive us to the train. Pulling up at the station, she pivots suddenly to face us and say sternly, 'Remember that there'll be a hundred pairs of eyes on everything you do on the train, particularly *himself* there,' glaring at Mack. 'I might be a housewife, but I'm not altogether daft.'

'How are you coping with all these eyes on you,' I ask Mack when our carriage chugs off, and we both laugh. The laughing kicks in again when Mack tells of his shock after climbing the town-pool fence at dusk on the last day of the season to search for a towel he left behind, only to come across a lifeguard pissing into the pool, behind the pump room.

'The dirty bastard just said, "Water shortage, young man, every bit counts," and left it out — *it was a helmet* — until he shook every last drop into the pool.'

When I tell Ashley about the poolie pissing into the pool, he says, 'The man deserves a medal — all pool workers pee in the pool on the last day of the season. It's an old superstition giving thanks for a year without a drowning.'

'Really?'

'At least they used to.'

EGGHEAD'S SILLY GAME

Every other Sunday since the end of the season, Laphead's dad, Egghead, has hosted Ashley and me for lunch at their dry few acres out of town. After cautiously eyeing each other's coaching efforts from opposite ends of the pool after we first hit town, the dads joined forces in midsummer to take turns training their instant team of two. Soon I was handing Egghead cryptic poolside coaching notes from Ashley, always in an envelope jokily addressed, 'To The Swimologist'. After a quick scan, Egghead would stuff the contents in his back pocket with a belly laugh. The pair obviously hit it off. (Egghead runs the local jail, and Ashley, of course, the drive-in theatre. 'I pull 'em in, and you haul 'em in,' was Ashley's take on their civic roles at our first lunch.) Training in Laphead's lane was fine, except in our lap breaks when he kept making these odd coughing-through-the-nose sounds, like the letter K had broken away from some word in there and he had to hack it out. When I asked, 'What's with the noises?', he told me that sportsmen were supposed to breathe in through the mouth and out through the nose. I'd heard this theory before, but only from coaches Ashley called *antediluvians*. Anyway, I felt Laphead took it way too far. He didn't use his nose only to exhale, but turned it into a double-barrelled snot-gun — you could hear those palate-ripping discharges coming underwater. He did the dry version when he ran.

The dads had contrasting coaching styles. Ashley strolled the side of the pool with hands clasped behind, gazing up, glancing sideways, whistling the odd ditty, flinging an occasional loose foot upwards. But when Egghead took us he was a statue at the end of the pool, his right hand in constant contact with the block, one foot resting up on the pool coping. Standing there in the low sun, he might have been General MacArthur if not for the baldness, singlet, and concrete-splashed thongs.

Their home's an old weatherboard workers' cottage on fat knee-high stumps, every surface painted white, Australiana bric-a-brac on every hook and shelf. Out on their paddock sit a few quaint drays and buggies which will soon be *earning their keep* as wedding-photo props. Mrs Egghead serves a formal lunch, bringing a pot of tea when we're all seated, then the main course, followed by more tea, accompanied this time by scones, cream, and jam. The whole operation runs well over an hour.

At first, Ashley enjoyed coming out. It was a chance for the town's new power-coaching duo to discuss conditioning and technique while basking in the company of champion sons. But lately he's been losing patience with always having to watch Laphead finish his running training in the hot sun before lunch; my lane mate's also a budding cross-country champion. 'We just come out for lunch, *for Christsake*,' Ashley spits through his teeth today after cheering Laphead into his final lap. Driving home after our previous visit, he even threatened to turn up half an hour late next time to teach Egghead a lesson, shaking his head and huffing, 'I'm tired of his silly game.' But today we arrived on time again because we're apparently giving them one last chance. And again we've waited twenty minutes in the sun; there is not one tree or shed near where Egghead stands in his terry-towelling hat, yelling, 'yip-yip-yip,' stopwatch in hand to keep his son honest. And of course Laphead must now shower after all that perspiring, so that's another wait *inside*.

In our last visit, Mrs Egghead proposed I go and join Laphead in the shower, and I wondered why she was so keen for me to hang starkers with her son for ten minutes. 'I swam a few hours ago, thanks,' I lied to her — I didn't train on Sundays. 'And that's my point,' she said tartly, either unaware or not even caring that I was lying. 'Chlorinated pool water's actually far cleaner than shower water,' I added helpfully, suspecting she knew I never washed; I began darting anxious glances at Ashley for backup. But she relented, leaving me free to dine in my lather of nervous sweat and eau de chlorine. Who does she think she is, I wondered angrily — *my mother?*

Another time, when I'd stupidly found myself alone with her, she stopped me halfway across the kitchen, set her jaw in a funny way, and said in some old-country accent, 'You know, my husband's a very good man.' There was no response to this that wouldn't have betrayed the panic of a first alien encounter, so I faked a reply to Ashley outside instead. 'Sorry, Dad, I'm coming right now,' I called, skipping out the back door.

'They must think we've nothing better to do on a Sunday, to keep us waiting for Laphead,' Ashley moans in the walk back to their cottage. I search hard to remember what's better, and it *is* nothing — a long hot one.

'As long as we're home in time for *Daniel Boone*, I don't mind,' I reassure him.

Today's lunch is a replica of all the others. I spend even more time ogling ancient showbiz posters tacked on their kitchen wall, once-glossy monochrome bills touting Egghead's previous gig as a stage magician. That's him with top hat, wand, and white gloves, his tuxedoed bust encircled by homemade glitter stars. He never lets on how he went from magician to jailer, but there you go: his final trick, perhaps. Through a window, I see his Black Maria van parked near the street, so everyone driving past can see this is where the tough prison boss lives.

When Egghead pours himself and Ashley a cold beer, Laphead and I pour tea from a Raj-era teapot in a blizzard-grade cosy. Ashley's always first to toast. *'Make your miserable lives happy,'* he roars. I've never heard this strange toast from anyone else's lips, and sneak a glance at Mr and Mrs Egghead for their reaction, but both smile famously as glasses clink across the table, so I suspect it's some quirky toast from his Singapore days, or a private joke between Egghead and Ashley (his other toasts are a simple 'Happy days' and 'Salud'). Egghead never seems to change out of his prison-guard uniform at home, a khaki drill-cotton ensemble of shorts and many-pocketed and pleated shirt. Sitting opposite, I can't help checking out his neck skin; it's loose, goosy, ruddy, and hairy. And yes, he's bald as an egg, with only the finest rusty down in certain light. Suddenly he decides there's been too long a pause in the conversation. Typically, at such awkward moments, he stiffens his back and stretches his arms under the table to declare in a grand, shiny voice, 'Aah, yes.' He must get three or four aah-yeses out with each lunch, the s left hissing like it's pissing out a fire, and I secretly treasure their strange reassurance as if even the most relaxed settings are a train wreck in the making.

For our next visit, Ashley finally makes good his threat to turn up half an hour late. The moment their paddock swings into view, he curses, 'Christalmighty, he's still got that kid out in the hot sun.' Pacing from the car, he apologises to Egghead for the flat tyre we didn't have, gushing, 'Poor Laphead must be nearly dead, you'd better get him inside.'

But Egghead scoffs, 'The boy's made of tougher stuff than that, and we've still two more laps!' (*We've?*) After pulling up, Laphead seems set to faint when he learns of his extra circuits and that they'll need to be done in two minutes apiece. His nose is now clacking out so many double-barrel K's that he greets us with a spittle-charged 'Ksh-hello' before flopping at the hips like an old wallet, hands planted on the ground in quadruped exhaustion.

Driving home, Ashley considers reducing the lunches to monthly. I find this odd because we recently moved out of town just to be near 'the Heads', as we now call them; I've even switched to Laphead's high school, where I'll start after the holidays. This time we've rented a front sleep-out from a German family in a Queenslander perched above a disused rail cutting. We cook breakfast on our portable stove — Ashley likes me to start the day with steak and eggs — but at night we eat inside with the family. Or at least *I* do, since he's at the drive-in till midnight.

We miss the next lunch with the Heads, partly because I've come down with bronchitis. Each evening while I'm bedridden, with Ashley at work, the German grandmother enters our room to feed me soup for dinner. '*Eat your zoop to be strong,*' she snaps with each spoonful, before stripping my bed of its damp sheets to replace them with clean ones. 'Gut night, zlip tight,' she calls, closing the door.

Now well enough to get around again, I'm seeing a Brisbane specialist after a local doctor detected a heart murmur. (Ashley's concerned because his brother had a hole in the heart.) After dabbing about with cold stethoscopes and palpitating every inch of my torso as I take jumbo breaths, the specialist beckons Ashley and me to his desk, where we're given a long lecture on advances in diagnostic technology and *heart* surgery, the mention of which makes mine sputter and race. But now he plants his hands grandly on the desk to pronounce my heart 'good as gold', and I don't care if this isn't a textbook diagnosis, as long as it gets me out of here. 'Yes, a little noisy,' he sighs, but apparently that's typical for young sportsmen like me, particularly after a bout of bronchitis.

A UNIFIED FIELD

Something weird happens between Laphead and me when I start at his school. Not only does he make a point of sitting at the far end of our train carriage, but at school I don't see him all day. Of course, he's a grade above me since he's nearly a year older, but even when I track him down at lunch he turns away to face his group if he sees me coming. But then I've never attended the school of my best — *only* — training mate before, so maybe this is what happens: different mates for pool and school.

Luckily I start getting on well with one of his classmates, Jack. That is, we sit together on the train. We must seem an odd pair, because I've just turned fourteen and don't even look it, while Jack is hilariously mistaken for a student teacher when his tie's off. One morning as we drift along with the train platform's usual tide of uniforms, two girls approach front-on to make us stop. Jack seems familiar with the one with frizzy red hair fanning her shoulders like some hellfire wimple, though there's no actual greeting. They're girls I've already noticed because they wear the shortest seersucker skirts in school. After we pull up, it's like a face-off until Jack breaks the ice with, 'Does your friend fuck?'

'Yeah,' parries the redhead without a blink.

Did he really just say … *fuck?* I wonder. *And did she really just say yes?* Not that I've … ever … *What on earth will the next voice say?*

When it comes, it's Jack again: 'Well, tell her to fuck off!' And we step around them. This is shocking, funny, crazy, and disappointing all in one. But I think Jack's words were only for show, and after school he'll probably be doing both of them behind some shed.

A fortnight later, Ashley and I still haven't been back to the Heads' for lunch. In the August school holidays, we quit the Germans for an old Tudor-style boarding house, much closer to Brisbane. It's only now that I twig there's been a serious falling-out between *the swimologists* and that the visits are over, though there seems no point asking. I still haven't trained since Mack and I caught the train for our first brief taste of winter training, but Ashley says I can start again at the Valley Pool, the site of my first state title win, when school resumes in September. I have no idea if Laphead will start back then too, or even where he'll train this season.

This new boarding house looks like it was once a normal home. Our room seems a recent addition, and juts like an internal promontory from the rear wall it shares with the house, into a vast dark lounge room and the comings and goings of patrons. Whenever Ashley and I head out, we have to pass in front of the communal TV, which is always running, always viewed by some of our sleazier fellow boarders slumped at odd angles like leeches across two battered floral lounges. If I'm passing alone and say, 'Excuse me,' I sometimes hear the low grumble, 'Yeah, piss off,' but don't look up to see who it is.

We soon move again, into a room — a burrow, really — in a brick wall holding up its end of a three-storey building in the Valley. An external staircase stitches the full height of that clay cliff past our room and up to a gambling den at the very top; Ashley says we got it cheap for him being on call for security duties. Because the staircase rail is made from old gal pipe, some of the drunk card players making their way down at dawn stumble and laugh and say things like, 'Bloody hell. First they fleece you and then they let you fall off the side of a building.'

When school resumes, I start at Brisbane State High; that afternoon, I complete my first training sets for the season at the Valley Pool under my new coach, Gordon Petersen. On my second school day, my new classmates have somehow scored an early edition of the afternoon *Telegraph*, whose entire front page is a photo of Australia's Ralph Doubell breasting the tape for the Mexico Olympics 800-metre running gold, and I have to pinch myself to believe he beat the Americans.

At the end of my first summer of training at the Valley Pool, I'm part of a celebratory bus trip to Sydney for Brisbane's top swimmers. Laphead stayed training alone in his dad's hired lane again, but he'll be on our bus because he made a point of registering in Brisbane at the start of the season. By season's end, I'd beaten him in everything but 50-metre sprints, where his size is still an advantage.

Most swimmers boarding the bus are my new training friends, and we immediately claim the rear bench seat for the best chance of a sleep during the overnight trip. The very last waiting to board is Laphead, who's wearing *black* jeans not blue, with coarse seam stitching probably run up by his mother, and chunky silver pocket zippers front and back. And he's in — *oh no* — tartan slippers, while everyone else wears Levi's and ugg boots. Everyone else, that is, but for the charmingly eccentric Nickname, who's in pearl-white Levi's and moccasins, and whose dad's a scientist. Nickname predicts one day he'll discover what Einstein couldn't, a *unified field theory*. At the moment, he's going crazy about some new take on matter called *string theory*. Whenever he tries to explain the physics he's in love with to me, he gives his index finger a mock professorial wag and says things like, 'So — let's imagine there's this kind of field,' and I have to cry out, 'Stop, you're going too fast.' The one and only annoying thing about Nickname is when he starts his explanations with 'So'. That one tiny word — so — followed by the usual pause long enough to say *once upon a time*, makes me feel even dumber. (Occasionally, to reassure him his efforts aren't totally wasted on me, I'll throw him a scientific conundrum like yesterday's, 'How can scientists be sure the planets are in orbit, and that it's not just an illusion caused by the sun itself spinning?') Nickname has officially replaced Laphead as my best swimming friend, and I've made some non-swimming mates, like Roland, Dale, Bruce, and Kent at Brisbane State High.

Now Laphead pauses on the front bus step to scan the seating arrangements, clutching his overnight bag and pillow. It's too bad about his fashion crimes and not really knowing anyone, but I can't risk losing my seat to go down and chat. Instead, I give a cheery wave, and he replies with a switch of his index finger before dropping onto the front seat for the night.

You know you're going to have fun when everyone laughs at your first lame joke. One that gets the giggles going is 'that Hitler dad', one of the goodbye dads I pointed out on the footpath, who just happened to have an index finger resting on his top lip as he raised his farewell arm in a perfect Fuhrer salute.

My best time all summer for the 400-metre freestyle was 4 minutes 42 seconds. But within an hour of disembarking our rollicking red-eye express the next morning at Forbes Carlile's ancient indoor 25-metre pool in Pymble, I climb from the bath-warm lanes to learn that I've not only trounced this time, but even bypassed the entire 4-minute-30s to win in 4 minutes 28. That's a fourteen-second PB! Sure, 25-metre pool times are officially five seconds faster than Olympic ones over 400 metres because of all the extra tumbles, but even allowing for this it's almost a ten-second jump. I'm over the moon to think I won't have to waste the entire next season wallowing through the 4-30s; apparently all it needed was a rowdy bus trip. And there are only two boys my age in Australia who have swum faster this season: Graham Windeatt and Graeme Romei. *'I'm up there!'* I silently rejoice all day, all week, all winter.

GROWTH SPURT

It's January 1969, I'm fourteen-and-a-half, and there are just two more sleeps before the Queensland championships. Tonight's so clammy that Ashley and I have only one sheet on, and all night there've been disturbances from the courtyard of our new New Farm boarding house: just muffled stuff down in the dark, but enough to keep us up — catcalls and the snapped-off heads and tails of obscenities ('ucken! — ssole! — slu'). Sometimes things go quiet and I think it's over, but then the cursing starts up again. Midnight can't be far off.

Now a bottle smashes shockingly close by, followed by a long howl fading to sobs, and at last it's all out in the open. 'That's it!' huffs Ashley, swinging his legs over his side of the bed, feet slapping the lino hard. He opens our door and strides onto everybody's balcony in his speedos, leaning on the rail to lecture the darkness near and far to 'Keep it down, I've got a champion in here.' That's me he's talking about, and I require my sleep.

Ten minutes later, it seems people do have respect for a champion in these parts, even if they've none for themselves, because it's all gone quiet. 'Oh, if only we'd known there was a kid in there with a big race coming up, we'd have taken our problems elsewhere,' seems the consensus.

In the morning, Ashley says it's unhealthy, our sharing a double bed here this past month. He's already told me the boarding house was a wartime hospital, its wide enclosing verandah servicing twenty dim rooms above a rubbly courtyard. *But what does he mean by unhealthy?* Is our mattress still contaminated with some old wartime gangrene or plague the nurses couldn't sponge out? 'We'll find some new digs after the state titles,' he promises.

The following day, it's my last free time before an intense four-day program of racing; I always take the day off everything before a big competition because it pays to dive into your race as fresh as you can possibly be. (For a while, I was even in the habit of eating an orange the night before race day because I'd once swum sensationally at club after an orange the previous night. But that was *before* I told Nickname and his brother, who both broke into fits of laughter and scoffed that the orange link was 'all in my mind' because my body would have had no trace of it or its energy by the next morning.) Stifling heat *again*, and only the double darkness of the verandah and our cavernous, one-tiny-windowed room can make a difference. There's a naked globe hanging high above our bed, but it barely throws a shadow from the pencil I'm using to draw the electric jug on my sketch pad. After a decent likeness, I lie flat on my back to work on my pretend powers of levitation, glaring hard into the high lime-green vaulted ceiling to imagine I'm actually looking down, to trick myself into falling up. But I can never make myself fully believe this ploy, and then decide it's probably a good thing because my fledgling skills might not be able to control a sudden fall. I often do this pretend levitating just for fun, but in my dreams I actually fly. (Those dream neighbours don't believe me when I excitedly run in to tell them I can fly for real — *not just dreaming this time!* But when they reluctantly file out and their faces strain up to see me flitting among the fruit bats and stars, you should see their expressions.)

Now bored by mere three-dimensional fantasies, I ponder what — and where — I'll be, far into the future. Let's take a round number like the year 2000, where I see myself — see myself doing

— no, I realise I can't see myself there at all. The world in 2000 is as empty as its zeros, my only presence there as the number forty-six, my age. As usual whenever I try to think about time, I've become so confused I'm even having trouble seeing it as something moving forwards. Maybe this means I can stay fourteen, or whatever the calendar says I am. In fact, I now decree this moment to be the ever-present centre of my life. Who'd want to be any older? My past and future can continue to knit right here, in some vague outward expansion of the present. If I'm still around in 2000, it'll be nothing to do with the supposed forward passage of time, or of me within it.

And now I give my new tree-ring existence its next growth spurt by wandering onto the verandah, where Ashley suns himself at the top of the rotting steps, shirt off, transistor on, sipping tea, and studying the form guide. Peering over his shoulder onto the *Courier-Mail* lift-out, I can see the jockey name Alan Cooper circled several times among the Doomben starters. Ashley follows this particular hoop on the *sign* of his surname alone. *Why*, I wonder, would a grown man believe a shared surname had anything to do with the outcome of a horse race? But there can be no surer bet than that he's had a few bob on Cooper's rides again today. Now a gust swats the slope of his old shoulder with the claw of a dead pawpaw leaf, and he brushes it off in fright as if it's a spider. When my half-a-head shadow darkens the Flemington field, he adjusts his reading glasses to look up.

'Drinking hot tea on such a scorcher might seem a little odd, but it draws the heat from the pores,' he exults, now handing me the page with Mac's Cartoon Tip on it. 'Go back inside and work out Mac's tip for the fifth at Doomben,' he says. Today's cartoon is a line drawing of a desert landscape, with a boy in the foreground seemingly set to dive into an oasis pond — or perhaps a mirage — under a blinding sun and barren sky. After barely a second examining

the image on our bed, I'm about to run out and tell Ashley that
Mac's big tip is Lonely Diver, when I find another starter, Desert
Sands, similarly fitting the bill. And over the following minute, I
discover almost every other runner is referenced in some cryptic
way, from Make a Splash to False Promise, Blue Skies, and even
Hesitate. Just when I'm certain the only nag that can't be linked
to the scene is Late Rains, I notice the faintest squiggle on the
horizon, hinting at an approaching squall. After I hand the page
back and tell Ashley, 'Mac tips the whole field,' he laughs till he
almost cries, braying, 'How about that!'

I'm not sure I like the songs I'm hearing in this creepy boarding
house. It's almost as if the stations have conspired to play hits only
about dysfunction, while we're stuck here in dysfunction-central.
First, there's this new manic-depressive number about some 'Eloise'
by Barry Ryan, which alternates between a screeching chorus of
obsession ('I've got to see her, yeah!') and an equally troubling dirge
of slow strings and wretched resignation ('but she's … not there'),
only to lurch back into the key of maniacal hope. And then there's
'Lily the Pink' by the Scaffold, a rollicking bar-room ditty seemingly
about some tragicomic alcoholic barmaid, while the real-life alco
lurking in the next room is anything but funny. I try hard not to
look in on her on my way to the bathroom and back, but can never
resist. (Why is her door wide open all day, every day?) And there she
is, glowering back from the edge of her bed where she sits stiffly in
puffy-shouldered, puffy-hipped, muslin shorty pyjamas, like some
ghostly hybrid of senior lingerie queen and conquistador. Even with
make-up on, it's clear she's quite old.

In the room along from her are Slow Man and Quickstep.
That's what Ashley calls them. Slow Man has one seriously mangled
eye from a machining accident down in the Valley, and Quickstep a
pronounced limp, though this doesn't stop him hobbling the streets

after he sets out at eight a.m. daily in his cowboy shirt and jeans. It's nothing to see Quickstep right across town — Newstead one day, Bulimba the next — forever banging fist on palm or doing crazy clickety-click things with his fingers. I always wave to him from the car, but he's never waved back yet; neither does he answer my hello on the verandah or in the bathroom. According to Ashley, Slow Man doesn't trust Quickstep one bit, and sleeps with a knife under his bed. (Ashley will talk to anyone here, and somehow gets them chatting about all sorts of things, even though he calls them *life's failures*.)

And it's taken me a while, but it's just occurred to me that what people here have in common is what they *don't* have — a family. You never see families at all, and it's as if the tens of thousands of generations that brought them to these walls, and the myriad phyla and strains that led to those, become extinct right here. Even the one boarder who has a steady job, the man whose every day begins and ends in 'Greensleeves' blaring from his Mr Whippy van, never has a visitor. When I ask Ashley why all these people haven't been able to get on with their families, he tells me that Tolstoy, 'or one of those Russian writers, said all happy families are the same, while unhappy families are all different'. Then he thinks on this, and says, 'Or maybe it's the other way round.' I try to help him out by saying that maybe families stay happy simply by deciding not to fight, and this makes them the same. But then he says it could be the unhappy families powerless *not* to fight who resemble each other, and we both give up on this bad Russian proverb.

SMOKE AND MIRRORS

Tomorrow's the Moon landing, yesterday I turned fifteen, and in between Ashley and I dock our cockpit-sized Torana at my mother's miniature, rouge-brick flat in Browne Street, New Farm. This is my first weekend sleepover here since we left New Farm for our new Edmondstone Street bedsit in South Brisbane, and only my fourth since the divorce. Booming through tie-dye curtains down their flat's narrow side is the big-dipper chorus of the 5th Dimension's 'Aquarius', my current favourite. 'THIS IS THE DAWNING OF THE AGE OF ...'

I'm always in two minds about coming here, but the divorce laws say I'm stuck for the weekend. *Things I'll have to put up with:* (a) My mother insisting my brothers would have been my match in swimming, *had they kept at it*. This is ridiculous, of course, because cuttings from all our club results are in our scrapbooks and not once did they qualify to compete beyond inter-club level. I don't gloat over this, but let's have the facts, please: my brothers are footballers, not swimmers. (b) If I go for another long run to escape my mother's interminable weekend soirees, I'll return exhausted and sweating, and risk her quipping sarcastically in front of her friends again, 'You can't be too fit by the look of all that puffing.' (She knows as little about exercise as car makes: Alfa-*Romero?*) (c) My older brother being seemingly incapable of uttering to me the words 'Dad' or 'our father' in conversation, but only *'your* father', even if he does think he's kidding. That's how much they miss him here. (d) Actually having to say goodnight. When I simply disappeared to the bedroom last time, my mother burst in five minutes later, turned the light on, and launched into a five-minute 'how-dare-you-in-my-house' rant. *House?*

Now she emerges from her dark front doorway in a tangle of sunlight and fly strips to greet me. *And* acknowledge my father. He, with no small talk at all, casually thrusts into her hands two packets of lima beans which *Brad must have* with meals for their remarkably high protein value (a day's soaking, hours of parboiling, and frying in an equal mass of butter are needed to magic those beige stones into edible forage). 'There's enough there for everyone,' he chirps. 'The extra protein wouldn't hurt the others either!'

She accepts the beans and condescension calmly, but as soon as we're inside she hurls the beans in the bin with a garnish of bile, huffing, 'Sorry, but I don't take orders on your nutrition, you'll have whatever's going!'

In the afternoon, it's her usual gathering of friends from all over. As they drift in, my brothers teach me the finer points of smoking in the laundry, but I can never do the drawback without a coughing fit. I'm sure my throat is too weak to ever be a smoker: even swallowing soft-drink fizz is like gulping tacks. And not just coughing now, but when my gullet clamps yet again, it's all splutter and retch into the sink. I now decide smoking's as clever as gargling petrol, and quit, telling my brothers I'll never learn and that I'm glad anyway.

When the party's in full swing, I watch her guests get drunk and drunker, the gags and jibes coarser by the swig. Now her long-time girlfriend, the brunette Dawn, leans across to slur to my brother that he'll soon be old enough for her to 'fix him up' with one of her 'younger friends' — sly chuckles all round. She's with another Saturday regular, the blocky building contractor who, when the talk turns to politics, will leap from his chair and march outside to fetch his Ayn Rand book from a ute glovebox.

Now my mother slips into her comedic staple: mocking her ex. She's on a stool at the end of the servery near the dips, and everyone seems drawn to watch when she swivels a half-turn to glare theatrically at a new couple, as if to say *don't you dare miss this one*. These newbies are not her typical guests. *Stodgy* is how she would describe their clothes, and their chuckles are more to themselves than the hearty head-jerking and leg-slapping of regulars. This time she's parodying the nightly chin exercises her mad husband used to do in their early years together; apparently Ashley always wanted a lantern jaw like the Hollywood actors whose blockbusters he promoted in Singapore. (Even now, his routine putdown of other men is 'chinless wonder'.) Most nights he supposedly sat at the foot of their marriage bed, robotically cranking his mandible in the dresser mirror to stimulate tissue and muscle growth. Several guests begin a low, bumpy chuckle as my mother's face turns from its pretend Ashley reflection and inches back, neck tendons flared like a frilled lizard, adoring eyes still glued to her 'image'. Suddenly she slaps her jowls, juts her chin, draws it back. More slaps. Jaw out, in, and out, pouting grotesquely at full thrust. Some are in tears she does this so well. '*Stop it*, Betty!' old Queenie snaps in encouragement.

Now it's the story I once found embarrassing, but which I've become used to: of the night I was apparently conceived aboard a cruise ship. My mother says she knew it was the equator when the deck crew 'started with all that King Neptune buffoonery'. From the midst of those oaths, tridents, and crowns, my father supposedly whisked her off to their cabin to make love. Even so early in the yarn, my mother can hardly breathe, seems barely able to continue, she is laughing so hard. *Are those tears?* 'And then, of all things,' she whines, 'get this: he says to me, "This baby will be the special one."'

Turning to me, she gasps, 'Sorry, darling, not mocking *you*, but can you imagine what was going through his head?' Her newer guests stare at her uncertainly, then across to me, as a courtesy perhaps, as if not to credit what they've heard. 'The special one!' she groans, flopping against the wall with a god-help-us-all sigh. 'Just like he's channelling some, some … Tibetan boy-priest, for goodness sake, within seconds of *the business* on the equator.'

Suddenly her demeanour's less trenchant, eyes evasive, as if she is momentarily rattled by the idea of her womb's role in that supposed calling, or self-conscious for having fallen for some loony twice her age. Yet there's still the odd giggle and laugh-weary sigh — nothing more — as we await the next twist. I've heard the story before, and would long ago have asked Ashley for his version but for the inevitable embarrassment. And it might also spoil things, because it's fun thinking I'm meant to be something special, even in one crazy man's mind or a bitter ex-wife's skewed recollection.

My mother usually has sharp timing, even when tipsy; she can easily sniff the souring of a theme, as in this case with the new couple's awkwardness at her seeming clash of satire and personal freight. She knows now to drop the hubby stuff for a while. Tapping her cigarette on the spring-loaded ashtray, her eyes flicker cunningly for a diversion: today's fashion crime, a spilled drink, an empty glass — she's onto it. The break in rhythm also lets me slip out unnoticed for my run. As I glance behind, her face tilts up again, features recharged to beam listeners back to the neglected present, her smile the quick 'whee' of a pigtailed girl leaning out from a carousel.

When I return an hour later, she's circled back to familiar turf, regaling a chosen few with the circumstances of her marriage. 'Well, I married my best friend's father, didn't I? *And don't think I haven't been wondering how it happened ever since.*' She's giggling now:

'It must sound creepy, but it's not as if my girlfriend was calling me Betty one minute and Mummy the next, though we naturally drifted apart.' Now, when two guests stand within seconds of each other and cite reasons to be home under threat of death, the party begins to peter out.

So today I won't get to hear of the night my germophobe father arrived home from a Singapore expat's bar, drenched in faeces after disastrously mistiming his usual tipsy leap across the *kampong* sewer drain. Supposedly he'd slammed open our front door to stand distraught in his saturated sharkskin suit, barking, 'Fill the bath with Dettol, I'm swimming in shit!' (Dettol had also been handy on their Indian honeymoon. He couldn't touch any surface beyond their motel room without immediately wiping his hands on a Dettol-dabbed rag.)

Or of the time he seized an antagonist's scrotum in a Singapore nightspot to roar in mock surprise, 'So you really are a man,' or Mum's visit to a soothsayer when she first fell pregnant: 'that Chinese tealeaf reader' who predicted three sons and a sporting champion in the family. Then her whimsy, at thirty, that the aforesaid champion was clearly her when she resurrected her teen tennis career on the Rockhampton ladies' scene. (That she'd seen fortune-telling as light entertainment was shown by her determination to hold out for a girl; she blames Ashley for 'ordering an end to the babies' after the third boy.) And then there's the story about my father taking his annual holiday to Australia with just one other family member — me, aged three. 'He adored you and wanted to show you off to his old Sydney friends,' she has often explained to me with crisp resignation. 'He loved taking guests into your cot to hear you laugh in your sleep.'

Although I think she was pretty dumb to allow that silly bonding holiday for a toddler, I never comment because I'm too flattered to care. I have my own special memories of the trip anyway. First there's a plane, recalled not as if I fully understand we're preparing for flight, but as a night-time crush of impressions in circling fairy lights and beaming towers, smells of well-made things, noises of irresistible power, and a sense of vast beginnings in the bumps of a slow, wide circling. Then I'm on a steep footpath holding my father's hand — I've never walked hills before — amid thrilling new building shapes in winding streets with chilling gusts; having my first taste of a musk stick; sharing a seat on a ferry in a fur-lined anorak; crying on a bed with persistent loud music when an adult enters to look me over before the door shuts again, the songs even louder.

Mum says when Dad and I returned from the Sydney holiday, I was a changed boy, now surly and taciturn. 'It took a while to get you smiling again,' she has often reminded me in that oddly accusing tone. 'That's when your temper started. Remember you used to tear up your brother's exercise books?' (How could I ever forget? Those moments of sudden mayhem were among the big thrills of my early life, even after deducting the cost of a smack and an apology.) I've replied once or twice that I also recall being badgered by Dad and her to smile in some backyard. Thinking they meant the breezy click-and-wink adult faces often shot at kids, I volleyed that, and was surprised when it made them laugh. Then I laughed.

We left Singapore for Rocky when I was four, and what it left me was smells and tastes, of Tiger Balm ointment, yeasty beer gardens, and pungent, jelly-like desserts. We must have dined out often because when I walk past restaurants now, there is often an exquisite waft, a fusion of heavily starched linen and fresh crust so intense that I've felt the odd momentary ache in my chest. It's such a reminder of life's fine things that it's hard to imagine a life without it. Matching that memory heaven are vast and fabulous night-time establishments, where I wander between walls of glass made dreamy with unforgettable slides and bursts of light, shadow, laughter, music, and mingling, and I think if I have children I'll take them dining as often as I can.

With only her most loyal or pissed friends left (her odd term for the alcohol-loosened is 'tight'), it's time for the mumbo-jumbo hour, when they huddle to debate puerile matters the sober and rational cringe at. If any sensible ones do stay — *sticks-in-the-mud*, she calls them, like smart-arse George with his engineering degree, and bone-dry, bachelor-grazier Bob — it's just to scoff or poke fun. And the discussions proceed not in logical lines of argument, but in hyphen-strewn declarations, nods, and squeals of 'me too', spanning subjects from alien contact to adultery, though not yet in the same breath. My mother's contribution today is to stumble through a recollection of the afternoon she rode the train from work as a young adult, scrutinising fellow commuters in some kind of awakening, when she 'suddenly saw we're all so unique — each face with enough information to start a new species — yet also identical — *sounds ridiculous now* — when I suddenly felt so free — a kind of grace — overwhelming — changed my life.'

'And how exactly did it change your life, Betty?' cow-cocky Bob yawns. My mother narrows her eyes, half a crease short of *fuck off*: 'Not that you'd understand in a hundred years of hanging with Herefords, but from that day, I could no longer be shy.' (I'm privately thrilled by her slap-down of this gangly crimson-faced redneck who recently confided in her that he found my handshake 'unmanly'. He's so goofy he doesn't get that there's no confiding in my mother, and that only masons, the mafia, and yokels like him think a male handshake is some golden mutual dick-squeeze.)

Mumbo-jumbo time is also the excuse for us boys to ride our

bikes to New Farm Park before it gets dark. Within a minute of arrival, my younger brother is in a fight with a boy over nothing more, it seems, than a mistimed blink in an exchange of territorial glances. For fun, my older brother and I cheer on the other kid, who quickly succumbs to my brother's manic windmill of arms resembling his old swimming style. In less than thirty seconds, the boy's taunts dissolve to a sob begging to go home, and when his bike rounds the first flower bed he yells back, 'Cunt.'

I arrive back at the flat before my brothers to find my mother sitting, now changed into singlet and ribbed sky-blue hot pants, on her new Welsh boyfriend's lap on the kitchen settee (I'm stunned to see she really does resemble Virginia McKenna, the actress she was once hired to double for — *only less horsey*, as she herself has put it). His arms engulf her affectionately from behind, with more than a hint of compromise. When neither makes an effort to adjust things, I realise it's one of those 'damned if you do or don't' moments, and they've gone with the *don't* to brazen it out.

My father would never be caught out like this: he still calls his current flame 'our housekeeper'. Most Sundays she takes the train from the town where he once employed her, lobbing at our bedsit after our return from swimming club around noon. The first thing she does is run a duster over our dresser and bedhead in a nod to her cover, before pulling up a kitchen chair to drink with Ashley until he drives her back to the station. Who are *they* kidding?

While I wait to be picked up, my mother asks me to pass on a message to Ashley.

'Tell your father I can do without his phone calls crowing about every swimming record you break, and asking me if *my kids* — MY kids, mind you — are still failing exams and running away from home, which he knows is utter garbage.'

'Sure,' I chirp, as I hear his car pull up. After a quick 'bye, thanks', I skip out to the car and we're off, but I'm keeping mum about what she said.

SHIT-STIRRERS

'That would be your father's wartime psychiatrist,' my mother quips in another sleepover when I mention Ashley's *old American friend* who gave him the book of Elbert Hubbard aphorisms I've been reading.

'So ...' I venture, 'you're saying it wasn't an old American friend who gave him that book?'

'Maybe they became friends, but the book was definitely a present from his military psychiatrist, who *was* American. Your father's unit might have been under American command in New Guinea.'

'Why would he have a psychiatrist?' I ask.

'Probably something to do with his breakdown at the end of the war when his first wife sprang a divorce on him.'

'But why would they treat him for something that wasn't caused by the war itself, and at the very end?' I persist. Typically, at such points in enquiries about my father when 2 and 2 could be 22 instead of 4, my mother breaks off irritably. But with a new burst of energy she spins from the stove: '*Look.* I could never follow his crazy past anyway, so maybe you should ask him yourself. And while you're at it, ask about the dumb scams he tried to pull off to get sent home, like swallowing huge wads of chewing gum before chest X-rays so they'd resemble tumours, and getting himself stung by swarms of bees in the jungle.' I reply I will, but know I won't.

Back in our bedsit on Sunday night, I'm browsing that old Hubbard hardback when I examine the words penned in the flyleaf,

'From your friend, Huxel Stuart': obviously by his army psychiatrist. And *Huxel* could only be American.

Elbert must have gone to great lengths to collect all these wise sayings, but one that always rubs me the wrong way goes, 'God will not look you over for medals, degrees, or diplomas, but for scars.' (I just can't see how some disaster-prone klutz should trump my medals, even if their scars are just figurative. It's not my fault I'm coordinated and driven.)

One of my father's long-time personal standards is also pretty flawed, and goes, *All things in moderation*. 'Isn't that a contradiction?' I ask in the kitchen where he's ogling the fierce blue glow of his new asbestos cooking plate. 'I mean, it's definitely going a bit overboard to want *all* things in moderation; in fact, I'd call that downright excessive!' The slap equivalent of a stiff jab shocks my cheek, followed by, 'Don't get smart, the exception proves the rule.' Another of his staples is, *A rolling stone gathers no moss*. I guess this explains our thirteen moves in eighteen months: we're the absolute anti-moss! And there's yet another: one I even find disturbing. Every now and then — I forget what triggers it — he'll blurt, 'You've got to belong.' When I hear this, I want to gawk around to see who else is here, because it seems meant for everyone, not just me. 'You've got to *beee*-long,' he repeats in a long, skinny whine. He's obviously talking about *beee*-longing to a swimming club, but I've never seen sport as some grim social measure. In fact, it's always been the exact opposite for me, a way of extricating yourself from the pack, while Ashley's 'belonging' spiel just makes it sound like some pitiful halfway house for endangered teen esteem, like we have to be fooled into who we are.

And maybe it's this moderation business that's started him drinking at home lately. Our fridges — if we had our own — were totally alcohol-free in our drifting days, but since we've now clocked up a marathon six months in South Brisbane he must feel entitled to a moderate homely tipple. Each Friday night, he turns up from work with two XXXX tallies in their brown paper bags and stashes them in the top tray of our prehistoric Pope fridge till Sunday. If his girlfriend, the fire-lipsticked widow Mrs O'Rogan, comes over, they drink them together. And even after she cancels today's visit on short notice, he opens one anyway, when, instead of a toast, he declares, 'I'd rather have a bottle in front of me than a frontal lobotomy.'

'Hey, that's in a Robert Lowell poem at school,' I interrupt.

'What's in a ... ?'

'*Lobotomy!* Some crime boss called Czar Lepke who shared a jail cell with Lowell was lobotomised, and one line went, "he drifted in a sheepish calm".'

Ashley drains his glass, eyes the dregs, and mutters out of the blue, 'I think your mother married me for the security. She was hanging with a bunch of young idiots and couldn't wait to get out.'

Huh? I think back — we never talk about *her*.

When his eyes search the dregs again, he predicts Mrs O'Rogan won't be back for a while because her just-married stock-car-champion son-in-law died of a twisted bowel from a crash this week. I hate stock cars, but I'm shocked and sorry too, because someone so cheerful doesn't deserve a death in the family.

On top of his new Sunday drinking, Ashley's never far from a bad mood either, and indulging alone can quickly join the dots: after a few solos last week, he accused me of stealing a two-dollar note off the dresser. Now, using my own money, I pretend to find it on the cracked, curled lino behind. Offering it from my patch of high moral ground, I suggest the fan blew it over.

'No, you keep it,' he decides.

But his once-weekly imbibing doesn't hold a candle to my

nightly glass of stout with dinner. 'It's to build you up,' he chirped the first night he placed it in front of me. Stout's as black as the Texas Tea that gushes from Jed Clampett's hillbilly well, and is so vile I think it's more to force me to gulp down a healthy chaser of vegetables to kill the taste. Between the stout, vegetables, and steak — on top of the lima beans, endless eggs, raw oats, Carnation milk, energy shakes, eggflips, V8 Vegetable Juice, and daily barbells — he's determined to build me up. Maybe he's never gotten over John Carew saying I was too skinny to be a champion.

Climbing our verandah stairs after the 5.30 bus from training, I find him dicing what looks like shit, with a chopstick, on a sheet of newspaper in an open cardboard box. *Maybe human shit.* 'What's that?' I ask with moderate indignation when I see him crouched on the decking in fading light. I'm told he swallowed a false tooth while chewing last night's dinner, something he calls a crown, with a sharp post on the end. Right now he's petrified his intestines were pierced by that spike as it surfed the peristaltic waves all night; he's getting pains. (I'd wondered why he was tossing and turning in the small hours.) It's obvious he's sweating on a result with all this frenzied stick-pushing, which leaves bright hieratic swirls on yesterday's news. He hasn't stopped while we've been talking, and the tooth hasn't surfaced yet, so maybe there'll be another tabloid-full waiting for us tomorrow night. And I can only imagine how much pride he's had to swallow by knowing he'll be putting that thing back in his mouth if he finds it. His normal hygiene paranoia demands the immediate binning of plates with even a hairline crack because cracks harbour germs, so I can see this tooth having an entire bottle of Dettol to itself for days. And it's a shared balcony, so I don't know what the neighbours think of turds ripening in the sun all day just metres from their door. Let's hope their little toddler didn't wander over to play in it, but maybe he's already found the crown.

(Ashley's not the only one with dental issues. Coincidentally my own baste-enamelled teeth have been undergoing an overhaul of fillings and extractions under the gorilla forearms of Dr Pappas down at West End. Whenever I'm due in his chair, the surgery door creaks slightly ajar before one of those hairy arms snakes out to begin a slow, ghoulish beckoning; he is the second Greek man to act the clown for me. And after his drill went halfway through my cheek last week when I jerked at a nerve strike, he said to tell Ashley there's no charge for the extra hole. 'Rokray,' I gurgled, watching my blood snake around the rinse bowl.)

Next evening I'm heading up Edmondstone Street again after the bus, wondering whom I prefer out of Judith Durham of the Seekers, and Mary from the folk trio, Peter, Paul, and Mary (who may just be among the world's last beatniks). I'm determined it won't be a parochial Australia vs America tease but a choice based on musical merit. I love Judith's voice, but she seems a little churchy for my liking, and there are a few religious songs among the hits, while PP&M seem more into secular civil rights. I saw Mary sing on TV, and her mouth has a life of its own; it's so huge that she just has to marry Mick Jagger so they can breed a tribe of the world's biggest rubber-mouths. She also has this gimmick of snappy head shakes whenever she whacks that tambourine, giving her long platinum hair a shimmy shock-wave from scalp to shoulder.

Mounting the verandah stairs, I'm relieved to find last night's newspaper and its cargo gone. Instead, I spy Ashley through the kitchen window cheerfully pushing a spatula across a pan of steaming brown rice. That's what I'm hoping, at least. I'm going with Judith. Better melodies.

When my Brisbane State High geography teacher Mr Zimmerman keeps us in after school on Friday, it rings this crazy little bell in my head. For months now, Ashley's been cursing such teachers who make me late for training. As well as being hugely unimpressed, he's told me several times to make sure I pass his contempt on to them. But I'd be stupid to carry out his wishes every time; it's my job as messenger to filter the hot air from the pragmatic content. My head has barely begun sorting these priorities this afternoon when I'm horrified to find my mouth already informing Mr Zimmerman, 'My father won't be impressed.' I usually don't mind this teacher: he's slim, fit, and chipper, and wears jumpers I approve of — today's in a busy diamond grid. And those black-rimmed glasses seem oddly to complement this impression of urbane athleticism. His reflexes are impeccable too, because Ashley's missive has barely reached his ears when his knees begin to tremble, his hands cup his face in mock horror, and he shrieks, 'Oh no, and what's he going to do to me?'

Although I'm glad to have established firm boundaries for the sharing of Ashley's diatribes, I also wonder how much raging blood my cheek capillaries can safely handle at such times. But one thing's certain: Ashley must never learn of Mr Zimmerman's response. As we wait to be let out, I fume about having a father who wants me to say things to get me into trouble.

Binning another egg carton on Monday night, Ashley rescues a leaflet with the bugle *free* on it. It seems the Egg Board is mailing out free microscopes to Australia's budding young scientists, and now Ashley asks if I'd like to join that new wave. 'It could be good for your studies,' he says, as if he's serious. Meaning *how lame*, I vacantly mouth yes, and a fortnight later there's nothing within a ten-minute radius of our bedsit that hasn't gone under its triple stalk-eyed lenses: scab, blood, lichen, phlegm, smegma of terrier, feathers of road kill. Some samples I view in isolation and others I prod or puree. There's a good few days' entertainment here before I've had my fill of being the local Galileo of shrunken infinities, and under the bed it goes for good, with Elbert's homespun wisdom.

THE MILITARY
INDUSTRIAL COMPLEX

My Sunday club times at Brisbane's Valley Pool were pathetic again this morning. Actually, two were almost Queensland records, but anything's pathetic these days because that's how my friend Nickname and his twin brother have begun describing their races. I still can't spit it out with the disgust they do, but I'm getting there. When my old Sydney club mate Jim Findlay turns up in Brisbane the following weekend for a carnival, he asks how my first race went. 'Fucken pathetic,' I spit back, expecting him to be up to speed on this *pathetic* business.

'Go easy on yourself,' he blurts, 'I heard it was your best time.'

At last! I think, I've nailed the tone, though I'm shocked at having been taken so literally: I'd hate him to think I don't enjoy racing because there's nothing I love more than finishing a club race and waiting expectantly for the timekeeper to chalk up my time. And as soon as I'm back in the stands, the first thing I do is check if Ashley entered it correctly in our logbook.

Nickname and his brother are from seriously clever stock. Not only is their dad a scientist, but Nickname's school even bumped him up a year because he embarrassed teachers with such *elegant* maths solutions. Thanks to hanging with geniuses like these, I can now denounce the long flat facade of Brisbane State High as *fascist*, and sneer that most people never honestly review their life choices but merely *rationalise*. Christmas, of course, is just a retail scam and not really Christian at all but, like Easter, an early Church theft of pagan dates. Nickname never tires of reminding me his brother is schizoid, verging on paranoid. But then the brother tells me Nickname himself is ultra-conservative, neurotic, and so insecure he dragged a hug-rug around till he was nine, and that his knock-knees and pronated feet, which collapse the inner walls of shoes within weeks of purchase, are 'biomechanical manifestations' of that insecurity. And then Nickname says his brother's streamlined, swimming-friendly ears were once *wing nuts* before a cosmetic procedure pinned them back when he was ten, and that those ears are now abused daily by weird musicians I've never heard of, like Frank Zappa, the Grateful Dead, and the Velvet Underground. The military industrial complex underpins every western economy, pulls the puppet strings of leaders, and has others assassinated.

Amused as I am by the brothers' merciless bickering, with its fictitious psycho slurs, it can still disappoint me because I'd always imagined brainy families to be above all that. Fighting was easy to live with in mine because we boys were getting boxing gloves for Christmas by our first year of school.

The only time I'm not tempted to mimic Nickname is when he offers me the latest book he's finished, *Slaughterhouse-Five*, by Kurt Vonnegut. I fully intend reading it until he lets slip that a major character time-travels. 'No thanks,' I groan, because I exhausted my suspension of disbelief by reading almost every superhero comic ever published after my parents separated, in those two crazy years when Ashley confused addresses with ping-pong bats. (The exception back then was Batman, because I'd refused to *unsuspend* my disbelief for two earthbound mummy's boys whose only advantages over Constable Plod were connections in city hall, high-tech gadgets, and designer capes.) If I read anything now, heroes must keep their feet on the ground. *Time travel?* Nickname should have known better.

Tonight I'm sleeping over at Nickname's home in leafy, petite-bourgeoisie Chelmer. When his parents go out, they're not off to meet friends, or to have drinks, but *to trip the light fantastic*. They won't be long, his mother assures us when they're leaving, because she's still recovering from *the dreaded lurgy*, and his father's been *in high dudgeon* all day. 'Oh, and don't forget to put the *moggy* in the laundry,' she reminds Nickname at the front door.

'They've actually gone to a concert,' Nickname translates when I ask about this *light fantastic* guff and other terms I've never heard before: 'My dad's favourites, Mahler and Sibelius, are being performed by a touring orchestra.' One of the games we play to keep occupied is one he grew up with, dictionary roulette, where we take turns to nominate a word to see who can find its listing with fewer page turns; bonus points when your opponent doesn't know at least two synonyms. We're pretty even on the page turns, but I'm killed on the synonyms.

They only give you life membership when your death membership's overdue, but our coach Gordon Petersen gave so much of his youth to a surf club that they cursed him with it in his thirties. Twenty years later, he's still running the Valley Pool to help swimmers like us. Apparently he had a go at boxing too, though he rates himself *just a journeyman*. And Gordon's actually his middle name; he told me he thought his real Christian name, Lindsay, a bit sissy, so he switched them. He says he was named after a famous poet, and you wouldn't see that in a million years with other coaches. There are also these great sayings on his office wall: *'You can tell the ones who could have … They did!'* Nickname likes it best, but my favourite is, *'Tomorrow's champion? He quit yesterday!'* A third advises, *'Never confuse promise with promises.'*

When Gordon's excited by impressive training, he can look like a snow skier launching from a jump ramp, angled staunchly over the end of the pool with chin thrust and hands clutching his buttocks instead of ski stocks. When it's stormy and he's carrying on like this in his yellow sou'-wester, it's a sight. Other times when he's fired up, he'll rake his fingers fiercely through his oily red hair, thickets flicking up like baby carrot spears. Dozens of kickboards, piled like an alley of mini skyscrapers along the end of the pool, serve two purposes: we kick laps on them, and use them as *cooling towers* on hot days by clasping a stack overhead for breeze-cooled water to drip down our backs. That was Shane Gould's idea. She wants a royalty, but we let her go first instead.

Whenever Nickname's brother baits Gordon about his supposed ignorance of technique or physiology, Gordon gives as good as he gets:

'What do you know about muscle memory, Gordon?'

'Enough to know yours have been given nothing to remember, boom-boom.' (There's always a boom-boom when he cracks a joke.) Yesterday's big comeback was, 'If theory's so important, jump out here and answer multiple-choice questions all afternoon.' His final word today is to jab petulantly at the pace clock and bark, 'In the end, kiddo, it's not technique that counts, but *tick*-nique. Get it? Tick-tick-tick-nique,' reminding us it's the best trainers who win races.

This afternoon, Shane and I are let out early to be interviewed by *the doyen* of Brisbane sports reporters, Frank O'Callaghan. High in the stands, Frank tells us we're both considered dark horses for the 1970 Commonwealth Games team, even though I'm only fifteen and Shane's just thirteen. Who could not like Frank, with his kindly, quizzical expression and craggy grin, firing off his questions? Snapping his notebook shut, he asks Gordon if he's thrilled to be coaching two of Australia's *genuine up-and-comers*. 'I couldn't wish for two better students,' Gordon answers, his eyes flashing back to the pool where a girl is accusing a boy of *fishing* her, and he's denying it.

'Yes you did!' she shrieks.

'In your dreams!' he scoffs back. Fishing supposedly happens in backstroke, the only stroke to make your hand pull wide into the adjacent lane, where it inevitably brushes against the odd passing swimmer. (If the by-catch includes sea slug, a disgusted 'arggh' is heard from both boys.) As Gordon scurries down to calm the situation, Frank wishes Shane and me good luck at the Commonwealth Trials, and ambles off.

I truly die a thousand deaths whenever Ashley calls at the pool on his way home to see how I'm training, as he has again today. It always seems to be when I'm doing backstroke, and once again I can't rid myself of this idiotic face-splitting smile from the moment I spot him. It's so unbearable that I have to bury my face sideways underwater to hide it. 'Go away, piss off,' I tell the imbecile grin, but whenever I come up for air it's still there. I just hope Gordon doesn't ask why my face is underwater all the time. Nickname's away today, so if I am asked, I'll say he told me it's a new technique his father found in an American journal. (That's not so ridiculous: every now and then there's some crazy coach teaching butterfly with *sideways* breathing.) When I'm at the wall in our next break, Ashley's gone, and my face is sane again.

We're in our HB Torana heading north to Redcliffe for the season's biggest non-championship carnival. As usual in our longer drives, Ashley's busy with *car gym*. This particular exercise is 'wheel-press', where he pushes against the steering wheel to bury himself into the backrest, a hundred reps to a set. 'Pecs, deltoids, and triceps, this one,' he grunts. If he's not doing proper car gym, he seems to be doing *thumb gym* by rubbing both thumbs agitatedly on the inside of the wheel. (When I told Nickname, he said this was a sure sign of an anxiety disorder.) On the rickety planks of the ancient Hornibrook Bridge, five minutes from the pool, Ashley asks for the soccer ball, which is always bumping around my passenger footwell. When I wedge it into the crook of his left arm, he cranks it with slow, dogged compressions. 'Biceps-traps-pecs,' he grimaces. With the left arm spent, he snaps it straight for the ball to bounce across the steering wheel into the crook of his right arm for another set, and all this without veering an inch off course.

At the Redcliffe pool, I'm gobsmacked by the number of inspirational mottos near the entrance, though none is as clever as the few pinned up discreetly in Gordon's office, and most are surely plagiarised. Nickname says the one I've found most lame, condemning 'the impostors of triumph and failure', sounds suspiciously like Kipling. I also find it offensive, since one of those two frauds is my guiding star. When I quip to Nickname, 'If failure and triumph get equal billing in this pool, let's cut our losses and go now,' he laughs and smacks haughtily, '*Indeed!*' Now he says he'd love to scribble his own maxim on the wall.

'What is it?' I insist.

'*Coaches find self-belief with other people's bodies!*' he fires back, and we both buckle over.

'Brilliant,' I roar, 'spot-on!'

In my second race, the open 200-metre backstroke, I'm ecstatic to find I haven't fallen my usual body-length behind the reigning state open champion, Arthur Shean, the swimmer Ashley has dubbed 'the Rolls-Royce of backstrokers'; with one-and-a-half laps to go, I'm at his ribs and gaining. Pushing out from the last turn, I put everything into an overtaking burst. Fifteen metres from the finish, I'm parked head and shoulders ahead of the Rolls-Royce and hold it to the wall. Nickname's dad is one of the three timekeepers for my lane, and when I glance up for my time he croaks in a quaver, 'Wonderful, wonderful swim, Brad,' a knuckle dabbing his leaking left eye: '2 minutes 14 point 7, a state record.' The timekeeping shift over, he accompanies me back to Nickname and Ashley for the lunch break.

After our next race, Nickname and I return to the stands to find our fathers gone. 'They must have taken a walk,' Nickname huffs (the pool's in a private Catholic school grounds). When the missing dads finally turn up near the end of the carnival, Mr Nickname seems uncharacteristically jovial, and a tad unsteady. It seems Ashley and his new mate have been sampling the hospitality of the Monsignor's temporary grog booth.

As we leave, Ashley and Gordon chat for a moment at the turnstiles before we head to the car park. Waiting at the crossing, I catch sight of Nickname standing at the driver's side of his dad's parked car up the street, and carping, 'You shouldn't drive, Dad, you shouldn't drive!' His dad, propped cheerfully in the plush leather driver's seat, could easily fly the car home. As we exit the car park, it occurs to me to ask Ashley if his new friend (and my old friend) will be okay, but the impulse dies when he toots the horn as we pass, signalling all's fine. Soon I begin a side-mirror vigil to check if they're safely following us, particularly along the rattling planks and bolts of the narrow Hornibrook Bridge, where a breezy hand on the wheel and an admiring glance at the bay could send a car through the rails in a flash. But I catch not even a glimpse of them in the receding distance, and, more importantly, no splash.

A few blocks after the bridge, we pull into an RSL club to celebrate my impressive performances: every race was a personal-best time. 'Gordon at least has you in good shape for the state and national titles,' Ashley declares, parking his keys and wallet on the table we've found. He always prefaces Gordon's contributions with 'at least', as if he's just managing to head off failure at every point. I'm not sure what Ashley thinks of Gordon. Sometimes it seems affectionate when he wistfully calls him *an old commie* (even Nickname thinks Gordon is 'a Maoist' because of his battered Gladstone bag and bland clothes) yet much less so when *old commie* becomes *old woman*.

As usual in our RSL celebrations, I sip a shandy under our section's gaudy resin light-shades while Ashley sinks a few middies, showing no sign of the many he must have downed at the pool. When requests are invited by the club's resident band, the Percolators, Ashley joins the trickle to the stage. I don't need to ask which song he'll ask for — it's the same wherever we go — and it soon booms through the auditorium: Neil Diamond's stirring 'Solitary Man'. But it's not my absolute favourite. I'd have chosen 'Itchycoo Park', 'Guantanamera', or 'Jennifer Juniper'. Now I'm suddenly wondering if Ashley can see the perfect irony that his favourite song could well be about him. 'Solitary Man' — what a neat coincidence! And he starts singing along, though far too loudly for my liking: '*I'll be what I am, sol-it-ar-y man,*' now beaming around conspicuously to see who else approves — '*I'll be what …*' After two more songs, we leave, arriving home just in time to watch *Daniel Boone*. It's been a near perfect day.

On Monday, thankfully, Nickname turns up still in one piece for our morning training session. I wouldn't mind knowing how the drive home went, but can't bring myself to ask.

At afternoon training, I'm about to push off during a set of 100-metre sprints when I notice that Ginger, who left a few places before me, has stopped swimming several metres out. I delay my own departure by five seconds because he's now completely hunched, seemingly tugging in angry frustration at his paddle straps, which probably loosened on push-off. I start my swim, but, after becoming the third to stroke around Ginger, I glance back to find him still tightly arched — except that those minor paddle-fiddling jerks are now seismic snaps of his entire body. Something's surely wrong, so I splash back and drag him to the side of the pool, where I hand him over to a lifeguard, my new karate-champion friend, Cyrus. When Gordon and a few parents finally have him cocooned in a blanket, Ginger drowsily responds to their shouts and shakes. By the time we're on our last lap of training, he's in his tracksuit and waiting outside the first-aid room for his parents.

After training, the squad stays back for our occasional game of water polo, renamed *walker polo* because our rules allow standing at the shallow end. Today there's a new player, Talkback, who's considering joining our squad. After she takes a pass and hogs the ball beyond the five-second limit, two boys pounce to reclaim possession. But she hugs her prize tightly to make them earn it, before slamming the ball on the surface with all her might. When the towering syllable 'NO' rings out, her challengers fall away as she lectures them: 'I totally understand boys having their bit of fun, but I don't appreciate your hands going *there* when you're supposed to be after the ball.' *Wow!* is all I can think to myself, not even sure what I'm so impressed by. After a half-hearted attempt to restart the game with a few self-conscious passes and goal feints, we all pack it in and go home.

The following day, after hearing I was the one who saved her only son from drowning in a fit, Ginger's mother traps me in the world's longest poolside hug. Over the next week, these grateful embraces continue, and although the gratitude's appreciated I'm secretly relieved when they eventually peter out to a big smile.

On Sunday, our entire lane turns up at Thor's birthday party. He's Thor because he was born in Scandinavia somewhere. We're playing Monopoly at his parents' imported dining table when he gets tetchy over a dice roll. This surprises no one since Thor is among the more highly strung of us, though he's really losing it this time. When his hands dive beneath the board, its entire contents explode upwards, and in an instant the ceiling fan has gunned dozens of plastic houses around the room from their former smug London holdings, the board itself flapping off like a headless pterodactyl as banknotes rain down. For the next five minutes, we scout around to prise dice and houses from exotic new addresses, from a stuffed polar bear's gaping jaw to the pelt of an arctic fox. When I find Thor in his bedroom ten minutes later, he's absorbed in drawing finely detailed images in one of his many sketchbooks, mostly full of mythical dragon and warrior scenes. 'They need you back out for Twister,' I tell him, and he says he'll be out soon.

LAB RATS

In the 1969 Christmas break, I hang at the Valley Pool each weekday while Ashley's at his new job as a Government Housing field officer, listening to tenants' gripes in the hot sun with a clipboard under his arm. ('I've the common touch for that line of work,' he boasts.) And somehow he's convinced Gordon I should do a midday training session on top of my usual morning and afternoon ones. Luckily Nickname has joined me *as an experiment*. With his scientific pedigree, he's always up for one of those.

On day one of our new regime, Nickname assures me the Hungarian national team trialled something similar before the last Olympics. They apparently trained three sessions a day for three consecutive days, followed it with a three-day break, and sustained this cycle for three months before the Olympics. And — this is the part Nickname seems to like — each session lasted three hours. 'All those threes!' he gasps.

'Three hours a session, three times a day, for three months!' I groan. 'But why the three days off?'

'They were trialling a new stress-rotation concept called *super-recovery*.'

'But wouldn't they ... leak a bit of fitness in three days off?'

'It's touch and go, but four would definitely have been taking things too far.'

'And how did they go at the Olympics?' I think to ask.

'Pretty much the same,' he shrugs, 'but one trial can't tell you too much.'

'Great!' I huff.

Something else Nickname tells me after training is far more interesting than an unproven fitness theory based on a number fetish. He claims there's this edgy new scientific concept called *morphic resonance*, which says that when a critical population of a species learns a new behaviour, members elsewhere on the planet soon mysteriously share it. 'It's not exactly mainstream science,' he adds, 'but its proponent has pretty good credentials — he's this Cambridge Royal Fellow in Botany, Rupert Sheldrake.' If I've understood Nickname, the theory was a chance outcome of experiments testing for Lamarckian heritability: thousands of American lab rats were repeatedly swum to exhaustion through mazes in giant vats to see if they passed adaptations on to offspring.

'The Lamarckian part proved inconclusive,' Nickname sighs, 'but they found an almost simultaneous improvement in swimming abilities of overseas lab rats.'

I ask if this explosive finding is ever cited to explain the relentless global improvement of human swimmers in *our* vats. 'Not that I've heard,' is all his scientific mind can offer. (I often wonder if there's anything Nickname doesn't know. I imagine him wandering his dad's lab each evening with unfettered access to microfiche libraries of every science journal ever published.)

By the end of our first week, I'm suspecting Gordon's heart isn't in this three-sessions-a-day caper. Our lunchtime training lasts hardly an hour, and most of that time he's in and out of his office, barely throwing us a sideways glance. Then he might disappear into the pump room as he did yesterday, emerging twenty minutes later with an ancient motor wrapped in newspaper under his arm, wires dangling forwards like a catfish he's caught for dinner.

Between sessions today, Nickname and I wander up Wickham Street for some pretend shopping. Crossing the road between

McWhirters and TC Beirne's, we catch sight of that famous old greaser Rock 'n' Roll George cruising up Brunswick Street in his notorious beige FX Holden, wheel discs painted red like some petrol-head gusset fantasy. Coming down the TC Beirne's elevator to our right as we're heading up is one of the swim-club dads, Mr Kitchell, wearing a suit. He looks as surprised as we are to be recognised, before he suddenly puts on a stern detective's voice to call across, 'I'm afraid I'll have to check the contents of that bag, boys,' and we all explode in laughter because there is no bag and Mr Kitchell is no detective. Other days we just hang at the pool and chat with some lively Bowen Hills girls who've been turning up lately. I can't believe Nickname's dorky confidence; the girls keep cooing that he's a dead ringer for a famous folk singer I've never heard of, Arlo Guthrie.

I've been coming home tired and hungry from my triplicate holiday sessions, though this has nothing to do with my new habit of leaping out of bed at night and telling Ashley I'm going into the kitchen for a biscuit. He knows I'm lying, because he asks if everything's okay. That's when I reply evasively, *'Yep, yeah,'* while the truth is that I'm freaking out after randomly thinking about death, eternity, and infinity in bed. *How can things just go on and on without end?* I wonder. And what can scientists mean when they say the universe is expanding? (I thought whatever it expanded into was already the universe.) I hadn't been totally ignorant my life would one day be over, but I'd obviously been avoiding placing myself at the scene. Suddenly, at a certain point, the only option is to jump out of bed before my racing heart explodes. That's when I'll tell Ashley I'm starving, but instead go out and pace the kitchen lino for a minute before cowering back to bed with an Iced VoVo to validate my alibi. It's been happening too often for my liking, so I hope it's only a phase like the one Mum says Ashley went through early in their marriage. (He'd apparently sit bolt-upright in bed in the middle of the night and keep yelling, 'I'm dead, I'm dead,' until she convinced him otherwise.) 'But it was just after his widowed mother died,' she explained recently. He supposedly stopped the 'I'm dead, I'm dead' stuff by the time he learned his mother had bequeathed their Blue Mountains family home to his sister.

Some days even swimming can seem a little futile in the face of seeing out the front end of eternity dead. Gordon doesn't help with his usual bleak quip when we train badly — 'That's a pretty poor imitation of a fish today, kiddo' — which makes all human swimming seem a pointless homage to fish, a dumb phylum unchanged for millions of years. *How demeaning for we supposed exemplars of evolutionary advance!* Almost as offensive was my younger brother claiming last week that the main reason I succeed is because I try harder than the rest. Until that point in our spat, I'd been ahead in the sledging, but his 'trying harder' slur knocked me flat because I'd felt accused of cheating. From a coach, of course, this would have been high praise, but coming from family somehow made it different. Only later did I see how silly it was to be accused of trying harder, because I train in a pool full of equally desperate try-hards; and how many lanes of us are there in Australia? I should have asked exactly how hard we're all meant to be trying, and who was doing the measuring: I wanted to be seen winning fairly, not just because I'd clinically engineered it with harder training. Then, after some thought, I realised I wouldn't want to win purely on presumed talent either. *What would that prove but privilege?* Yes, there was still real glory in winning a tight contest, but not if that heroism could be traced back to inevitable causes. And then I felt a little confused because there suddenly seemed no perfect way to aspire, and I wondered if I'd fallen for some monstrous con to have become a sportsman in the first place. And now I suspect it's too late to change anyway, because the only alternative seems not to try, and that's a sorcery even Nickname steers clear of. Or maybe I could just try at the usual things that make a go of life — school and career. But that wouldn't impress Ashley. 'Half the world gets to pass an exam,' is the way he sees it. Besides, swimming's been in our family for centuries if you can believe him, so it's something we do, win or lose.

As if the week couldn't get any more whacky, today's *Weekend Australian* has this spiteful Murray Hedgcock opinion piece where he totally unloads on swimming, claiming the only stroke deserving to call itself a legitimate sport is freestyle. 'Butterfly,' he writes, 'resembles some undignified picnic sack race', and backstroke 'would only make sense as an egg and spoon contest'. By the time he's dumping on breaststroke, I've stopped reading in acute embarrassment. (But then, even Gordon's been known to crack the odd breaststroke joke. 'What's a medley relay?' he loves asking, before self-answering, 'Three swimmers and a breaststroker. *Boom-boom!*')

I feel like quitting for days after the Hedgcock rant, until it dawns on me that all sports are completely arbitrary challenges. I mean — who uses javelins or bows and arrows to catch dinner these days? Or hops, steps, and jumps to the office? And it's not as if anything real happens anyway. Even the so-called results are concocted news, the reportage value founded entirely on someone having once said 'let's race' or 'let's play', the outcomes a kind of embellished coin toss: dog-bites-man on one side, man-bites-dog on the other. 'So how's a coin toss news when it's designed specifically to create news?' I ask Nickname as we sun ourselves in the stands after another session.

But he seems almost not to listen, volleying deadpan, 'The only way to understand sport is as a play where the characters get to change the script: if a play's worth a review, sport's worth a write-up too.' I give this some thought and concede he has a great point. In fact, I can't help repeating *a play where you can change the script* over and over in my head, deciding it's the cleverest line ever spoken about sport. Suddenly sport's much more interesting than a dead play — as different as photos and movies. And now he says anyone wanting a meaningful justification is barking up the wrong tree anyway. 'Sport's all about the peacock feathers,' he quips. 'The human brain's pretty sophisticated, but there's still loads of Jurassic wiring hanging around for dumb stuff like showing off.' Nickname predicts there's at least another 100,000 years of 'reptilian display behaviour' to play out.

'Then what?' I ask.

'Eternal peace and happiness,' he laughs, and I laugh.

Seeing yourself as a peacock with a prefrontal cortex doesn't seem to bother the brightest boy I've ever known, but I'm still left uneasy. In fact, the more knowledgeable I become under his mentorship, the more fragile the world seems. Soon he's explaining how we never engage with the outside world anyway; all we know is our own sensory data. So now I'm just a processing automaton, interacting exclusively with myself via some drip-fed facsimile of reality, filtering just enough information to avoid walking off cliffs or being eaten by lions. How lonely this sounds! Not that it doesn't make perfect sense, but I was happier deluded the world I saw was really out there.

Seemingly as an afterthought, Nickname lets me in on a personal secret: that some other friend of his developed a weird illness after spending too much time on this line of thought. He apparently told his parents he was just some dumb, soggy machine, and everything he touched had this dead, rubbery feel, particularly himself. Then he started refusing to get out of bed and saying life was pointless and now he's in hospital. Suddenly I wonder if just knowing Nickname is a health hazard. *Maybe he's the one responsible for my leaping out of bed at night!* The only consolation is that despite all the soul-destroying stuff Nickname knows, he's still upbeat about his own second-rate existence.

A month later, the night panics disappear as abruptly as they started. Despite the obvious relief, I now find myself cautiously trying to think my way back into them, as if they're an insight I'm scared I'll never have again. Yet as hard as I try, I can no longer find the groove.

GRIZZLY VS LION

Ashley and I watch the Sunday-night news from adjacent beds in our cramped South Brisbane bedsit, itself sandwiched between the huge white loaves of the Greek *un*-Orthodox church (as we now call it) and the 'Belvedere' flats. We're a week into the new school year, and my 1970 Queensland titles start in a fortnight. Commonwealth Games selection trials are a month off in Sydney.

The buttery waft of a slow fry, our typical rice and diced-vegetable dinner, fills the room. Ashley's hands are clasped behind sixty-year-old salt-and-pepper hair pressed deep into two pillows. His right knee is drawn up, left ankle slung across, with calf muscle yolk-loose under scaly, puckered skin. Through the ad breaks, I've been doing my usual *bed gym*, this particular routine requiring me to reach up and push against the middle rail of the bedhead to bury myself into the mattress a hundred times: *triceps, traps, pecs, and deltoids*. Other times I pull myself up instead: *biceps, lats, teres major, rhomboids*.

'Best car, Dad?' I ask, to break our usual silence.

'Rolls-Royce, of course.'

'Best camera?'

'Rolleiflex. Remember ours?'

'Best watch?'

'Rolex.'

'Why do so many luxury brands begin with *Roll*?'

'Dunno. Maybe the marketing people think it rolls better off the tongue.'

Ashley's Rolex is in the top dresser drawer, under our socks, sitting on old yellowed newsprint covering Harold Holt's disappearance. The particular model is an 'Oyster Perpetual Datejust', though it clammed up itself after a decade of Singapore sweat and steam supposedly entered the seals. And though it's now nothing more than a timeless sculpture barely glimpsed as we fish for socks, I'm more in awe than ever. One day I'll have a Rolex on my wrist.

'Best singer?'

'Cliff Richard. *No. Make that Roy Orbison* — he's had a lot of tragedy in his life.'

Changing the subject slightly, I ask, 'What wins between grizzly and lion?'

'That's a close one. Cashed-up miners pitted them in the California gold fields when they had nothing better to do than ship the odd lion over.'

'*Really?* Leopard and gorilla?'

'Leopard, if the gorilla can't quickly break its back.'

'Doberman and Alsatian?'

'It's the fight in the dog, not the dog in the fight.'

Next day I'm hoping Nickname's dad will have all the facts — not just opinions — on animal winners. It'll help that he's a scientist, though his lab specialty is only in the micro-predation of free radicals on cell membranes. In their car on the way to training, I ask, 'Leopard or gorilla, who wins, Mr Nickname?'

He darts me a raised eyebrow in the rear-vision mirror. 'I doubt they'd meet. Are we talking highland or lowland gorilla?'

'The one closer to leopards,' I volley, tempted to exclaim, *Duh!*

'I don't think either would risk injury,' he drones. 'They might give each other a wide berth.'

'Grizzly and lion?' I persist, adding for his benefit: 'Apparently the miners fought them in the Californian gold rush.'

'Never heard that one.'

For a biologist, Mr Nickname's apathy about inter-species conflict is nothing short of scandalous, though I could never hold it against him, because his is the most relaxed and friendly face of all the swim-club dads. In fact, he could easily double for the sleepily charming *Skippy* dad, the actor Ed Devereaux; it's just too bad about animal champions. Maybe I'll have to ask our landlord, Mr Cowley. Landlords might be more in tune with the law of the jungle.

My father calls Mr Cowley a devout Catholic, while we apparently call ourselves Calithumpians (is this is an *Ashley joke* about some creed of thumping people, or a real religion?). Originally from Lismore, Mr Cowley lives in the big front unit with his wife and two little boys, and looks far too young to own a block of flats. In the driveway on Sunday morning when he's off to church in his squire's hat and I'm off to swim club, he and my father chat. Mr Cowley seems willing to talk for as long as required, even as he squirms and tugs at his collar and tie in the midmorning sun with the smile of a boy trying to grin his way out of trouble. When I ask how much he earns from the flats, to see if it beats Ashley's wage, both men are suddenly tongue-tied until Ashley quips, 'That's entirely between Mr Cowley and his accountant,' after which Mr Cowley protests that he doesn't mind one bit. But a minute later when we're waving goodbye, I realise he still hasn't let on.

Without fail these days, whenever my father talks about him, it's 'nice Mr Cowley' this, and 'nice Mr Cowley' that. I've never heard him call any god-botherer 'nice Mr *Anything*' before, even a top-notch edition like my Uncle Martyn, who almost became a priest after years as a brother in some religious order yet who has recently, according to my mother, 'finally put all that behind him'. He now appears in toothpaste and beer ads on TV, does a midnight-to-dawn DJ shift on commercial radio, writes love poems he hand-delivers in pink envelopes to new girlfriends, lifts heavy weights daily, is halfway through a sociology degree, and is at this very moment cooling his heels at Mum's place after supposedly 'breaking a Yugoslav's jaw' in a Sydney road-rage incident. He also has one of those winning, lopsided actor's smiles, and currently gets around with his balding head looking like it's been wearing an octopus, its strips of raw, fleshy plugs courtesy of pioneering follicle grafts to reverse male-pattern baldness.

So special is Mr Cowley these days that if I wake early on Sundays, Ashley has me under strict orders of silence, as if all the Cowleys are deep in warm-up sacraments for mass. And neither do I ever seem able to pin him down about animal winners, though he at least has a feisty little Fox Terrier, which, on this rent day, has again darted into our kitchen to clasp its legs around my shin to deposit its usual filthy dollop of smegma. 'His calling card,' my father chirps, and we all laugh to see the dog tear back into the dark hallway.

Mr Cowley and Uncle Martyn are as close as we ever come to discussing religion, if you don't count Ashley's jokey opinion on who gets to heaven and who doesn't. 'Even priests and the pious get there eventually,' he says, 'but the idiot will never be let in.' Whenever he says *the idiot* (which he pronounces *eejit*), he means the French mathematician and theologian Blaise Pascal, whose famous proposition 'Pascal's Wager' advises believing in God in case he turns out to be real.

'As if an all-seeing creator won't spot that scam coming through the gates,' Ashley scoffs. 'A billion heathens will be let in before the eejit,' he roars, as if the smart each-way money's on atheism.

We discuss history even less often. When I ask about Australian history, with a school essay due at the end of the month, Ashley says he knows 'the long and short of it', but insists I'll have to decide between those two versions to hear any. When I choose *the short*, he quips, 'Guns beat spears.'

'Is the long much longer?' I ask.

'Significantly,' he says, but recites it anyway: '*And then there were shops.*'

Other times he'll just say, 'Nothing's happened since the Romans.' As pithy and funny as I find these accounts, I'll be padding my essay with the usual stuff on settlement, Federation, prime ministers, and the economy. And of course the wars, which Ashley won't talk about anyway, even though he served in New Guinea on cipher breaking, and his father was gassed in France.

On Wednesday when our essays on a more contemporary topic, 'The Generation Gap', are handed back by our English teacher, I'm stunned when she singles mine out with special praise for being the only one to have taken an impartial position. This is embarrassing enough, but it seems she's going to — *oh no* — she's actually reading from it: '*Whether the phenomenon is global, or restricted to the west, is unclear. It is not known, for instance, if there is such a thing as The Generation Gap in Communist China. Perhaps a Confucian respect for parents prevents such attitudes taking hold, and it is unlikely that pop music and its irreverent influences have reached there. But with so little information coming out of Mao's China, we can't be sure.*'

Labouring her point to the class, she scoffs, 'With the exception of Brad, everyone used the essay to take a cheap shot at your parents.' Now almost terminally self-conscious about my sudden star status — star betrayer, that is — I wonder why I'm the odd one out, the odd, happy, gap-less one. Is it because Ashley's old enough to be my grandfather, so he doesn't count? Or perhaps my generation gap is with my mother, whom I'd forgotten to even consider. Neither do I understand the teacher's harsh tone with my classmates, whose gritty despatches from the front lines of the conflict seem worthy enough.

When those Queensland championships eventually roll around, I'm well on the way to an anticipated handful of wins on my first night, the first two in quick succession. Nickname's third place in one of my finals narrowly guarantees him qualification for Nationals — at least as one of the *paying* entrants — so I'm hoping he'll be in Sydney with me for the Commonwealth Games Trials. On the second night, Ashley's trialling a new mail-order cushion purchased specially for his piles, its forgiving doughnut shape mercifully muted within a busy floral sleeve; you'd need to gawk pretty hard to see the haemorrhoid connection.

In the stands nearby is the young firebrand Townsville coach Laurie Lawrence. He's been running and skipping along the bottom rail all night to wave a battered program at his swimmers in angry gusts of encouragement, two fingers of the other hand shoved in his mouth for ear-piercing whistles. Between races he sees me and rushes over to tell Ashley he's a big fan of my backstroke; he loves the way my head swings from side to side. 'It's like he's pumping his shoulders with all that head movement,' he gushes in big, friendly, outback vowels. Neither Ashley nor I respond to this, while Laurie keeps his excited expression in my face until distracted by his assistant coach.

When Nickname finds us, he nods discreetly in Laurie's direction and whispers, 'I see you've found *Manny*' — this is the moniker Laurie was given in our training lane's contest to think up jokey code names for various coaches. Most of them got saddled with notorious historical figures, but with Laurie we went for alliteration to mimic his name: Laurie Lawrence, meet Manny Manson.

Half an hour later, Nickname's back with news that *Manny* threw a swimmer's silver medal over the pool fence onto the train tracks. 'I saw it happen!' he gasps. 'The girl was showing it to him after her race and he just went bananas, saying silver isn't good enough if she expects to make the Edinburgh Games team at next month's trials. Then he just turfed it over the fence.'

The girl is Helen Gray, a Townsville distance swimmer. Neither Ashley nor I can quite believe all this until we see the jerky skating of torchlight ovals along the sleepers, maroon-coated officials dimly attached, and someone like Manny checking the ballast. Over the next twenty-four hours, Laurie's medal-chuck is big news, his poolside detractors and defenders equally strident.

After my successful state titles campaign, I'm back into my normal morning bedsit routine, preparing for school. Ashley left for work half an hour ago, and now it's my usual time to check on the lady next door in her ground-floor bedroom of the 'Belvedere', a white suburb-grade tissue-box of rooms with Tudor trim, overlooked by our bedsit. Once or twice weekly around this time, she crouches below a large open window in her short tunic to reach forwards beneath a double bed in a dextrous display of spring cleaning. Under and back, under ... and ... back, in long slow stretches with the dustpan. It's usually a great show for that minute or so, but evidently not today. Now, with a guilty shudder, I hear a knock on our door. Who could it be but Mr Cowley, possibly — hopefully — just looking for my father? I open it, but the hallway's empty. *Did I imagine this?* I have tinnitus, but that's never knocking, merely *ringing* in the ears ('Never pick up!' Ashley cautions). A minute later, I'm combing my hair in the dresser mirror when there's another rap. I walk over, open up, and again no one. On impulse I stroll a lap of the hallway in an eerie goosebump inspection, pausing briefly at the three doors on the other side and two on ours, unsure exactly what to check for, or even which senses to use. Soon I'm back waiting at our kitchen table with a glass of milk, in the unlikely event of a third knock. When it comes, I slam the glass down and fly across the lino, but all I see when I open the door is a wing of bouncy curls almost guillotined by a slamming door in the full glare of the street end of the hall. *Aha!* I suddenly realise: *the church girl* who lives with the single mother the Cowleys have recently taken under their wing. She must be in there alone with nothing better to do than play knock-and-run games on my door. I have to leave for school now, but if she tries it another day when I have more time, I might just walk down and knock on *her* door until she answers. I've no idea what would happen then. Not that I'm at all interested, because there are other girls I know who don't have to play those games, and whose parents never have to be taken under someone's wing. And there's something odd about a girl my age who rarely goes to school.

I'm glad we're at swimming club Sunday mornings because I'd hate to be home when Ray Stevens' sad song 'Sunday Morning Coming Down' is on the radio. It reminds me too much of the alcos sleeping it off in Musgrave Park across the road, and all the dead local streets. Fortunately we're not home from club till around one, when Sunday morning's well and truly gone down and we're settling on our beds to read the papers or watch *Daniel Boone* and *Uptight* on TV. They can play it all they like then, and it's actually not such a bad tune, though it's got nothing on Perry Como's 'The Bluest Skies You've Ever Seen Are in Seattle'. Ashley calls Como 'an old crooner', whatever that is.

In the evening, when there's an old clip of the Mamas and the Papas singing 'Creeque Alley' on *The Ed Sullivan Show*, Ashley barks, 'Look carefully, because you might just see the exact point in history when beatniks became hippies, right there in John Phillips' big silly fur hat; the very moment beatniks shaved off their goatees and grew long hair, swapped their turtlenecks for tie-dye, daddy-os for groovy, and bongo drums for love-ins. Except that beatniks read books.'

And then there's this Jose Feliciano character. How's a blind Puerto Rican with an acoustic guitar fit in to all this psychedelic mayhem? His 'Light My Fire' hit certainly brings something new to the Doors' version, though all those pitch acrobatics stretch the melody too far out of shape for my liking. Jim Morrison's version is tighter, darker, scarier, and suits the times.

GOOD NEWS

It's late March 1970, I'm fifteen-and-a-half, and these are my first Australian open championships, at Sydney's Drummoyne pool; actually, my first Australian championships of any kind, since I wasn't old enough for last year's Juniors. This year, of course, they double as Commonwealth Games Trials. Shane, Talkback, and Nickname are also here with Gordon's other top swimmers, and we're having fun being carted around in big Valiant hire cars in our new Queensland tracksuits in crisp Sydney weather.

This morning Nickname and I are first to arrive at a daily briefing in the room of one of our drivers, in this case a coach nicknamed MS. Since it's anybody's guess what those letters stand for — they're not his initials — my stab is *monster set*, because he's reputed to have dished out the longest training set known to swimmingdom, at least the Queensland version of it: forty times 100 metres freestyle, leaving on 1 minute 20 seconds. Pausing conspicuously at MS's half-open Travelodge room door, we find him sprawled on his back on his bed, and on the phone, a chicken wing waving over the mouthpiece like a baton in his free hand. Without acknowledging us, he tilts the wing at a few plastic chairs for our benefit while continuing his conversation, evidently with a fellow coach: 'Yeah, this new ten-year-old I've got can already do his 50s on the 45,' he informs the other end. 'No-no, that's the medley kid,' he spits back. '*He's* been eating 400-metre medleys for breakfast since he was eight.' Now Nickname nudges me and whispers, 'What about the six-year-old who finishes training and freestyles out across the car park to his mother's waiting car.' To which I add, 'And the foetus doing its hundred laps of the uterus every morning.' We're both sniggering when MS frowns our way and hangs up, as more swimmers file in. The wing, now sucked to the bone, is dropped into a waste-paper bin before MS licks his fingers and stands to organise today's car pool.

On the first night of the championships, I can hardly believe I'm leading my 100-metre open backstroke final down the first lap. *This is me, the best in Australia,* I tell myself the moment I'm sure of it. But after I glance over my shoulder to judge the turn, my world goes black. When I'm certain all my body parts are still in motion, I realise I haven't experienced some sort of mental blackout — not a total one, anyway — and do my best to turn where the wall *should* be, but miss it altogether. I stretch my toes in case I'm a millimetre off, but still no wall, so I swim off from a dead start and try to find top gear as quickly as possible. My slight lead is now a metre deficit to the new leader, Neil Rogers, and I'm still wondering what happened back there in the black. I try my hardest to swim him down in the last 25 metres, only to be beaten to the wall by two tenths of a second. I'm disqualified, of course, for not touching at the turn, and soon learn that my puzzling 'blackout' came from a bag of black dye tossed into the pool by anti-apartheid demonstrators protesting the selection of a small team to tour South Africa next month, the dye a symbolic gesture. I'm reassured by Queensland officials that selectors will take the dye bomb into account when they pick the Games team, so it's fingers crossed.

Shane's been talked up in the papers, but her best effort so far is to make the odd final. She's *having a quiet carnival* as they say, but at thirteen she's years younger than any other finalist. As a swimmer lucky even to qualify, Nickname never anticipated getting past the heats and he's been on the money every time. Talkback was an outside chance to make the odd final with slight improvement, but, like the vast majority of qualifiers, she'll go home without that honour; and she's been oddly distracted the whole time, so that can't have helped.

I'm shocked to discover Ashley here at Nationals; there was never any talk of him coming down. I was playing poker on the mezzanine deck yesterday, slouched in a mess of mats and sleeping bags with my head down, when he walked by. By the time I convinced myself it was really him, he'd started down the stairs, and because I was sweating on a picture card I let him go. Then I felt guilty and avoided him the rest of the day, leaving me even guiltier today. So, naturally, I've been dodging him like the plague ever since. But that's not hard, because his eyesight isn't too flash these days.

A few of us are watching TV in my motel room after our fourth night of finals when there's a rattle on the flyscreen door. It's Laurie Lawrence, or, as Nickname whispers, 'Uh-oh, Manny Manson.' I let him in, and, typically, he's soon bouncing around and telling us we're all swimming *fan-tastic*, and flattering the girls. 'Youse girls scrub up great,' he cranks in that fierce nasal Strine. (*Scrub up*, I wonder, *in tracksuits?* But why isn't he with his own swimmers? He has five down here.) There's a guitar strapped over his shoulder, so it looks like we're in for a song or two.

I'd always heard of national championships doubling as trade fairs for coaches who turned up at dorms to invite swimmers to come and train in their 'part of the world' ('The Coorong? *Sure, I'm there every other school break!*'). It made sense though, because years of frustration coaching hapless juniors could be redeemed with one fortuitous burst of killer charm on a ready-made champion. But Laurie himself seems a cut above such oafish overtures when he arranges himself on the lounge to tune his guitar.

Nickname and I exchange a sly grimace because Laurie barely knows any of us, and now we're expected to drop everything to listen to *Laurie the troubadour*. And we do so without protest because he's a coach and we're only swimmers, even though we're not his swimmers. I just hope he won't take too long. After a few Bob Dylan numbers which he absolutely murders while forcing a cloying eye contact on at least one of us through each verse, he leaps to his feet and clownishly demands to know what sort of hosts we are, not to offer him even a coffee. Nickname and I volunteer like rockets, and as soon as we're in the kitchen fall about in vomiting theatrics. But when we return with the coffees, he's gone. 'He thought you were taking too long,' Shane informs us, 'and he had some swimmers to check on.'

'Yeah, his own for a change,' I laugh.

'What an ordeal,' Nickname groans in the girls' direction, before Talkback leaps to Laurie's defence.

'I thought it was … *kind of cute*,' she says, and when I shoot Nickname a despairing glance, he salutes the door to bark, 'Mission accomplished, Manny.'

After morning heats the following day, I return to the motel to find Nickname in his room reading the Bible. It's no musty Gideon exhumed from a motel bedside drawer, but one he's brought down with him, and titled, worryingly, 'Good News for Modern Man'. Possibly sensing my disdain ('Is that a friggin' Bible you're reading?'), he insists it's not the stuffy old King James version, but a special new edition in modern idiom. I can also see it's full of cartoon line drawings, most likely a pitch for the comics market. Still finding it cringe-worthy that someone so smart could stoop to Bible reading, I give him the only benefit of the doubt to offer a shred of dignity: that he's swotting for quotes to impress Talkback and Shane, whose families are known to be churchy. But surely no one's that cynical, even under the spell of hormones!

'You should have a read, Brad!' he urges shamelessly. 'You don't have to swallow all that resurrection and trinity stuff, or even believe in God.' Nickname says he reads the Bible purely for its *beautiful parables*. 'It's like any other literature, and as much a part of the western canon as Shakespeare.'

Although Nickname's selective engagement with the Gospels seems on the same curve as going Mormon for the polygamy, I open the Bible to keep him happy, and can't believe my luck when I'm struck by a thunderbolt within a few random page turns. 'Hey, Nickname,' I call out. When his head pops around the servery, I tell him Manny Manson even barges into rooms in the Bible.

'What are you on about?' he snorts, approaching cagily as I prepare Manny's entry for perusal.

'It's true,' I insist, tapping at the particular verse in John. 'Right here!'

Nickname scans the verse to read haltingly, 'In my father's house ... are ... *Manny Mansons*,' and breaks into hysterics. 'Good one, Brad,' he roars, repeating the line before whining, 'And good grief, there's more than one of him!'

In midafternoon Talkback wanders in to join Nickname and me watching TV, settling surprisingly close to me on the lounge. When our bare thighs press firmly together and stay glued for minutes, it's like two entire telephone exchanges have been hooked up. Whatever garbled words proposed this, we're now on someone's bed and all she has left on her venetian-shadowed curves is a bikini. We've carelessly left the door open, and Nickname occasionally wanders across the lounge room, but we don't care. And now we're kissing. I've heard of this pashing business before: Nickname and Talkback supposedly once set a kissing record, huddling for an entire hour in a wardrobe at one of their parents' dinner parties. It really is the most intimate thrill, though Talkback's efforts are definitely on the sloppy side. And now, she too finds fault with the technicalities of snogging when she squirms, pulls away, and, in a surprisingly tetchy tone, insists on another attempt. *What's there to lose?* I'm thinking, even as her renewed efforts bring more lip chaos. Not only this, but her tongue has now shockingly breached *my* pucker to take up residence within my mouth, where it frantically explores its unfamiliar back-to-front surroundings. Of course — and to my eternal embarrassment — I suddenly grasp that this is real kissing, and it's disgracefully crude and exciting. When Nickname pauses at the door, he says, 'I think that's our driver about to leave without us,' and barely a minute later we three are in the back of another Valiant gliding to the finals.

When the Games team is announced, neither Shane nor I are mentioned. This doesn't bother me, because we were only ever long shots, and I've come away rated Australia's number-two backstroker, at least for black-dye races. With continued improvement, I'm a shoo-in for the next team. Among the few non-Sydney selections is Helen Gray, the girl Laurie Lawrence predicted wouldn't be good enough to make the team. But that was *before* her medal hit the tracks at the Queensland titles, and now I have to wonder if that stunt was a stroke of coaching genius.

In the days after I return to our 'digs', as Ashley calls our Edmondstone Street bedsit, he asks if I've given any thought to training in Sydney. 'It's obvious now,' he begins solemnly, 'Sydney's where the best training is.' By Sydney, he means Don Talbot or Forbes Carlile; in my case, Talbot.

'There'll be no more taking winters off down there,' he chirps, before reeling off familiar Brisbane names already in Sydney or moving soon, including Shane and Talkback with their families. Shockingly the list includes most of Gordon's top lane. 'I wouldn't go with you, of course,' he adds. 'We'd have to find you a family to board with.' Soon I find myself in total agreement, and it's such a big move that I can't see the point of mulling over what else it entails. It now enters my head that this is what he'd been up to in Sydney — sounding out coaches and interviewing potential billets, for me to train under Talbot. (Did my avoiding him help make up his mind?) Soon Graham Windeatt makes an unexpected appearance in my dreams, weirdly taking the form of two boys.

My very next thought about my Sydney future is when I'm actually in it, one surprisingly mild April evening a month later when our Torana slows outside a block of blood-red brick units in Maroubra. Ashley jerks the handbrake and pulls an address from the glove box before stating the obvious: 'This is it.' Somewhere in that four-storey cube, behind its curtain-muted flashings of quiz shows, is my new home. About the only Brisbane swimmer I *won't* see down here is Nickname. After his pathetic Nationals performance, he said his moving down 'would be overcapitalising'.

When the father of my new host family greets us, he takes my butterfly barbells from me the moment I've pulled them from the boot. Now he's cramming them in a back corner of a dark little garage under all the units, slamming its tilting door down as if a dog's been dropped off at the pound, and I have a sense I'll never use them again.

BODY PARTS

'Coaches work better without body parts,' Ashley quips when I mention the shark-bite-sized scar above my new coach Don Talbot's right hip where a rank kidney was once plucked in a hurry. It's our first chat since he drove me down six months ago — trunk calls aren't cheap — but I urgently need him to settle a passport hitch before I can be considered for coming representative tours.

I knew nothing of Talbot's missing kidney until I asked his son Jon why two crates of soda water turn up on their back step every Tuesday. 'He drinks nothing but tap or soda water,' Jon said from his bunk, crouched with a flick-knife to trim proud tinea flesh between his toes. 'It's better for his kidney.'

'Don't you mean kidneys, plural?' I corrected.

'No,' Jon replied, 'check his scar next time his shirt's off.' (That's easy because the shirt's started coming off at training, now summer's almost here.)

Never one to be outdone, Ashley asks if I'm aware Laurie Lawrence has only one lung.

'No way!' I exclaim. 'What's Gordon missing?' I shoot back, hoping he measures up.

'His curse is to have all organs intact, if you don't count the charm bypass.'

'Forbes Carlile?'

'He only has one ... *head* — Bye,' he laughs on the time pips, hanging up.

When swimmers address Talbot, we're meant to call him *coach*, except that I can't; it has this fake American ring and after all this time I'm yet to utter it. (I don't even call my dad *Dad* half the time, so I'm not starting with this *coach* business now.) Yet his swimmers use it every day and seem to like it, even those who tower over him and whack hardest in the change rooms when we boys take turns to *run the gauntlet* through a tunnel of thumping arms and lashing legs after training. This is at Talbot's heated Hurstville winter pool, aka *Hurts*-ville, where the ceiling's lined in a thick, grey layer of asbestos fibre with dents and gouges because kids with a death wish have frisbeed thongs up, and where we're supplied with salt tablets because the water's kept at a bath-like thirty-three degrees for babies' classes. A sign high on the wall at one end says, '*A winner never quits and a quitter never wins.*' At the opposite end, its evil twin posits, '*A diamond is only a piece of coal that stuck with it.*' When Talbot switches on the fluorescent lights at five a.m., you can't see the other side for the mist. Then he makes a coffee from the plastic espresso bar in the foyer, drinks half, then, probably remembering his kidney, flicks the rest into the pool, where I watch its beige clouds hang about for ages. So many bodies churn up and down these shallow lanes that once we're wedged in file there's no speeding up or slowing down: it's a caterpillar chain circling itself for kilometres with only the briefest breaks. Sometimes we wear huge masonite paddles; their edges will soften but there's always the odd new set passing the other way to nick your exposed fingers, and when those cuts heal they're like extra knuckle creases.

I've been with the Talbots a month, after my first Sydney boarding stint ended badly. *They* lived three floors up on a patch of cement an Olympic runner could flash across in a second neat, housing seven of us in three tiny bedrooms in a kind of double-bunk bedlam. God knows why they thought they could take a boarder: generous, of course, but doomed. Their only swimmer, Rupert, was my age and trained with Talbot. I suspect he'd lost heart after falling well off the pace last season, so perhaps his parents thought rooming with someone on the up, like me, would breathe life into his tired gills — he'd been quite the super-fish in his young days. Maybe he was too small, anyway — five foot nine compared to my six foot. (As Gordon always said, 'Shorter swimmer, longer pool!')

Space was also a problem in the outside world — too much of it. Even without traffic, Talbot's pools were a thirty-minute hike across town. Catching most red lights as he carted us through empty pre-dawn Sydney, Rupert's poor dad was forever impatiently reversing over embedded signal strips to trip them green again. His balding pate was rarely sighted from behind, but on every red light his left arm hooked fiercely over the seat back and those black-rimmed glasses exploded above his shoulder on a face contorted with frustration as he gunned us backwards.

There was no sign of trouble for a month or so. 'Just tell us if there's anything you want,' Rupert's mum parroted through the first week. *I just want out of this 24/7 living in each other's pockets*, I thought-bubbled deafeningly in reply. And ominously, even the songs were disappointing: 'Airport Love Theme', 'Yellow River', 'My Little Green Bag' — each in its own musically mutant way. ('El Condor Pasa' was passably pretty.) And there was one song I didn't know whether I loathed or loved. Always on the radio on our way to morning training, 'My Baby Loves Lovin'' seemed all chorus, and so catchy it might have been stamped out by a machine to perfectly mock the sense of bleak enterprise I felt I'd sentenced myself to in that cross-town stupor. (What kept it from being pure bubble-gum was a slow refrain in the middle with a tiny sigh of soul.) A month later, when a stinging sensation turned up in my right side after every porridge breakfast, I hoped it wasn't the start of an ulcer like the one that sometimes gnawed at Ashley.

It wasn't that I couldn't admire the way this family strived. Each parent held down two jobs — few dinners saw both at home — and the kids were strapped so tight into a school-and-study juggernaut that, barring derailment, it couldn't fail them. Yet none of this diligence could make them see that you couldn't be a straight-A student *and* a swimmer, or that Rupert's decline in the pool was terminal. They had the drive of migrants and few callers to distract them: at least none came in my normal hours there. (In this at least, it was a seamless transition from my Ashley days, except that we'd lacked even a phone for people not to ring.) And despite being high off the ground, the atmosphere was subterranean, ant-like.

Unlike them, I'd given up on school: this was my fifth interstate syllabus shock. In my first week at Hardwick High, I wasn't even sure I was attending the right class. The school obviously received its fair quota of daylight, but my memories now seem framed in a gloomy cloud; I sat alone every lunch hour for three months. (I'd mistakenly presumed friendship on my first day when a classmate assigned to explain our compulsory school diary guffawed at my first entry under the index heading 'Contact in case of accident', where I'd chosen to scrawl *ambulance*.) The school highlights at this point were a visit by the almost-centenarian former premier Jack Lang, and everyone getting fingerprinted.

It was the first school where I actually embraced this level of popularity, and only once was I threatened with meaningful interaction. Sitting against a chalky demountable at lunch, I'd bitten into a sandwich when jarred by a loud bang barely a metre from my head, as a cricket ball ricocheted from cladding to bitumen. Only when it hit the ground in a bounceless grainy lump did I find it was a chunk of sandstone and not an unlikely six from the sports oval. After I glanced up to see a nearby gang of Greek boys laughing, one peeled off with a kind of power waddle in my direction before settling beside me, his face an impish and pasty duplicate of the Munsters' grandad. Planting a foot heavily on the next bench, he rolled his sock down to expose a hairy calf with a waxy pallor. 'See my calves?' he asked without the scorn of his recent collective mirth. 'My ancestors the Spartans marched to battle on these.' There was no reply to guarantee his marching back to his current phalanx, so I said nothing, though relieved his ominous approach had ended in such an infantile boast; I almost liked him now. His raw ancestral pride even had me about to share similar tidings, since I too boasted anatomy passed down from heroic times: my great-grandfather had been swimming champion — *grand champion* was Ashley's term — of the British fleet in the days of sail. Then I hesitated, unsure it would measure up to the Classical sensibility of my new brother in myth. I was spared that trouble when he suddenly stretched the sock back over his calf, fastidiously levelled it, and waddled back to his gang, who eyed me menacingly before drifting off.

Rupert's parents' attitude towards me soured terminally when his swimming showed no sign of improvement, his acne enjoyed a bumper season, and I showed no sign of tackling homework. His mother kept her head wrapped day and night in a tight pink scarf, rollers bulging beneath like smuggled munitions, and she never wore anything dressier than a faded shift. Add gumboots and shovel, and, in my unkinder moments, I could see her in a Soviet tractor poster; she wasn't one for airs and graces. (In all that time, I saw her hair out of the scarf only a few times, and was startled each time by how full and wavy it was.)

One day Rupert's mum opened our bedroom door — she rarely knocked — and shook a new pair of speedos at Rupert before tossing them across with a stiff, 'Try them on.' Now she might have put herself in reverse and shut the door, but she wasn't going anywhere. With Rupert's shorts and undies suddenly around his ankles, my disbelieving gaze zeroed in on his sweaty post-school tackle for confirmation. And now I suspected the tiniest effort to avert my eyes might bring *me* unwanted attention, as Rupert's free-hanging school shirt alternately displayed and curtained everything through his fumbling, adding burlesque to bollocks. *Is this okay*, I wondered, *for mothers to see their fifteen-year-old in the altogether?* I was a bit rusty on this sort of entitlement because I hadn't lived with my mum since I was eleven. (*For all I know, this could go on for life*, I pondered — and maybe she just hadn't thought things through before entering, expecting to find just Rupert in there.) This was *their* business, of course, but there was also my present situation — of being within a metre or so of both a grown woman and youthful manhood. If there was an algebraic indecency going on, I was unsure of the equation. When I could no longer resist turning to Rupert's mother, her pupils were still lasered on her son, now trudging dutifully through the speedo leg holes. After he tied the drawstring, the togs were mutually deemed 'on the small side' and would need exchanging, which seemed an oddly precious concern under the circumstances. When he handed them back, his mother left and closed the door as if privacy mattered.

The crunch came at the dinner table. Rupert's younger brother had never liked me, and I couldn't blame him. I'd been given his bunk with Rupert, forcing him to room with teenage sisters (was this a twelve-year-old boy's version of hell?). We were seated opposite when he began kicking my shins under the table: just casual, swinging pot-shots. I took these with good grace until he found his range and let go a hard one. When I growled, 'Don't!', his parents glowered in my direction, though I was confident they'd tell him to stop because blind Freddy could have seen that he'd slid down his chair for reach, his shoulders still dancing in counterbalance. But when they said nothing, the boy smiled like a Cheshire cat.

After another direct hit, I croaked, '*Fuck off*', and now I'm with the Talbots, and Rupert no longer swims.

The day I collected my things, Talbot said I should offer an apology to Rupert's dad. But there was no way he deserved one after sitting back while I became the family pinata, so I merely told him Talbot said I had to apologise. 'It's not a case of having to,' he volleyed testily.

'Okay, fine,' I replied, facetiously taking his counsel for a pardon: he didn't *have* to tell his son to stop kicking me either, and he hadn't, so now we were even. I walked out as bitter as on the night in question, biting my lip so as not to let go another serve.

By the next day, I knew I'd been in the wrong to swear, and felt terrible. *How did I manage to start the victim and come out the villain?* I kept pondering. Here I was, a thousand kilometres from home and taking a big punt in life, and some little so-and-so was allowed to get one of his first big thrills by kicking and baiting a genuine trier, like a hunting pup being blooded on tethered game. At least, this was how I'd felt. I should have calmly told his parents, 'If you won't tell your son to stop kicking me, I'll ask for somewhere else to stay.' And then it would have been them doing the explaining! *How easily the world turns on the right response*, I marvelled, particularly if you're not in your own home. *And if that's the way the world works*, I told myself, *I'll come out on top next time.*

A few days later, I realised I'd left my barbells behind. But I'd never gone down to their tiny garage to exercise anyway, so I left them as a sacrifice, too proud to waste another word on them.

PLANES, TRAINING, AND AUTOMOBILES

Too many cars could never be enough for Talbot. Most Saturday nights he crams us into the Kombi to cruise Parramatta Road car yards, pulling up here and there for us to spill out and ogle new models. As a young man (according to Jon) he hung with a petrol-head crew thrashing hotted-up Holdens and reworked Porsches on deserted Western Sydney speedways.

A friend of Talbot's with a dealership has loaned him a new prototype micro-car to test-drive. The motor's so small that Talbot dubbed it a lawn-mower on steroids, but that doesn't stop him red-lining it all the way home from the pool this morning with swimmers pressed against every window.

On the first day of the 1970–71 school holidays, Jon shows me a letter he's just received from Laurie Lawrence, inviting him to train in Townsville for a week. It's full of cheesy 'channelled' taunts from some of Jon's elite backstroke rivals, the first from a national champion in Jon's age, the Carlile swimmer Rob Williams. Laurie calls Williams 'Rob the Wriggler' for his famously jerky backstroke. *'Hi Jon, it's Rob-The-Wriggler here, and I'm going to smash you right out of the pool again this summer,'* is Williams' cheerio to Jon, via Laurie's handwriting. I can only assume this lively invitation comes with Talbot's blessing, since both coaches surely know each other. In fact, I'm now thinking that the whole thing has to be Talbot's idea, since coaching your own must be tricky, and no coach's kids become champions. Besides, Jon seems to have lost interest lately, and a change of scenery might gee him up.

I think nothing more of Laurie's letter, even on Sunday morning when Talbot asks several times, with increasing testiness, if I've seen Jon. Then I overhear, if not the exact words, the jarring notes of a succession of interrogative phone calls. By midafternoon Talbot's back on the blower, when his grilling tone fades to the tedium of airline bookings. I'm only now beginning to suspect Jon took up Laurie's offer, because I've just noticed his guitar missing from its corner resting place. But the idea's so unlikely, I'm still doubtful. As I walk down the driveway for school on Tuesday morning, Talbot squeals past in his Beamer, and when he returns in the evening, Jon's with him. In our room after dinner I'm nonplussed when Jon makes no mention of his shock disappearance or parents' concern, but instead blithely raves about his several training sessions in Townsville and private guitar sessions with Laurie. (I'm desperate to know what happened when his father turned up at Laurie's pool, but don't want to rub his nose in it — just yet!) Now Jon's head jerks back with a snort even a pig wouldn't own up to, when he recalls the Townsville swimmers' many colourful *deep north* sayings, particularly one describing a rowdy, unpopular swimmer as *uglier than a hat full of arseholes*. 'A hat full — of arseholes!' he cackles. 'How exactly do arseholes get in a hat anyway? And who makes up lines like that?' Suddenly there's new colour pumping through his recently pasty cheeks as he gags and sniffs on high-octane hilarity. He can't stop laughing. 'Fucken Laurie. He's crazy. They're all crazy up there.'

Once school's in full swing in the new year, the annual Combined High Schools state championships loom. School events normally don't rate on the swim calendar, because they're basically exhibition swims, and we never sharpen up for them; some timekeepers are just students. But the squad buzz says Windeatt's training well enough for a crack at the world 800-metre record, and in the lead-up week he and Talbot are seen in huddled discussion. Although the 800-metre is rated a 'trainer wheels' record because it's not an Olympic event, any world mark will do for a young swimmer on the rise. Soon the papers get wind of this poorly kept secret and the pressure's on.

This is what happens when you race. No, I'll start with what *doesn't* happen. It's definitely not the way deluded sportscasters say. Instead of training and competing when they were young, deluded commentators must have been reading Biggles stories about saving the day with imaginary biplane swoops and other acts of bucolic upper-middle-class childhood fantasy-daring. They'll tell you that truly worthy sportsmen find themselves crippled with exhaustion halfway through a race before suddenly surging through the field on pure monster balls to win, as if their opponents were bribed to daydream of strawberries and cream. In reality, however, the only swimmers crippled with exhaustion are fresh-from-lessons five-year-olds who sometimes have to be rescued in tears by their parents. For experienced swimmers, the thing you dive in most focused on is not winning or losing, but how close you can stay to the greatest sustainable pain for every moment of the race.

You might have found this calibration through past trial and error, but when those gambles didn't pay off you still finished the race, though perhaps a little off the pace because your overspending attracted some compound interest. Yet unless you take those punts occasionally, you'll just be guessing about your limits. Another thing you learn by trial and error is never to discuss pacing with Talbot, no matter how interesting you find the subject — unless he initiates it of course — because he'll just throw it back at you as another example of your self-doubt.

Did I mention second wind? Excuse me for laughing, but

when commentators mention this arcane whimsy you should stop listening because they're insulting your intelligence. Second wind only happened back in the days when even top athletes trained just a few times a week, and only if morning tea didn't interfere. It might have seemed real in Victorian times because they were so unfit that they'd often misjudge their early pace and have to pull back so severely that sooner or later in that pedestrian convalescence they began to feel chipper again, mistaking this sensation for some sort of heroic vitality they coined 'second wind'. That was it. Whenever I wonder how a poor trainer like me can be one of Australia's best sportsmen, I just have to remind myself how many athletes are fed this sort of feverish locker-room make-believe.

On the national scene I'm the top backstroker and sometimes medal in freestyle, but down at NSW-school level today I'm the clear number two to Windeatt for our sixteen-years 800-metre freestyle final. After finishing my usual fifteen seconds behind him, I look to Talbot in the stands for any hint if the world record fell, but apart from a slicing gesture directed vaguely at the pool, it seems there's nothing worth sharing. Ten minutes later, a mildly chuffed announcer proclaims Windeatt's new mark, though it's by the merest margin of two tenths of a second. All in all, it's been a strangely muted triumph.

Soon after we're driven home, Jon says his dad wants me in his office, *pronto*. 'You wanted to see me?' I ask, peering around Talbot's door after lightly knocking. He's at his desk, but jumps to his feet.

'Yeah, come in. I wondered if there was anything wrong with you today.'

'Why?'

'You were never close to Graham at any stage — never close enough to really push him — and you'd have known he was chasing the record.' *He broke it, didn't he?* I thought-bubble back. Now he leans over the desk, propped on knuckles, elbows out: 'So — ah — were you sick or something?' Studying that bristly dome, that mohair jumper, and those mohair-clad upper legs straddling the desk, I tell myself this is the wrong time to start seeing a tarantula, and suggest my swim wasn't so bad. But I also sense something is brewing between us, or at least between him and me, and that I should watch my words.

Now he takes it further, the tone brisk and forensic. 'Okay — *look* — so we've established you weren't sick, but maybe you didn't give it your all. Is that possible?' At this point, fibbing's justified: either I'll remember I *was* a little off colour, or, if it makes him happy, I'm not too proud to admit to the possibility of a minuscule drop of unused petrol. What honest swimmer wouldn't? It's not as if a firing squad awaits anyone who hasn't tried to kill himself. Can he be certain even Windeatt gave it everything? Maybe it's Windeatt who should be on the end of this grilling for *nearly failing to break a world record*. How ridiculous!

I go with the petrol. 'It's possible I might have gone harder, but that could be said about any race.' And now he does something I've never seen before: his head drops like a tendon's been severed, and hangs over the desk for two, three, four seconds. When it's connected again, his raised eyebrows have jammed those two meaty ridges of his forehead into a rack of murderous intent, and he skirts the desk perimeter until we're at arm's length. '*You bastard!*' he blasts, with a chest poke for good measure. Now it's two more angry jabs to the office door as I stumble backwards, another 'You bastard' at the door, then poke after poke down the hall. I'm still shuffling backwards through the sunroom where we breakfast and play records, before a last 'You bastard' at the back door, which is slammed in my face.

I sit on the steps to stop shaking, trying to process the spiralling hostility that led to this. I'm angry with myself too, for lying to appease Talbot. A real lie is for gain, but I was just trying to help the prick out; the lie itself was a lie. I *had* tried, and Talbot hadn't even discussed the record attempt with me, let alone designated me pacemaker; I'd never finished closer to Windeatt than today's fifteen seconds. My admission to uncertainty about my effort was a philosophical doubt, not the confession of a slacker. And Windeatt's one of the world's top distance swimmers, while I'm a backstroker who just happens to be cursed with being a better freestyler than my backstroke rivals.

Soon we're all in the Kombi headed for training, and to get my mind off Talbot I'm pondering *bastard*'s exact place in the profanity rankings, with the c- and f-bombs up on their own at number one, and cartoon curses like *drat* and *gadzooks* at the very bottom. I eventually rate *bastard* a four, easily one up from *jerk*, *tosser*, and *moron* (themselves above the almost genteel *blighter* and *bugger*), but lacking the anatomical crudity to challenge *prick* above it.

SWIMMING THE MING

I'm cruising in style through gritty Ashfield in the passenger seat of Talbot's big beige BMW. I've been his demonstrator at a clinic across town. This bad-boy Beamer is the most powerful model they make; his wife has a smaller one, and both are near new. Suddenly Talbot's left arm unfurls across the windscreen in a blur of mohair as he cries, 'Look, a red Ferrari!'

My response, a half-hearted, 'Yep, I see it,' must sound patronising, because he seems to take exception.

'*So*. A sports car like that doesn't do anything for you?'

'Not, um, too much,' I hesitate.

'And the colour *red* doesn't mean speed and excitement?'

So I tell him the terrible truth: 'I kind of get red, the symbolism and stuff, but I really love grey cars; we owned a mid-grey Holden when I was eight, and I still glaze over when I see them now.'

Talbot shakes his head and frowns across his arm's reflection at sooty shopfronts, when it suddenly strikes me that my inquisitor on colour theory this past minute has been a man in a beige mohair jumper and beige slacks, driving a beige car to a waiting beige house.

It seems I'll be able to stay with the Talbots until the middle of the year, maybe longer; Talbot says it 'all depends'. So many swimmers have called this mansion home that it's become known as 'the Ming Hilton', since the press dubs Talbot himself 'Ming the Merciless'. Back in Brisbane, the whole boarding experience got called 'Swimming the Ming', and people would actually ask how you felt about the prospect. It sounded exotic, like we were heading off to conquer some fabled Asian river, except that Ming's river is just one lap long, and what you eventually found yourself in was more pit than river — a freezing hole in the ground for a quarter of the season.

Recently I've begun to think of us going up and down along our lane as if we're scanning the same line of a book, ad infinitum, to know it better than any line's ever been learned before. Of course, learning just one line — and a blank one at that — won't do wonders for your vocabulary, but maybe repeating it 300 times a day, 340 days a year, makes it seep into parts of the brain that have never seen a line before, and suddenly your limbic system, parietal lobe, and cortex can't stop playing with it and passing it around like kids with a crazy mongoose, because the human brain won't waste its brief time on earth without a good play. And just maybe one day you'll be out in the world somewhere and some wizened old-timer will spot you and say, 'I'll be blowed if yonder kid ain't knowed just one darn line in its entire life, but what I wouldn't give to know a line so deep.'

Yet there's even more to knowing a pool lane than this. Under your seventh stroke at Auburn is the chipped tile. Under your twelfth, the crack. Getting deeper, at twenty-four strokes, some genius has had the time and cunning to scratch the first two letters of a mystery word, 'FU', onto a tile. And because today's training set is such an eternity, I finish that word off underwater at the top of my lungs, but am suddenly horrified that it might have escaped fully loaded into the sky as I breathed, so that when we're back at the wall, Talbot says, 'Who was that?' and we all look at each other in surprise to mutter, 'Who was what?' before he quips, 'You know, whoever you are.' And I know, whoever I am.

The next day when I casually ask Jon how much his dad's

worth, he shocks me with a flat, 'Not much.'

'*How can that be*,' I gasp, 'if your parents drive the latest luxury cars and live in a double-storey, five-bedroom house with a pool? Not to mention your Hawaiian-themed billiards shack and Kombi.'

'Everything's leased,' he explains.

'What's *leased*, exactly?'

'A tricky sort of renting,' Jon says tiredly. 'Everything's, like, *rented*, except the indoor pool, which the bank basically owns. Anyway, rich people don't watch TV from bean bags and pine furniture, or sleep in bunks.'

'Okay,' I reply, knowing he's lost interest.

Jon and I get on so well; I've been studying his art textbooks daily since I arrived, and am smitten. 'I should have taken art,' I tell him, 'I love these pictures.' Jon says my favourite, Kandinsky, was already painting 'pure form and colour when his peers were still glorying in late impressionism'.

'Christ, I love that art talk too,' I gush, and we're laughing. Soon I find more favourites in Dufy and Gorky. Especially Gorky, since his biomorphic forms and occasional thin vertical lines hint at the dangling light-shades of boarding rooms that Ashley and I shared. Except that Gorky's full of colour too, like someone gashed those fusty dosshouse walls to bleed rainbows. And whenever I skip down the many stairwells at Homebush Boys High, I now see my rat-a-tat feet through the strobed blur of Duchamp's *Nude Descending a Staircase*.

Jon surprises me the next day when he says he knows where his parents have plenty of money: 'There's all this leftover bread from a pool they leased years ago, at the top of the cupboard under the stairs.' With his parents out for an hour on Sunday, he fetches a stepladder and torch to show me two small dusty calico bags spilling with silver and copper. It's hardly the cache I imagined — more like someone forgot to roll the last day's coin. 'I just grab a bunch of fifty-cent pieces if I need serious dosh quickly, and replace them when I can,' he explains. 'They haven't checked it in years.' Jon says his next withdrawal will be this weekend when his dad's interstate, so we can visit Kings Cross for a strip show. Our great escape will necessitate tying bedsheets together to climb down the front of their house from our upstairs bunk room, or else his mother might hear the floorboards creak as we creep past her bedroom. Hal will be part of our big night. Hal's an absolute scream, with his sayings like, 'That's funnier than Art Garfunkel's underpants,' 'I'm so hungry I could eat the cunt out of a low-flying duck,' and his quaint way of refusing an offer by groaning, 'No, *please!*'

Our big night comes and goes. The easiest thing to remember is abseiling down the front of the house like pirates. The tricky part was being prevented from climbing out directly over our sheet-rope after we closed the big centre window to anchor the last knot. We squeezed instead through an offset side bay, reaching around the pillar to grip the sheet with our left hand before nervously letting go of the sash for the double grip. Thankfully we made terra firma without putting a leg through the ground-floor window or being shredded by waiting rose thorns. In town we saw the horror movie *Dr Phibes* before downing a bottle of plonk in Hyde Park. Then it was the strip club, a few more drinks, and the train home. We must have been talking loudly on the train because a huge man came up the aisle and said a few threatening words. His ultimatum was confusing, though one part implied the possibility of staying pain-free and included the phrase 'the next station'. Obviously too sloshed for the required algebra of '*if*', we each got a whack in the eye as we sat there pondering. My next memory is of Hal blacking out in the walk from the station, Jon and me then trying to carry him, but mostly dragging him along the verge. (The gravel massage woke Hal up long enough to stumble with our help for a while.) I forget how we made it up to our bunks, but it can't have been the way we left. *Wait* — Mrs Talbot's face floats in and out of that last thought, at the back door. That's right, because it was the only time I'd seen her in pyjamas, *men's* blue-striped pyjamas, and that was a sight.

It's pitch black on our block when Talbot rouses us Monday morning with a typically sharp foot tug at the end of every bunk. Before that yank is dreamed into shark bite or amputation, he's revving the life out of the Kombi downstairs, and soon eight blanket- and towel-flapping silhouettes converge on its open side door. Out on the highway after Talbot sprays the drive with gravel, the tyres are slapping on concrete joins to the beat of the Rolling Stones' 'Brown Sugar' on the radio. (Talbot's musical taste is limited to Buddy Rich drum solos and his one Nana Mouskouri album, but he doesn't mind proper music in the Kombi.) Soon, I find my right elbow's been bumping a loose counterpoint against a girl's left breast, and it's either been liking this or is numb with the cold as we bounce across the Cumberland plain. Is Mick Jagger singing 'How come you *dance* so good?' or 'How come you *taste* so good?' *Is anyone else thinking this?* As I drowsily scope whatever the fog gives up under passing orange shrouds of streetlight, I fleetingly wonder who on earth could feel happier or more resolute at this crazy hour.

Now, up ahead, the mist releases a hitchhiker in jeans and blue flannel shirt, and lugging an army-disposals backpack. He looks vaguely familiar from behind, so I twist for a better look as we pass. *What the … ?* I'm sure it's the gaunt face and long blond locks of Neil Gynther from Brisbane; I almost thought 'swimmer' from Brisbane, only he's a breaststroker from a legendary Queensland water-polo family. But why on earth would he be hitching a thousand kilometres from home like an apparition on a freezing

Western Sydney freeway before dawn? I should ask Talbot to stop, but it's too bizarre to be true. And what if it wasn't him? Of course it can't be, so I keep quiet.

An hour on, I glance up from my freezing lane at Auburn pool and there's Gynther in that flannel shirt and backpack, talking to Talbot: *another Queenslander down south for the big miles!* I want to call out that I was the only one to see him hitching, but he'd probably ask why I didn't make us stop. Next day I expect him in squad but he doesn't turn up. Nor the following day, nor the following week. It now seems Talbot didn't want a breaststroker, or maybe Gynther couldn't convince him he was genuine, despite the spectacular gesture of hitching in the cold dark to join the world's toughest swim squad. Jon's always said that for every Queenslander in the pool, two are turned away, and now I believe him! I've also heard of others begging for a spot on Ming's team, only to insist they can do just eight of his eleven weekly sessions, they must always be let out exactly on time, or they have to return to Brisbane every holiday and birthday. I can only imagine Talbot's response. Who turns up on the doorstep of the lion of world coaching with a bunch of demands to make him a pussycat?

But every rule has its exception, and the exception to Queensland wannabes with a sense of entitlement was Max Tavasci, a distance specialist reportedly taught to swim by his cane-farmer dad in taipan-infested irrigation drains. After his Ming stint last year, Max almost toppled Windeatt as the world's top junior distance swimmer with a close silver to him in the Commonwealth Games 1500-metre. Jon remembers Max with near-disbelief and awe. 'You'd better sit down because I'm going to shock you,' he warns, shaking his head and snorting. 'This ... Max ... used to ask Dad if he could — *wait for it* — do extra training after we finished!' A fit of cackles later, he whines, 'How crazy's that?' Max's no-nonsense attitude apparently carried through to life after the Games, when he quit to start a business venture with his sister. I often glimpsed Max across the foggy lanes of my first indoor months with Talbot. I loved his deceptively lazy, loping stroke, and how his head stayed down low when he rolled to breathe, as if his body was on a rotisserie skewer — the exact opposite of Windeatt's lofty but equally impressive head carriage. And now that I know Max is the only one ever to have begged Ming the Merciless for more, he's my all-time favourite.

Saturdays we train later; it's almost daylight when we leave. A few blocks out, we pick up a new swimmer, or at least a new *old* one, the double Commonwealth Games medley champion Denise Langford. It seems she's on a comeback, and now I see why the front passenger seat was left vacant: so she could sit beside Talbot on her first trip back. We rear passengers get only the slightest nod when she climbs in, her lively eyes not quite meeting ours, as if she can't quite believe we're her peers, so fast is the churn of talent now. Talbot must be a little warm from thrashing the Kombi, because he asks Denise to help remove his jumper, raising an arm for her to yank it over his head. But after it snags on his chin, he's driving blind and we're all over the road until he hits the brakes, the Kombi bucking to a squealing stop. Now he coolly raises both arms for her to complete the job, but Denise seems visibly shaken by her role in nearly killing us all, and after training we don't see her again.

THE KEYS TO EXCESS

At Auburn pool I'm seeing a key-ring jangle an arc through the cold night air, its long dark keys in shaggy orbit. When all that metal slams into Talbot's upheld palm, the departing manager calls, unnecessarily, 'There, Don, let yourself out.' The only other person now left at the pool with Talbot is me. I've already been in the water an hour since the last swimmer went home, making it three-and-a-half hours since I dived in. And there's another to go, if I've read his mood. This afternoon's session was apparently a squad record for total distance covered, almost eleven kilometres, and that was before I was kept back. I've just passed fifteen kilometres.

Most people have no idea what swimmers do for regular training besides that meaningless term 'laps'; have no idea that each lap's a tiny link in a tightly regulated and time-managed *set* of a repeated distance, the set itself lasting anything from forty-five minutes to over two hours. Sometimes sets are so long that they need breaking up into identical subsets separated by a token break like tonight's 200-metre kick on a kickboard. We're often asked how much rest we get after every single repeat of a given distance, as if a guaranteed pause separates each swim. But there's no standard break: it's whatever time scraps are left of the fixed interval we have to leave on after we stroke in to the wall. Tonight's push-off interval of 2 minutes 30 seconds for each 200-metre freestyle left around ten seconds' break for most of us. It's not the sort of training the average Joe could ever dream of doing, but when you've been swimming since you were six, you know to the very second what time you'll see at the wall. It's like the precision of a gymnast working the beam, except that *our* beam — our exacting plane between execution and failure — is time itself. And our only defences against an undignified landing are fitness and pacing.

None of which fully explains why I'm still here well after dark with just one pole of floodlights left glaring down, long after everyone's gone home proud of their record session, their eyes now glued to some TV sitcom as they eat dinner. I miscounted, that's all. I guess it's pretty hard to lose count when you're only doing four laps at a time, but there you go; I was falling behind too. I was so far behind I was getting lapped, and thought Talbot mightn't notice if I got it wrong. Did I mention I was beyond caring? But he must have been watching and counting, and near the end of our third of a designated six cycles of eight by 200 metres, he told me to start over from scratch. So here we are. There's no way he'll wait around till I'm finished: that'd be well past nine p.m. At least that's what I'm counting on.

When Talbot huffs, 'Come on, let's go,' at 8.45, I've clocked seventeen kilometres, all rubbish. But he's made his point, and now there's a smouldering extra-nothing to talk about on the drive home. It's been almost five hours since I jumped in, three hours since the sun went down, and when we get home everyone will be asleep, so I'm hoping for some cold leftovers to wolf down.

The following day, it's our Homebush Boys High swimming carnival at Ashfield pool. I always wonder why they bother with school carnivals, since everyone knows who's going to win. But you have to admire the kids who turn up in board shorts hoping those few afternoons they trained half their lives back might fluke a medal. Midway through the program, a classmate tells me some boys from the senior drama group at the top of the stands are taking the piss out of my warm-up drills. 'I don't mind,' I tell him. 'They're probably bored shitless, so good luck to them.' In fact, if I were parodying me I'd focus on the single arm swings I'm always doing behind the blocks. I'd spin that arm so fast it'd come clean off, and then I'd have to pretend-dive into the pretend-pool to pretend-retrieve it. Maybe that's exactly the sort of gag they're doing up there.

When we're milling around the buses to be taken back to school afterwards, I'm almost speechless with appreciation when one of my alleged satirists, Neil, approaches me to offer assistance with homework. 'You're strapped for time with all the swimming, I guess,' he says, 'but if you ever need help, let me know.' I tell him I'm so far behind that I've given up, but *thanks just the same*.

The following day, Neil and I sit beside each other in English. Our teacher Mr McManus is fielding a question about colloquial usage from Mark, another brilliant drama student known to cheerfully take the piss out of himself for being raised under his mum's progressive-but-kooky Dr Benjamin Spock methods. Mr McManus has been telling him — and now, seemingly, the rest of us — that there is no such word as *poser*, in the sense we boys use it, to mean *exhibitionist*. 'The correct word, *poseur*, is of French derivation,' he insists with a haughty head wiggle of mock snobbery. Even more theatrically, he repeats *poseur* with the accent firmly on the second syllable: 'So, boys, it's actually po-*seur*, this *poser* of yours,' before screwing his lips into an absurdly Gallic pout to torture the *seur* into a gravelly *zyeer*. 'Po-ZYEER, po-ZYEER,' he suddenly bawls like some frog town-crier, relishing his burlesque.

I've had my hand up a while to ask Mr McManus if the e-u sound in 'seur' counts as a diphthong, when, from the corner of my eye, I notice Neil's head turning my way. After I lower my arm self-consciously to return gaze, his anodised bronze bifocal rims stay trained on me. I've seen this odd stare when he talks to other students: the focal lock of a prodigy whose prose pieces in the school magazine are almost beyond critique because they're entirely in Latin. He's not looking down his nose or anything; there's just this odd narrowing of the eyes above a tickled mobilising of that vast upper lip. He could be appraising an insect collection, and maybe this is the kind of cataloguing lens you use on everything when you're one of these genius drama types, because they're being trained to observe people, not pool lines. It's like that poem we recently studied by Alexander Pope, where he says, 'The proper study of mankind is man.' I normally resent being scrutinised, but because that weird artsy condescension is a cut above your moronic sporty eyeballing, I disengage and zero back in on Mr McManus hamming his way through the language.

Tonight the Talbot kids, Hal, and I are riveted to a current-affairs presenter touting the prospect of a live on-air debate between Shane Gould's dad and her coach, Forbes Carlile, to settle the current strife between the two men, when Talbot walks in and switches the TV off. (Talbot takes his chief-household-censor role seriously: last week he had his wife remove their daughters' copy of the new teen magazine *Dolly* from our room because it led with the article 'To Bra or Not to Bra', though our sole interest had been our pride in former swimming champion Ilsa Konrads' founding editorial role.)

Carlile and Mr Gould are totally at each other's throats in the media these days over the conflicting demands of swim training and education. Tensions sky-rocketed when Mr Gould told the papers Shane will skip the Munich Olympics if it means missing too much school, a totally unthinkable prospect for Australia now that she's threatening a new world mark with every swim. And of course, I'm totally on Mr Gould's side, though I think he's a bit slow off the mark. I found out as soon as I came to Sydney that school's indispensable — as a restful cipher between two killer training sessions (the less it intrudes the better!). Last week Jon and I even used a vacant classroom at Homebush High for a kip because we were sick of traipsing to the golf course for a private scrap of shade to snooze in. Dragging some desks together, we fashioned a bed each, wedged a chair-back under the doorknob to block entry, and waited for the zeds. We eventually woke to a class lined up outside with a teacher banging on the window.

Talbot hates all this negative publicity from the bad blood between the Goulds and Carliles. At last weekend's carnival at Auburn pool, he ordered us not to fill out a questionnaire some university was handing out. But I'd already read the questions and they were pretty pointed, like 'Does swimming satisfy all your social needs?' and 'Are you generally happy, or only when you race well?' They read like someone from that benign institution was reaching out to us, and I was ready to sound the alarm with the right answers. No wonder Talbot banned them.

OSLO'S BEST BAD

April 1971. After my wins in the 100-metre and 200-metre backstroke at Nationals in Hobart in February — no dye bombs to contend with this time — I'm on a small team for a one-month European tour. *My first trip.* Apart from a pair of Victorians, our dozen members are all Talbot and Carlile swimmers; Talbot's the coach.

Four hours into the flight, we bank sharply right; through the window, there's no trace of sky, cloud, or horizon, just a carpet of glowing ochre. *Are planes supposed to tilt this sharply?* I wonder. And is the desert meant to be so astonishingly vast, featureless, and without texture that it loses all scale, and looks to be barely an office block down? *Maybe we're in trouble*, I think, before I feel the world correct itself, the darkening horizon sliding back down my window like a blind.

I settle back, close my eyes, and soon dream about flying, where I'm persuaded against my better judgement to board a particular plane. Very soon, my worst fears come true when the right engine catches fire and we're spiralling down to crash. I'm bracing for the inevitable when I'm inexplicably excused from a big chunk of the dream, and once I'm back inside it I find, to my elation, that the pilot has us parked safely on some tarmac. When a calm, petrified voice orders us to relax and stay put while workmen replace the charred engine, my brain is suddenly the world's biggest prefrontal neon billboard, pulsing, 'No. Fucking. Way.' I activate the emergency exit and dive-bounce-flip-roll-cartwheel down the inflated ramp, then sprint for the terminal, where I leap turnstiles, brush aside passport demands and security guards, and stride across screeching car bonnets until I'm lost in the safety of the dark alleyways of whatever city I'm in, where I collapse and hug the ground. Then I'm up and walking, just because my feet are meant to walk, not fly, and because I'll never give another incompetent fool the chance to mess with the one life I've been given on this earth.

Stepping out into the sauna blast of Singapore from the cabin chill, we're soon strolling the airport's cool duty-free stores and coveting seductive new gadgets during our first stopover. Only a few hours later, we're all aghast-but-chuckling to find ourselves squashed together on clapped-out floral lounges our grandmothers would have discarded years ago, but in this case they're the only comfort Karachi Airport can offer.

From Heathrow, we're bussed to a weird-but-wonderful timber-panelled skyscraper dorm adjoining the sprawling Crystal Palace sports complex. Well, maybe not quite a skyscraper, though the brooding sky seems low enough to be impaled by our twelve-storey vertical hobbit shaft. Down in the dining area, aluminium urns dispense endless cups of milk-based coffee, a real treat when you're about to head out at midday across the car park, where we're told it'll be six degrees, the coldest daytime temperature I'll have experienced — exciting though!

I win my 100-metre backstroke race at the Crystal Palace pool in midafternoon, but it's Shane who stuns everyone by equalling Dawn Fraser's 100-metre freestyle world record — and this was supposed to be our warm-up meet! Almost as if to answer Shane's arrival on the world stage, Karen Moras then breaks the world 400-metre freestyle record.

When you thought the day couldn't hold any more surprises, in walks Rolf Harris, and I instantly wonder if he's been hired as some kind of zany novelty motivator. I'm flabbergasted to think our little team has this kind of clout, and wonder why his presence hasn't been formally announced, though it seems he's happy enough to float among us for a casual chinwag. Maybe someone told him world records were in the air today. Soon he's telling me that he too was a backstroker 'back in the day', apparently winning a Junior National 100-metre backstroke title in the 1940s, and it's suddenly like I'm just chewing the fat with another teammate. When he wanders off after barely an hour among us, I'm still stunned to think he had the time to share his modest boast and take in a nostalgic whiff of chlorine.

After the swimming, there's a disco, where my usual excuses for not dancing are interrupted by the chaperone, Mrs D, who wonders if there's been 'a falling-out, or something, *maybe nothing at all*' among the girls, because a few, including Shane, have gone to their rooms early. Several of us are delegated to 'go and knock on a few doors', and, since I'm an old training mate of Shane's, I'm allocated hers. Confident she's retired early to rest after the excitement of joining the ranks of Dawn Fraser, I wince to make myself knock once on her door before asking haltingly, 'Everything … *okay?*' When I think I hear the faint reply, 'Just scribbling in my diary,' I decide it makes perfect sense because all the Carlile girls seem maniacal diary-keepers, on top of the special training logbooks they're meant to fill out and submit for weekly perusal by the Carliles. 'Make sure you scribble this in,' I joke back, but silence tells me I'm unheard. When the door swings open a moment later, Shane looks tired but is keen to head back to the celebrations, so off we go.

The pace continues and soon after we hit Rome we're all over the Spanish Steps. 'Come and see the steps-a,' proclaims the

butterflier, Hiccup, as if he's our tour guide. 'Step up, step up-a,' he
bawls in a mock accent, doubling over. 'Which a-step you like to
see? So beautiful, a-step-a number three. *Touch if you like-a*, watch
the ant-a crawl-a.' And now I think he's probably lucky Talbot's not
here right now to touch *him*. I've read somewhere that the poet
John Keats had a pad adjoining these famous steps, but I can't go
off searching. Next, it's a brief stop at the Colosseum, where people
played sport to the death, its encircling wall like a richly textured
biscuit chomped on by gargoyles every other century.

On our third night in Rome, I'm momentarily nodding off in
the stands of a cramped indoor pool in my new Australian tracksuit
with its flashy, jagged-cut yellow stripes along the arms, when
someone calls from above, 'Hey, Bradford.' I look up in amused,
sleepy irritation, half-blinded by a flash. 'This photo make you
famous,' the voice from the black continues, and I think back,
I don't-a think so-a.

On our last day in Rome, we're sharing a bus with the Italian
team, and I've never met more talkative girls. Their English is so
good that it's almost impossible to keep up with the flow of words
and gestures, but if you miss a beat they lose interest and head
for the nearest fun. One comments sharply that I 'look German',
suggestive of some undecipherable overtone. Confused, I stammer,
'W-what? *No good?*' and for some reason they find this hilarious and
at last I've something in the bank.

The pools in Marseilles are the filthiest in the world, we all
joke, or else why would we be heading off in a bus for a *Piscine*. The
bus driver calls over his shoulder that the annual cost of swim-club
membership at this spectacular headland piscine we're competing
in tonight is well over a thousand dollars. No one swims well;
it's almost as if the shocking price of being a swimmer here has
overwhelmed our amateur ethos into a passivity that even Talbot

understands — no one cops the dressing-down you'd expect. The additional fact of there being so few spectators makes it the most unsatisfying racing of the tour.

The following day in Aix-en-Provence, I'm halfway through a warm-down when I start itching. Not just itching for a scratch here and there, but absolutely all over, and I jump from the pool barely able to believe an itch could send you crazy, though that's where I'm headed if the manager can't find a doctor. Luckily one soon arrives with his black bag of tricks and I receive an injection, making me settle within minutes. 'Bed bugs,' the manager tells me. Luckily too, we'll be in new beds in Paris tonight.

Another day, and we're up on the Eiffel Tower, a few girls nudging up against boys on each platform because it's cold and they must think they have to — Paris being the city of love — but down there in the arrondissements, banks, and quarters, it all looks oddly uninspiring. Yet on the way back to the motel, our minibus wends through a charming little cobblestone loop, and the flower shop that swings around to fill the dappled screen is the prettiest I've ever seen.

At lunch, Mrs D is the centre of attention at the far end of the motel dining table. She's just returned from a trim at the hairdresser, where her sympathetic snip-snip gesticulations to show she wanted only a tiny bit cut off were somehow misinterpreted to mean only a tiny bit *left on*. She makes no bones about how upset she is, tugging at her remaining hair and rolling her eyes while searching for the right words. 'I am so. I am *so*. Absolutely. *Distraught*. I'm just devastated. By this.' Tears welling. Anybody — anybody but the manager, that is — could see that the last thing she wants to hear is, 'It'll grow back,' to which she sniffs, 'So will the Sahara one day,' before heading briskly for her room, pulling her neck scarf over that sorry lawn.

We visit every Scandinavian capital except Helsinki. *Are Finns*

Scandinavian? I've heard they're in a different language group, but they look similar in photos. I love Stockholm. Volvos everywhere, even the taxis. I'm in the very back of a station-wagon cab with three Swedish girls and we can't stop laughing. Maybe it's because the driver takes the corners hard enough to make us roll together as one big lump. Or is it that we just happen to be the planet's four funniest people at this moment? We haven't even been drinking — not since we've been in the cab, anyway. I'm not sure when we're getting out, but I want it to be the longest not-yet ever.

All the pools in Norway are Bad. At least, that's what it says over each entry — *Bad* being Norwegian for *Baths*. By far the best Bad is in the woods outside Oslo: this towering Euclidean riff of glass triangles, leaning in then out, the odd nip and tuck of aluminium, and red plastic for calculated Bauhaus rhythm. You look through the glass sections and see even more wedges of bright colours in the massive stands. We dive in for the warm-up and suddenly I could be back at Auburn, the black line pulling me down from our Bauhaus bubble like I'm some soldier being woken for exercise drill.

We're here today not for aqua-boot-camp, but for a friendly session with Oslo's best, and we soon discover an unforgivable deficiency in the Norwegian swimming program: they are all squirt-illiterate. Every Australian swimmer knows at least three of the five hand squirts we're always doing to annoy each other at the end of the pool between sets. There's the front and reverse double-hand pray squirt, the cross-hand forward, and the single-hand front and reverse. A few of us chip in to help our new Norwegian friends — Anja, Lisbet, Erik, and Alex — correct this personal failing by positioning their fingers and palms as they clumsily compress their squirt-less hands. Lisbet suddenly cracks it for a single-hand front, then reverse — a full metre of squirt, getting Erik square in the eye. She's quickly chaired on the shoulders of teammates like a new national hero, and Talbot hasn't a clue what's going on when he looks over, but doesn't want to cause an international incident by ripping into us in front of the local coaches.

Last of all, Bonn: the embassy, with its manicured grounds, minor topiary, and hedge-enclosed pool, where we strip to our togs to see who can go the most consecutive laps underwater. My best is six — it's only a 12-metre pool, and the push-offs alone get you halfway. The winner, Hiccup, hits ten, pushes off for the eleventh, and nearly blacks out as he lunges up through the surface like some purple sky-busting marlin. We all laugh. He spends thirty stationary seconds groaning on the side of the pool. We laugh harder. 'No. Fucken. *Really!*' he sputters. We laugh again and finally he does too. And coughs.

Three weeks after our return, there's a rumour that several girls from the tour are set to quit. One already has. Reportedly they had such a good time that they're having trouble settling down, already sick of the twice-daily slog and nothing new on the horizon. But when Talbot overhears the names we're throwing around in the Kombi, he's all over it, scoffing over his shoulder that this is the usual post-tour 'scuttlebutt' and he 'frankly doubts' any of the girls will be permanently 'lost to swimming'.

Lost to swimming? I ponder. *Swimming*: a gerund describing the efforts of animals (in this case, humans) to move through water? And the movement of the word itself, *swimming* — just a vibration of the vocal cords, sculpted to meaning by lips and tongue, its momentary puff of air leaving no trace in the atmosphere?

But who knows what Talbot's thinking when he says *swimming* with that definitive look and tone, like swimming's the animal itself, navigating itself through his thought processes. If anything's lost, it won't be these girls to swimming, but swimming to them — that's if they care.

RETREATING LADIES

It seems all Sydney — except for the Talbot household — has been talking about Shane and her challenges balancing her hectic life. Now my Homebush High Indonesian teacher Mrs Thomas stops me in the corridor outside her half-opened staffroom door, just to ask if I know Shane. It's the teacher who discovered Jon and me asleep in the classroom (I still can't believe she let us scamper out, scot-free). 'Shane and I have been friends for years,' I volley a little too keenly. I like this teacher, with her ski-slope nose, sympathetic eyes, and long platform boots. Her hair is in a fashionably long fringe today, a feathered dovetail fanning the back of a chic reverse collar on her flute-breasted rayon blouse. 'So, what do you think of her?' she continues, snapping me out of my fashion reverie, as if Shane's been the hot-button topic at today's staff lunch. Feeling suddenly put upon, I need to sound convincing.

'She's really ... *um* ... quite well-adjusted, and smart,' I answer in my most clipped tone. Having heard so many adults use 'well-adjusted' lately, I'd been busting to give it a spin myself. And Shane really is smart. At the consulate in Bonn, I waited in line for minutes while she and the ambassador chinwagged about rising Australian nationalism; she was barely fourteen! But Mrs Thomas' indulgent smile hints that these aren't quite the pickings she's after, before she reverse-wiggles through the staffroom doorway like a moray eel with its wispy scrap. What I didn't share with her was my surprise in the Goulds' car a fortnight ago when Shane had bridled at her mother's mention of *yet another* magazine reporter waiting at home for them. They'd only seconds before picked me up for a picnic. (*I'm always overjoyed to be interviewed, but evidently there's a limit.*) Shane was so testy about having journalists continually snooping around that I expected to hear a reprimand, but her mother just kept this cool conversational tone to suggest she try some patience. And it worked, because Shane suddenly eased up, and that was surely a clinic in modern parenting.

I begin to think about Shane's dad and his highly publicised conflict with Carlile. When you look at Mr Gould and Mr Windeatt, it's hard to imagine two more different stewards for the two best swimmers of their generation. Mr Windeatt is a company man through and through. Seeing his family's apparent composure (one boy already in America on a swimming scholarship, the other methodically inching his way to seemingly predestined Olympic glory almost from the cot), you'd never guess there was the imminent threat of a hippie and communist takeover on our doorstep. No Vietnam War, no draft dodgers, no anti-war protests, and no drug crisis, just the Australian franchise of the American dream under the watchful eye of the military industrial complex.

A week later when Mrs Talbot shows me an invitation to fly to a country town to address some Rotary sport dinner, I keenly accept. I also accept that it's incumbent on me to put a shoulder to the wheel in the Goulds' crusade against coaching tyranny, by taking their message to far-flung parents who are but dimly aware of the perils of choosing their children's sporting career. NOT SWIMMING IF YOU CAN HELP IT will be the general tone of my polemic. Not that anybody in their right mind should take me seriously, because I gave up on school a year ago, if you don't count all my hours in the school library pretending to read everything from Shakespeare to the Letters of Pliny the Younger — and isn't he the pompous one? — while mostly nodding off with my face in my palms. But my audience is not to know.

I give the speech not another moment's thought until I reflect with blanching unease, resting on chenille bedding in this distant town's plushest pokey motel room, that it's only an hour away. Shockingly, until now, I was incapable of seeing myself standing before rows of aftershave-reeking businessmen in some lit-up auditorium, attended by waiters positioning entrees along dazzling linen-clad tables. It wasn't until twenty minutes ago when two larger-than-life Rotarians met me at the airport, reaching out from their big cattle-auction bellies and monogrammed pockets to crush my hand, that I first attached a human form to their kind. The only thing now is to bolt across to the bottle-o for a stubby or two, then jot down a few bullet points with one hand while pouring Tooheys down my throat with the other.

After being introduced by a diminutive, unassuming life member who is nonetheless perfectly at ease with a microphone in these parts, I stumble through my talk, glancing everywhere but at my audience, blinking idiot-quick to recall the notes I made. (I'd intended slyly referencing these in my cupped hand, but pocketed them when I feared this might be cheating.) Surely no one has ever strained as hard to scrutinise their own words, as mine stagger from my lips like lexical zombies; for entire sentences I seem to speak across my own echoes in a panicked equivalent of blurred vision. But mercifully it's question time, and it's as if a Cessna flown upside down and blind in a cyclone has miraculously found itself taxiing on a runway: this answering-questions caper is a million times better than just standing there and saying shit.

'How many kilometres do you do for training?'

'Too easy. Good day or bad?'

'What do swimmers have for breakfast?'

'Do you have an hour?'

'Would you recommend swimming as a sport?'

'As I said in my talk, not as things currently stand.'

A few days later I'm still riding the weirdest high, as if all post-speech existence is some ecstatic reverse orbit of reprieve around that public vivisection. And now, before school, Mrs Talbot beckons me to the foot of the hallway stairs. Guessing the newspaper banners she's toting are all about my recent Commonwealth backstroke record, I jog over expectantly. If you've seen a rococo painting of those bonneted ladies leaning on swings or strolling under parasols in lush Regency gardens, you've glimpsed Mrs Talbot. Those cheeks have a permanent boudoir flush, her hair all bouffant and ringlet. She's a thoroughly sympathetic, though worryingly passive, presence in the Talbot household, and, unlike her husband, has a charmingly self-effacing wit. ('What's an actuary, Mum?' one of her girls asked yesterday. 'Well, *actuary*, I don't know,' she sweetly parried.)

'What the hell did you think you were getting at in that speech?' she demands hotly, shaking those newspapers at me. (Hell? *Only her husband says hell.*) Rattled by her transformation from demure matron to domestic demagogue, I focus on the fluttering headlines, one of which shouts back, *'Swim Champ Says School and Pool Poor Mix'.*

And now she gets to the point. 'You've been given this incredible opportunity with your swimming, and you — *you* — go and poison it to good country people who pay your airfare.' I now see there is no explanation for this outrage that the wife of *the enemy* could understand, and fall mute until she finishes rattling *The Examiner* in my face and withdraws up the steps with her ravaged souvenirs. *She and Talbot hardly speak to each other these days,* I tell myself to somehow discredit her reprimand, before congratulating myself with a smirk of *mission accomplished.*

But within minutes, I also find myself seething at her use of 'incredible opportunity' to describe my barracks-like existence in her home, where I'm expected to simultaneously cope with school and the world's toughest sports training regime, not to mention my sweatshop Sunday afternoons assembling Ming's line of exercise equipment with her two boys, whose idea of a regular family holiday is to recall what they've heard of their father's most recent overseas coaching assignment.

DOLPHINESE

*Hi Nickname. I thought it about time I dropped you a line. Hope all's
well. You're so lucky you're still up there in that constant 26 degree
Valley Pool water: when we left the indoor pool last September for the
outdoor (unheated) pool at Auburn, the water was 17 degrees. So, one
day we're in a wilting 33 degrees in Talbot's indoor Hurstville pool
(apparently they need it that hot for babies' classes) and the next we're
in those freezing outdoor lanes at Auburn. Now that was a shock and
a half.*

*You can't throw your body into such cold water without feeling
you've seriously betrayed it, particularly when you know there's two
hours to go! And this Talbot doesn't put up with 'namby pambies'
slinking in via the steps with a squeal for every inch: it has to be a
running jump. And after hitting the water, we're all bouncing around
on tiptoes with arms above heads, blowing quick half breaths and
shouting 'phwa, shit, Christ!' As long as we don't take this show too
far, Talbot says everything will be 'hunky dory'. If you haven't guessed,
two of his favourite expressions are namby pamby and hunky dory. Oh,
and I almost forgot Creeping Jesus. You're definitely a Creeping Jesus
if you always tag on the end of the line, hoping he won't notice you
draughting on everyone. (When my friend Hal finished a 1500-metre
yesterday, Talbot reached down, grabbed his skinny wrist, hauled him
out of the pool like an underfed seal pup he was about to club to death
and barked, 'Listen, you little Creeping Jesus.' Hal's always going last.)*

*Your body never warms up in 17 degrees. After morning training I
was still shivering through breakfast 20 minutes later, losing cereal off*

every shaky spoonful. On a sunny day the water picked up a tad, but overnight it dropped again.

In my first week in the outdoor pool I kept hearing the high pitched whine of an outboard motor. Either this, I thought, or my usual tinnitus had hit a new frequency from some sort of eardrum frost bite. Then one day a lane-mate asked why I never replied to their cheerios. 'What cheerios?' I asked.

'The ones we give when we're passing each other,' he said (and I was getting passed a lot in my first few weeks).

'Dolphinese!' one girl laughed. 'Surely you've heard our underwater dolphin squeals.' And that was my outboard motor whine. Now I speak fluent Dolphinese!

Talbot and Gordon are dead opposites. Both get angry, of course, though Gordon's age made him a kind of lovable 'C man': crotchety, crabby, cranky. But Talbot's definitely your 'A man' — adversarial, abrupt, authoritarian — and he's decades younger than Gordon. He's built like the nuggetty drill instructor in Gomer Pyle, with the same flat-top crewcut but minus Sergeant Carter's man-boobs and conflicted lapses into pastoral concern. And he's always saying 'hell': 'That was a hell of a swim — you'll have hell to pay — you can go to hell.' If it's not hell, it's backsides. 'He needs a kick in the backside — my backside you're getting out — as long as your backside points to the ground you'll never ...'

When you're in trouble with Talbot he'll order you out of the pool for a good chest poking, though some new recruits oddly look forward to this. After their first taste of it, they turn up the next day proud of the bruise rosette on their chest, but after it yellows out they never want another. (And get this. A kid in my lane, my old Maroubra club mate Jim Findlay, developed a crush on one of Talbot's daughters. But Talbot was onto it and told him in front of everyone, 'If I see you anywhere near my place I'll break both your legs.')

Now, prepare to be amazed: I'm known as a bit of a maths genius down here. Stop laughing. It just so happens that one of our regular longer swims is a kind of pyramid where we do one lap fast, one slow, then two fast, two slow, and so on, non-stop, right up to wherever Talbot wants it to stop; it can go as high as 13, and that's a 9km continuous swim. To calculate the total, everyone would stand around adding up the numbers (you know, plus 6, carry the one!) Then one day I thought there had to be a short cut, and began multiplying and squaring numbers at random until I found that by multiplying the set's top number by the number above, I got the right total each time. Even Talbot was impressed, and he was a maths teacher!

If you want revenge on Talbot, you have to wait for Christmas eve. Apparently he'll be halfway through telling us he's going to do something ridiculous, like keep us in till midnight, before spinning on his heel to take off onto the spectator hill. Almost instantly, all the boys know to jump out and give chase, eventually tackling him onto the grass before laying into him with fists and kicks. Apparently that's his Christmas present to us. Two years ago he picked up a broken rib in that scramble. Crazy, isn't it? (I can't wait — NOT.)

As I expected, Windeatt's treated like a god here. But oddly, his nickname's Grub! It must be some sort of ironic nod to his decidedly un-grubby demeanour. And there is actually a weird gravitas to him that gets everyone's respect. He's pretty straight; a tad aloof too, but no one minds because he can take a ribbing.

Shane and I keep in touch. I've even had a sleepover, training with her coach Forbes Carlile the next morning. (I'm surprised Talbot approved, because coaches are always stealing swimmers off each other down here. At carnivals, they greet boys from other squads with compliments like 'Hi, muscles,' and the girls with 'Cute cossies, luv,' though Carlile himself seems a cut above all that.)

Most Talbot swimmers call Carlile a 'girls' coach', and the boys who train under him 'mummy's boys'. They could be right, because the lane I swam in had an Alastair, Jonathon, James, Roger, and Buddy, while in Talbot's alpha lane there's just this monosyllable proletariat of Dave, Hal, Mike, Greg, Rick, Jim, Rob, Grub, and me. (I was actually christened Bradford, but Brad will do for now!)

It's weird: Carlile and Talbot have these really striking voices, so maybe that's what's needed to be a top coach down here. Carlile's is what your dad might call donnish — he was a physiology professor before coaching — and it resonates like it's knocked on every skull cavity on its way out. Talbot's is part bull's roar, part Satchmo, part exhaust note. And it's the first voice I've heard to make that supposed female fascination with the male larynx almost believable.

If you don't train with either of these coaches, you're just not serious about the Olympics. And if you're any good and live north of the Harbour Bridge, you'll train with Carlile, but in the south or west you're with Talbot. (Nothing happens at all in the east unless you count a couple of private schools where stodgy old-boys mentor relay sides for their full blue, or a few hired lanes here and there where oddballs in cravats coach a handful of rich kids.)

It's all about the big k's down here now. As you know, Gordon never gave us more than 4km, except for Saturdays when it trickled to a 'heroic' 5km. But with Talbot, the bare minimum's 8. (I still wonder why Gordon didn't bump us up to 8 when so many were thinking of heading south. He must have known he'd lose them. Has he increased the k's yet? Please let me know.)

I'm usually in Talbot's bad books because of my erratic training, so that's a turnaround from Brisbane (whenever Gordon was quoted in the papers, he'd say, 'There's no better lad!') Of course, I wasn't such an up-and-down trainer back then because of the easy work, but you've no idea how tired this training makes you: last week we clocked 100km in our 11 sessions. That's 24 hours in the water! When Talbot gets sick of me being lapped by swimmers I beat in races, he boots me over to the junior lanes for a day or three. This is on a fortnightly basis! But I don't fudge deliberately. I just get this deep fatigue in my gut and it soon radiates into my neck and limbs, like it's taunting me with 'quitter, quitter!' and after fifteen minutes of that, I stop caring. The only thing that makes me smile sometimes if I'm going up and back like a zombie is that old joke — 'Mummy, Mummy, I don't want to go to New Zealand,' when the mum says, 'Shut up and keep swimming.' (A month of Talbot's training could actually get you to Auckland!) But every now and then I strike a good day, and that's when I'll train near race speed for as long as I hear those trumpets, to make up for all my crappy laps.)

But one day — get this — Talbot's assistant Ruth has a quiet word with me and says not to worry about my inconsistency. 'It pisses Donny right off,' she quipped, (Donny??) before suggesting my topsy-turvy laps might be a blessing in disguise. She says they mimic recent research on energy cycling. Apparently the body adapts better with varied training stress (she listed half a dozen metabolic processes enhanced by this cycling — things like enzyme reactions, glycogen and lipid fat metabolism, blah-blah aerobic and blah-blah anaerobic — the sort of stuff you know about.) I'm still not totally convinced my fecklessness is exactly what those exercise boffins had in mind, but our little chat made me feel better.

This Ruth's actually a bit of a card. Doesn't care much for appearances and never wears a dress — just these old navy gabardine flares and a plain old button-and-collar shirt. And there's always a little tongue of tucked-in shirt poking through the top of her trouser zipper. She has a kind of slow-talking, coy manner with us, but if any of the parents are getting on Talbot's goat, he'll send in Ruthy (that's what the Talbot kids call her) to sort them out.

Talbot himself is a 'hands-on' coach. If he's not poking you in the chest, he's got a very firm clasp of your wrist in a pep talk, and that's creepy. The older boys say he's got a Napoleon complex, though his shortness had completely escaped me till now (I guess I was too busy reading the warning on the overall package: 'Beware!') But there's definitely something gratuitous in his endless rebukes. On tour with him recently, our bus stopped at Rome's famous Trevi fountain where the kitschy tourist thing to do was to throw a coin in. Later, back on the bus, Talbot asked if I'd tossed one in for myself, and when I said no, you should have heard him tear strips off me. It was embarrassing for the whole bus. What a turd! You could understand it if I'd missed seeing a famous Titian or Breughel, but not some bogan make-a-wish community piggy-bank fountain. Now get this: after Talbot's rant, the first motel we passed was the 'Hotel Napoleon'. I rest my case!

And something whacky happened when I got home from that tour. I went back to Talbot's with him from the plane at 9am, had a bite to eat, then a nap. I woke in the afternoon starving, and after going downstairs to cook a jaffle I noticed the Talbot kids gawking like they were playing a joke. 'Do you know what time it is?' Jon finally asked. I looked at the wall clock, replied, '5pm obviously,' and shrugged, 'I must have been tired, hey?' Then he said I must have been more than tired, because it was the following day. I'd slept 30 hours!

The girl I'm seeing at the moment is Esther, a tall blonde. That is, I 'see' her twice daily in squad, but at carnivals we actually hang together. And if Talbot's son Jon can steal or con the Kombi keys off his dad, some of us pair up and head out for a serious discourse on race strategy on the Kombi benches, nudge-wink!

Esther's cool, but I'll let you in on something odd. She surprised me yesterday when she said a few of the girls think Talbot's 'a bit of a sexy beast'.

'Sexy beast??' I laughed and laughed. That's when she told me one of her friends dropped a tampon onto the end of the pool last week.

Anyway, Talbot snapped it up and asked if it had an owner. When it went unclaimed (surely the owner should have jumped up and down, shouting … ME ME … I've just checked and it's definitely my spare!) he announced it'd be in his pocket if required. So there you go. Don't tell me I never give you tips on how to be a sexy beast.

I don't know what's on the English syllabus up there, but at Homebush High we're studying the Auden poem 'Musee De Beaux Arts', which basically says that if you've high aspirations you'll fly too close to the sun and melt your wings before plopping into the ocean unnoticed (based on the Icarus myth, apparently, as illustrated by Breughel). And then there's Shelley's Ozymandias, which says that no matter how important you become, all your monuments will end up old stones buried under sand.

So, how are they for a couple of inspiring poems? Don't you think it's a bit rich for two famous writers to be telling us not to be try-hards? I mean, how much time and effort must they have put into learning their craft? (Maybe the education system really has been overrun by Marxists, like you used to say.)

Got to hit the sack now. Write back! Bye and good luck, Brad.

P.S. I forgot to mention this new kid in squad, Bobo. You'd find him an absolute scream. He's actually some sort of budding surf ironman, but when he started beating pool swimmers in his home town, his coach suggested he give the pool a good crack under Talbot. (Apparently that coach also once trained under Talbot, and she and Talbot now run clinics together.) Bobo walks — waddles — like a penguin with a dislocated neck, and wears the shittiest old sloppy-joes full of holes. He only joined us a month ago, so I'll keep you posted.

P.P.S. What's an ulcer supposed to feel like? You always seemed to know lots of medical stuff, so I thought I'd run this past you. When I was staying with my first boarding family down here, I'd get a kind of stinging sensation high in the right side of my stomach after breakfast. It usually went away by midmorning, but the rest of the day there was a queasy discomfort. Now that I'm with the Talbots, the stinging's gone, but it's still uncomfortable in there.

P.P.P.S. Do you remember me saying I liked swimming because it was one of the few sports where you could actually lie down on the job? Well, cancel that, 'cos down here with Talbot cracking the whip, it's more like we're prostrating ourselves to our stalag guard.

P.P.P.P.P.P.S. (Just kidding.)

LEADING EDGE

The two Talbot boys and I are on our usual unpaid Sunday-afternoon shift, fabricating exercise equipment in Ming's downstairs home office; Hal's gone home for the weekend. While Jon's brother and I box and tape finished units for shipping, Jon takes a break and leans back grandly in his dad's swivel chair to read letters from this week's in-tray. His feet are up on the desk, and if he found a cigar to puff on he'd be lighting it right now. One letter he begins reading aloud is from John Devitt, the Rome Olympic 100-metre freestyle champion. It sounds too polite, almost fawning, to my discerning ears, and goes, *'Hi coach, trust you and yours are well. It seems you haven't got that writing arm out of plaster yet.'*

Jon chuckles at this last comment, 'Dad hardly ever writes back.' And now he resumes reading because he's clearly proud that old legends think his father's still worth the odd line, a reminder he was actually named after Devitt. (Or was it Konrads? No — make that Henricks, because I'm sure he's the only three-letter Jon of this illustrious trio.) As he reads, I tune in and out while leafing through a surprisingly spiffy brochure I've pulled from the same tray. It's from Indiana University, where the famous 'Doc' Counsilman trains Mark Spitz, who won some medals in Mexico and is tipped for far bigger things in Munich.

The booklet's frontispiece declares that Counsilman's made a stunning breakthrough in describing how swimmers *generate propulsive forces* underwater. With the help of his university's fluid-mechanics boffins and photography department, he filmed hours of underwater footage of freestyle arms pulling in darkened pools, with luminous bands on wrists to graphically trace patterns. In the booklet, photos show those pulling sequences like glow-worm blips in the black. What Counsilman discovered was that champions don't pull in straight lines, as once supposed, but in 'sequenced sweeps' and 'elliptical patterns' — an undulating continuum of multi-planar slices. All this fancy movement is dictated by three things: the laws of fluid mechanics, the complex interaction of the arm–shoulder system, and a swimmer's natural *proprioceptive* talent (neuro-sensory feedback that helps swimmers respond powerfully and accurately to their body's motion). Counsilman claims the hand acts as a foil, like the leading edge of a plane wing, as it generates 'lift forces' through changing direction, pitch, and accelerative bursts. But this is all a little confusing because I can't see how the shape of a hand has any 'leading edge' like the rounded top profile of a wing, unless you count the crude offset bulge of the thumb muscle — and that's a stretch. I glance down at my own hand and see only a slab of wrinkled meat with one end shredded into banded sausages. And anyway, the leading edge of a plane wing is a passive, fixed structure, while a swimmer's hand is active. But what *is* crystal clear and absolutely hilarious to me is when Counsilman claims good swimmers have always instinctively pulled this way, even with coaches barking at them to pull in straight lines. Seemingly to excuse these past errors of his profession, he insists those coaches could never accurately observe underwater movements from above anyway, due to the water's choppiness and refractive error. (*Then why did they advocate straight pulling?* I wonder.) But at least he seems happy to admit past champions succeeded *despite* their coaching, not because of it. Maybe we're still doing that.

For several days I wait keenly for Talbot to announce Counsilman's radical findings, since time is surely of the essence and the brochure's already been in his in-tray a week; he must be itching to tell us. But a week later when there still have been no meetings, no revelations, I start my own experiments by waving my hands this way and that, lap after lap, making my arms even more tired than usual. But instead of going faster, I'm slower. I'm *so* slow, even by my worst standards — it now takes twice as long to pull my arm through — that Talbot boots me over to the junior lanes again. There's always a two-day wait with the little kids before he'll even consider my return, as if to show that you don't stuff around with Donny and come swanning straight back. But being back in the shame lanes gives me more time to experiment. There *must* be some secret to unlock in these crazy curves I'm doing, though my eyes have at least been opened to the fact that my arms already had their own sweeps, like Counsilman said. My native curves seem most dynamic after halfway, though to my surprise I've also discovered my left hand goes limp near the finish, sort of crumples up before pulling out short. It's obvious that if the hand is limp, not even the most rigorous sweeps can be transmitted as force: *fairy-floss could shift more water!* I decide, finally, to abandon my oversized Zorro zig-zags under Counsilman's channelled mentorship, and concentrate instead on keeping my wussy left hand flat and firm to the end.

By the time I'm back in the top lane, my left tricep has been throbbing non-stop for twenty-four hours from repeatedly sweeping back with a firm hand until it extends well past my togs on exit. But I don't let up, the jolting pain proof I've given things a big shake-up. Even a week later the tricep is tender from all those buckets of extra water I've been throwing down my leg, though nothing like the first few days' ordeal. The difference now is that my hand has done it so many thousands of times that it's no longer a conscious effort.

For the first time in my career, stroking with fully functioning equipment, I begin staying with Windeatt through entire training sets. In the third week of the school holidays, I beat him in an 800-metre race, going within a few seconds of his world mark from the Combined High Schools titles. A week later I beat him by half the pool in a 1500-metre race at Birrong when I massacre thirty seconds off my best time. He hasn't even come within a body-length of me in several 400-metre freestyle trials we've raced in training. (He still kills me in the one-lap sprints Talbot occasionally dishes out after training, but those sprinting arms are useless after the first lap of a race anyway.) Although I'm a little disappointed all this new power hasn't come directly from my Counsilman sleuthing, I'm still indebted for the intense scrutiny his theory prompted. If I've bridged the gap with Windeatt after just a few weeks of my renovated freestyle, just imagine where I'll be by the time we're back at school. *I've made it!* I repeat over and over in my head.

One night after training a month later, lying about in the settling water of my lane, I overhear a candid discussion between Talbot and Windeatt at the wall. *Don't they know I'm here?* Talbot's voice is alternately consoling, then raspy and carping. It seems he's telling Graham how past champions did it, mistakes they corrected and qualities that got them through — that sort of guff. 'You know, Graham,' he coos through the wall and gutter slaps, crouching closer, 'even champions try only as hard as required for success, or whatever passes for success at the time, and within a few years their records can look shabby. *You following?*' Windeatt nods obediently before Talbot strikes an upward note. 'What I'm actually saying, Graham, is that every swimmer is keeping something in reserve. Always! Even you.'

Well hello, I'm thinking — what had he thought champions did? I mean, if you're lucky enough to draw an empty chamber at Russian roulette, you're hardly going to risk another turn just to call yourself the two-chamber champ. And of course new generations of swimmers will come along and trounce a champion's times. They're from a much bigger town called the future, for goodness sake, with fresh talent and the momentum of chasing those ever-receding marks from their first races.

Is that all they've got? I ask myself: just some platitude about champions not wanting to kill themselves if they can possibly help it? Now they glance across as if they're listening back; I've come too close. I nod, smile, and jump out.

A month into the new school year, it seems Windeatt's struggling with his health. One week it's sinuses; the next, a trace-element deficiency. And now it could be simple fatigue; nobody knows for sure. What *is* clear is that his father has turned up twice recently with a sheet of blood stats, which he and Talbot pored over for minutes at a time. They're thinking there *has* to be some explanation for Graham's recent lack of improvement, for someone like me — *a backstroker from Queensland* — beating him. I like his dad. He never lurks in a tracksuit like some of the others, just to chew the fat over their kids going up and back. Mr Windeatt's only here if it's important, and otherwise prefers to let Talbot get on with his job. He's the manager of some big hardware store in town — Nock and Kirby's rings a bell — and gets along with a rolling limp some kids say is from childhood polio.

Today Windeatt gives us all a laugh when he jumps in the pool and quips that the only deficiency found in his latest test is chlorine. I didn't even know chlorine was meant to be in our blood, despite our skins soaking in it for five hours a day. Maybe he means *chloride* — I think that's a kind of trace element — or perhaps his sinus blockage confused the two sounds. Anyway, everyone thinks it's a scream that his blood's lacking the very substance we're pickled in for a third of our waking hours.

BELIEVERS

Do buzz-cut Talbot, crew-cut Carlile, and any-cut Lawrence even know hippies exist? I don't get it: Talbot lets his boys play their hippie albums by Country Joe, Blind Faith, Cream, Santana, and Jimi Hendrix, but every month he marches them to his carport to clip their hair to a stubble with electric shears. *Doesn't he read the papers?* — everyone at school has hair well past their collars, even the prefects. But not his boys, who turn up looking like kids from the migrant hostels. And a music teacher in a band called Blackfeather even has hair to his backside.

I'd never so much as listened to an album in Brisbane, and gave record shops a wide berth because they made me nervous, especially if I smelled incense — my only songs courtesy of our battered Hitachi on sink or bedhead. Playing records still seems such a decadent thing to do, but at least I've learned some great new songs. The big radio hits right now are 'Maggie May' by Rod Stewart and 'Your Song' by Elton John. (There's no separating these for favourites, making it the first time I've had to award a tie since 'Norwegian Wood' and 'Guantanamera', way back in Kenmore.)

Hippies reject competition because it's toxic to the flowering of human potential. They wouldn't know what a sporting trophy was, and if they found one would probably melt it down into charming trinkets for their womenfolk. To get by, they fish from streams and harvest their own produce, which grows more wholesomely when sown by harmonious hippie hands. They also reject possessions because ownership is anathema to the spirit, and live mostly in teepees or log cabins erected by communal labour. At the end of each day, wrapped in Indian shawls by a fire, they compose haikus into the night. Hippie mums breastfeed on demand in open sight without the slightest hesitation, so that their toddlers grow up without the hang-ups of *our* uptight world.

That's American hippies, at least; I'm not sure Australia even has any yet. I can't imagine it. And to be honest, I'm hoping the inevitable counterculture takeover is still a few years off because I'd hate to miss my chance to swim at the Olympics and beyond. Can you imagine hippies hanging on to the Olympics once they're in charge? They'd die laughing.

And what would any swimming coach know, for that matter, about flower power and escaping the slavery of the military industrial complex? They're far too busy inviting themselves into motel rooms and ingratiating themselves to swimmers some other coach has put a lifetime of work into, knowing that sooner or later they'll hit the jackpot when some pissed-off pimple pole dumps his own coach and gives them a try.

Some nights my eyes are so itchy from the chlorine, I can't sleep. Swimmers in other squads use goggles all the time now, but Talbot says there's still too much fiddling around for them to seal properly. 'Next season, when the technology's better,' is his usual comeback if anyone dares ask (though Jon says he let swimmers trial them last season until some boy disappeared to the medley lane to check out girl breaststrokers from behind for an hour). My eyes are so sore tonight I haven't stopped rubbing them. If I keep it up they'll bleed for sure, so I'm putting clothes on and sneaking out the back door for a stroll. I'll pretend it's a practice walk for when I run away to live in San Francisco and pitch a tent at *The Hate Ashbury*, whatever that is. (Strange name for the supposed global nerve centre of free love, The *Hate*!)

I head south to the end of Abbotsford Road and take a right until I find a highway, which I follow, and follow. At midnight I'm passing a cemetery that goes on forever. If this is the famous Rookwood, I think it's where my grandmother is buried, though I've never visited her there and wasn't aware she'd died until months later. I'm still headed south or south-east, though my direction's irrelevant because it's only a dry run for The Hate. Now that I've hit my stride, I feel like walking forever, just to see what it would take to make me stop. (And that would be a very hip and natural thing to do.)

Another hour, and it's good news: my eyes are better, so I turn back. I should hit Talbot's by three, leaving plenty of time before anyone stirs for training. At two, I haven't seen a car for ages: it must be the quietest hour on the roads, deader than the Augathella morgue at dawn, as they say. Any cars that do come along now, I hear them so far off there's time to look over my shoulder in case it's a sinister one up to no good. Truth be known, it's creepy being out at this hour. Now a car's whistling up the last hill and I glance back to see a roofline inching above the apex; it's almost the beige of Talbot's. Seconds later the entire car's visible, though still a hundred metres off. Coincidentally, it's a Beamer, and it slows behind me; the cemetery's alongside again for me to scramble through the headstones if anyone from the car tries to jump me. Now it eases to the kerb, the driver straining across for a closer peek at this halfwit walking the streets. *Shit, it's Talbot.* I've got my parka hood on, but surely he recognises me and the game's up. I keep my head down and affect a homeless person's shuffle, though I'm also thinking up fantastic excuses, ready to hop in if he calls. But after he heaves back to the wheel and roars off, I'm almost disappointed. God knows where he's been at this hour: apart from his coaching commitments, he's never at home these days, but I still wonder why he didn't stop. Maybe he thought to himself, *That looks like Cooper, but it can't be; I'm just tired.* An hour later I'm tiptoeing through the back door, and as soon as I put my head on the pillow I know I'll be asleep in one minute.

According to Talbot, our swimming fates are limited only by the strength of our self-belief. After hearing this mantra all season, it's only after our latest pep talk that I suddenly grasp self-belief's absolute primacy in Talbot's universe. *How have I been so dumb for so long?* By insisting it's *our* self-belief always on the line, Talbot totally excuses himself from the liability loop. *It's pure genius:* if we swimmers make a small gain, it's but a glimpse of what's possible with truckloads of the stuff, while any setback is a sign we're wallowing in self-doubt again. And guess the identity of the grand wizard of self-belief, whose reputation stays unsullied by our crappy racing? *No prizes.* It's also pure evil, of course. But then I remember a Brisbane coach who nobly conceded a mistake he *might have made* in his team's doomed state-championship preparation. Within days of that gesture, his top girl left him. Then the girl who'd relied on her for pacing jumped ship too. Within a month, that domino nudge had emptied his entire top lane. The coach then had a breakdown and was last seen selling cars for a living. Talbot lives for cars, but he'll never have to work in a car yard, because he has too much self-belief.

Friday afternoon there's a new swimmer to pick up on the way to training. Jon's given me all the goss on this kid, who's trained before under Talbot and lives only a few blocks away. The father's some transport magnate, who, after tiring of his teenager arriving home each night bitching about Talbot, decided to build him his own backyard heated pool. But after a few months shuttling up and down those brand-new lanes under his dad's proud gaze, the kid shot through. A few days later, with police only hours away from giving the sensational story to the papers, he turned up again, and today's his first day back in squad. When Talbot pulls up outside their home's surprisingly modest exterior, we slide the Kombi door open and the kid hops in with a sly grin to share a joke with Jon, as if his long absence was just a pause for breath. The dad, in his home-office casuals and olive cardigan, saunters to the front of the Kombi, where Talbot's arm hangs over the door. He murmurs a barely audible greeting through a tight smile as he clasps Talbot's arm. 'Don't know how to thank you, Don,' he says firmly, when for a split second his face is a sucky, blubbery sump before flexing back to a damp moon-face. He turns away and gives Talbot's shoulder a squeeze, and we're off.

We're waiting for Talbot to announce the next set on Monday afternoon when word gets round of 'a lifter'. Lifters are totally clueless on how to react when getting poked in the chest by Talbot. Instead of their heads bowing and chests sinking, lifters' chins jut in defiance and chests rise as if Talbot's index finger's a bike pump (it's *that* thick). You see those chests puff higher on every pump-stab, and just when you think there's no more lift left, something's sucked from deep in the gut and up it goes again. Sooner or later there must be an explosion. They're in the middle of this crazy brinkmanship right now, and it's why we're still waiting for the next set; Ruth would normally step in to tell us, but she must have gone to the loo. Talbot has his lifter boxed into a shady corner of the louvre-brick wall at the end of the pool and looks unfazed, his head at this relaxed cocky angle showing he's very, very interested in the psychology of his victim's next move, but not the least in how this ends.

Real swimmers never, ever lift. We know to keep humble, and we're all super-flat-chested anyway. In fact, we're flat and wide right through, the paper cut-outs of the sporting world: we don't even have proper bottoms, just a hole in the lower back. But this lifter's a chunky footballer, chunkier than even Talbot, and three inches taller. (He's only here because his footy coach told him to swim in his off-season for discipline. He's not good enough to train anywhere near the top lane, and I'm sure I noticed his boxy hull floundering among twelve-year-olds in my last stint in the shame lanes.)

At long last, Ruthy's headed back, tucking her shirt into her flares as if appearances matter. She stops for a brief word with 'Donny', stays another moment to look the lifter up and down like he's some agricultural exhibit, and strolls over to tell us what's next.

When we finish our set, the lifter's nowhere in sight: not in the pool, and nowhere near Talbot, who's scribbling on a notebook resting on his thigh. But there he is now — in his car on the other side of the louvre-bricks, where he drops the clutch to smoke all the way down the street, never to lift again.

Another day, another two sessions — and this afternoon, Talbot's complaining that we might as well give our routine set of training 50s the big flick from now on. They're too easy; we get too much rest. Doing 50s leaving every 40 seconds is apparently 'a hell of a waste of time'.

We don't refer to our training as *laps*. Lap swimmers call their laps laps because they lap non-stop up and back for half an hour. No, we do 50s, or 100s, or 200s, or 400s, or 800s, or 1600s, or 3200s, and without ever saying the 'metres' afterwards, because it's understood that it *is* metres and not ants, galaxies, or cashews. And all those saved metric syllables will obviously go into some energy store to make life fractionally easier or more productive somewhere down the track. Even more economically, from 200 up we don't even say the 'hundred'. They're just 2s, 4s, 8s, etc. If we have to do six 800s, for example, it's 'six eights'. Neither do we say 'seconds' or 'minutes' to describe the push-off interval. So it's never so-many 50 metres leaving on 40 seconds, just 50s on 40. Likewise, it's 2s on 2,30, 4s on 5, 8s on 10. If syllables were an endangered species, we'd be up for a team knighthood.

These are all race distances, of course, these noun-denuded and syllable-shaved 50s, 100s, 200s, doubling with each ascending distance (except for the 1600, of course, which was cut to 1500 for some arcane historical reason to do with the difference between metre and yard pools). When Talbot orders us to do any of these distances in training, it's at a slower pace than races because we repeat them many times over, not just once. The greatest number of repeats, of course, belongs to the shortest distance, the 50s. We usually do sixty of these, though we've been known to do as many as a hundred — always pushing off every 40 seconds on the clock.

But it's this 40 interval that's begun to fiercely exercise Talbot today, because almost everyone in our top lane will average 33 seconds, giving us a whopping seven seconds' rest. And because we depart five seconds apart, this 33 seconds gets you to the wall two seconds before the swimmer ahead leaves; and then the swimmer behind you strokes in two seconds before *you* go, leaving you only one second alone at the wall. In that brief overlap with each, you might get a few words out. Not a sentence, mind you, let alone a proper conversation, but the odd snatched phrase and a grunt for *okay* or *really?* If there was something of riveting importance you had to tell someone, say, Hal, who's always at the very end of the line — maybe something about a girl — you might use this wall overlap to quickly tell the swimmer behind you, 'Ask Hal what her name is, *pass it on.*' So it'll be sent down from swimmer to swimmer, and twenty or so 50s later, you'll have your reply back up the chain from Hal saying '*Huh?*' or whatever response he's given.

But tiny embers of conversation kept alive by heavy breathing aren't Talbot's main concern about these 50s. It's only the disproportionate rest. He thinks the whole idea of 'interval training' (where you break up really long distances into really small units for 'an anaerobic threshold effect' — *but that's another story*) is effective only when you're getting five seconds' rest or less. So seven's obviously way too much — a 'namby-pamby holiday', as he calls it.

So today he has a bright idea. He's going to fix things. Apparently we're to have a go at leaving on the 35 seconds instead of 40. It has to be this jump of exactly five seconds because the clock is marked in five-second numerical indices. You can't just leave on, say, every 38 seconds (though this two-second interval reduction would be the most logical and humane adjustment) because the 38 won't 'cycle' on the fives or zeros required to follow the clock.

It's not too hard to grasp what a challenge this is going to be, if only because all those 33s were made possible only because of that huge rest. Therefore, if we'll be getting *less* than seven seconds' rest — in this case, a whopping five seconds less — it's more than a fair bet that we won't maintain our 33s for long. It would be no exaggeration at all to suggest that very soon after we start, our speed will rapidly fall off to two seconds slower, and two seconds slower will be 35, meaning we'll have no rest at all. *Then* meaning we won't actually be doing 50s, but a continuous swim. And if we know there'll be no rest at the wall, why wouldn't we tumble and keep going? Which is precisely what happens in our longer distances — say 400s — where we actually do repeat continuous 35-second laps with tumbles and no rest, though nobody pretends that those 400s are 50s leaving on the 35 because they *are* 400s. In other words, Talbot's gone crazy.

A short while later, if Talbot had longer hair, he'd have pulled it all out by now, because our first attempt at doing these wildly optimistic 50s on the 35 lasts barely three minutes. Windeatt led off. He'll always lead for Talbot. The first 50 went well. Very well. Everyone in 31 seconds: four seconds' rest — enough time to think *but not say*, 'Great start, Brad' (or Grub, or Jim, or Rick, or Greg, or Mike). The next one in 32 — enough break to check the clock, note the time, savour three breaths, and go. Then 33 — *the old standard* — but only enough rest to touch the wall, lean back, and set yourself up to go. Then *bingo* — 35, and we started missing the interval. Half a second over, then one over, two, and so on, and Talbot was dancing about at the far end under the clock like some wild buzz-cut, mohair-clad leprechaun ranting, '*Stop. Stop.* Come back, *stop.*'

Now peace is restored and we're to have another go, because Talbot's a believer in mental preparation, and suspects we weren't fully focused for the first attempt. It could be that simple. Our failure could have been 'all in the mind' because the mind's such a powerful thing when you're up there calling the shots and not doing the actual failing. We *have* to believe we can do it this time because nobody achieves anything without believing it first, and we're all *okay* with this. 'Okay,' 'Righto,' 'Sure,' 'Yep,' 'Fine', and no dissenters. We put on a show that we're in the mood this time when we mimic strapping ourselves in and buckling up for a white-knuckle seat on the believers' express, and here goes. But it's exactly the same train wreck all over again, and now Talbot's become very dark — telling us that the twenty minutes of our lives we've wasted on our hopeless attempts at his new interval has just cost us each a state championship. It's that simple.

Of course, there are other things Talbot could have done if he thought swimming 33 seconds on the 40 wasn't challenging enough. He could simply have insisted that we swim 32 instead. One second faster doesn't sound much, but when you think it's a second faster than the old 33s that even Windeatt thought had its challenges, well, it's a bit like instantly improving your best race time by one second for every lap. And nobody ever does that. (In fact, it's common knowledge that for every second of reduction, there's an algebraic fatigue penalty — meaning you need far more than that additional second's rest to compensate. Taken to its logical extreme, the penalty for doing, say, seven seconds faster — in other words, your best 50 time of 25 seconds — would be to have to lie down on the side of the pool gasping for air and not being able to swim another stroke for ten minutes.)

Talbot could even enforce this new 32 standard with stiff sanctions for anyone randomly caught going slower, but this would involve someone — namely me — suggesting it to him in the first place. Also, if he accepted it, there would need to be monitoring, and maybe even *informing* on each other, and then someone might dispute their time and there'd have to be another poolside poking or someone storming out or quitting for good. So for the rest of the afternoon it's back to doing 100s on 1,15, which is about the closest you can get to doing 50s on the 35, because it's double 37.5 to do both 50s. And 1,15 cycles very simply on the clock, like points on the compass: depart the first on the 0 for north; leave for the second on the 15 for east; the 30 for south; 45 for west; and so on, repeating and repeating the quadrant. And because we rarely have much more than five seconds' rest in these, Talbot's almost happy.

QUINIDINE

I'm in the North Sydney Olympic Pool showers looking down on Talbot's heavy shoulders and busy right hand; he's crouched awkwardly at my thighs. We're in a hurry because these are the 1972 NSW championships and I'm meant to be waiting behind the blocks for what's become my best event, the 400-metre freestyle. (After noticing I hadn't bothered shaving down for this first big test of the Olympic year, Talbot's decided to embarrass me with a hurried once-over in the showers.) Up and down my thigh sprints his razor, forehand down and backhand up, a mini-snowplough spreading foam clods either side of a tan runway. Tiny red bulbs ooze and bloom along the odd nick line.

Moments ago Talbot was furious, but he now seems warmed to his task like a bossy hen with its chickens finally in line. As he hacks away, I'm thinking how much tripe this shaving-down caper is: one of the sham rituals greasing the coach–swimmer hegemony. And swimmers are such suckers for coaching palaver. As soon as there's any hint of boffin-babble (*Reduces the drag coefficient! Exposes the nerve ends!*), their eyes glaze over as if it's an edict from God's lab. But as if a few mangy hairs could slow down a design already as flawed as the human form in water. I mean, what proper hull ever had a big wobbly ball up front, shoulders, hips, and a gooey adipose lining? (The jargon for those particular liabilities is *form drag*.) Worrying about a bit of leg fuzz slowing you down is the idiocy-equivalent of a snail fretting about the drag of a dewy shell.

At last, I'm back out behind the blocks on glossy new pins in a murky slick of floodlight on damp concrete, bodies, and decaying dive towers; the smell is rust and salt. Under swaying lamps and fine drizzle, I swing my arms in counter-rotation, half in athletic pageantry and half wondering if there's a point. Straight ahead is the darkening arch of the Harbour Bridge, with its inching headlights; over my right shoulder, the ritzy turrets of Luna Park.

With any luck there are now only the tiniest spots of shaving foam left on the back of my legs, because the Mexico Olympic bronze medallist Karen Moras is directly behind me, leaning back nonchalantly in a row of plastic chairs. She's stretched almost flat now across her chair's hollow, arms joined coat-hanger cool behind her head, waiting for her own 400-metre final. At eighteen, Karen's less than a year older than me, but in girls this can be an extra decade in maturity; and now I can almost feel her inquisitive gaze counting foam flecks on my hammies. But suddenly I'm in luck when one of her club mates jogs past to the girl beside Karen and asks her to check for something on the back of *her* legs. There's a hushed urgency with the request, and by the hurried half-pirouette to face away from her appraiser, I can tell it's for higher stakes than the odd scrap of shaving foam. When she's given the thumbs-up, she trots back to her chair almost whinnying with enthusiasm.

I don't know how Karen can look so cool, knowing Shane is the new world record holder, and that they'll be splashing it out straight after me. In fact, Shane now holds the complete suite of freestyle world records, from 100-metre to 1500-metre, a feat once thought impossible. But silly me — I now see one girl's rise explains the other's resignation. The spotlight's shifted.

People don't mind Karen. She has these big never-miss-a-trick doll's eyes and an expression always seemingly braced for banter. Her family's a team: Mrs Moras can often be seen fussing over her parka-clad daughters between races, diving into bags or twisting thermos caps. You know you're at something big with her around.

'What time you gonna do, Brad?' Karen asks flatly from behind, as officials fuss over another hitch in the starting trolley. (*She spoke my name*, I marvel; maybe she saw me smash Windeatt's world 800-metre record last night.) In the same automatic tone, I turn and reply, 'Hmmm … exactly 4 minutes 4.7 seconds, Karen,' and she's all chuckles at this mild parody.

After finishing two body-lengths clear of Windeatt, I glance up to see Karen quizzing my timekeepers in the light rain, nudging in under their umbrella; now she returns my gaze, suddenly hands-on-mouth, to cackle, 'It's … oh my god … 4 minutes 4.7.' I'm thrilled such a freakish fluke has impressed Karen.

As Karen's final is called to the blocks, I crow, 'Good luck,' divining that she will lose to Shane.

The next night I'm leading my 1500-metre freestyle final when, six laps from the finish, something snags in my gut and I stop breathing. I hug myself into a ball to relieve whatever's making my insides feel like a gaffed fish, before treading water across to the lane-divider, where I throw an arm over its beaded discs. Thirty seconds later, with my breathing relaxing and heart rate slowing, I continue the race, though now a lap behind the new leader, Graham Windeatt. At the finish I find my time almost a minute slower than I'd hoped for when I dived in.

A day later I'm sitting across the desk from a doctor Talbot has scheduled for me at a sports-medicine clinic, and I'm slightly embarrassed he should be pondering a whacky ailment which has intruded on my entire life perhaps a dozen times, and only in swimming races. By his strange harrumphing I suspect he has his doubts, and who can blame him? Hang on — he's actually putting pen to paper for a prescription. *But I'm not really sick*, I feel like protesting as he rips out the scrip and pushes it into my hand before

seeing me to the door. In his brief muttering of a diagnosis, I hear
the term 'diaphragm spasticity', and marvel that there could be such
a thing. Visiting a pharmacy on the way home, I pick up a course
of quinidine tablets. When I phone my father in the evening, he
asks, 'Isn't quinidine some sort of drug for heart problems?' I reply
that the GP merely called it a muscle relaxant, and insist he must
have known his stuff because he was from the Lewisham Sports
Medicine Clinic. I take my first tablet before bed, but the following
day I throw the whole bottle away in disgust because I don't want
to take drugs just for sport, recalling Ashley's past disparagement of
prescription users. ('Christalmighty,' he'd gasped in the car when I
was nine, having apparently peered into the bathroom cabinet of
friends we'd visited. *They had a pill for every sniffle and a cream for
every crack!'* And when he wasn't putting on a show of mild outrage,
he'd simply call such people 'lab rats'.)

A month later at the Olympic Trials in Brisbane, I break
the world record for 400-metre freestyle, beating my NSW
championship time by three seconds, and without the help of
prophecy. This makes me the swimmer to beat in Munich for
the event. I also win the 1500-metre in a time just two tenths
outside the world mark. With additional wins in the 100-metre and
200-metre backstroke, I'm a shoo-in for the team, having taken
nearly a quarter of the men's individual gold medals on offer. I'd also
have won the 800-metre and likely beaten my own recent world
record, had Talbot not instructed me to attempt a further lowering
of my new 400-metre mark en route (records can be set during
longer distances, with foot contact at the wall at the designated
tumble a legal touch). But I failed that attempt narrowly and was
so exhausted that I fell back through the field, rallying towards the
end to finish second to Windeatt.

I begin wondering about this strange ploy that probably cost me a world mark and another title, and wonder if Talbot merely wanted me hamstrung to guarantee Windeatt the win to secure his spot on the team. But then, maybe he really convinced himself I had a better 400-metre in me, even that I'd be the first under four minutes; the sky's always the limit with him. He thinks we're cars that have to be constantly red-lined to get the most out of them. From his perspective, at least, there was nothing to lose and everything to gain.

But it wasn't my perspective. I'd have liked another world record. As the hours pass, I find it increasingly hard — no, *impossible* — to believe that someone of Talbot's experience could think that after giving my all to break one of the toughest records in the books, I could do even better just twenty-four hours later. What an insult! In my mind, he told me to *throw* a race, to betray the whole idea of competing, just for *his* plans, whatever they were.

My dreaded breathing problem showed no sign of a return during the trials. But then, they were at the Valley Pool, where I'd trained and competed for several years, trouble-free. It's one of my 'friendly' pools.

TURF WARS

Today I'm catching the train from Burwood to be interviewed at an Epping TV studio for the Munich Olympics. The station's just a few blocks from the home of my new host family, the Dickmans, who've come down from Grafton to give their fourteen-year-old son David a shot at swimming glory under Talbot. They're a great family, so I've no idea why I got it in my head to shoot through last weekend: I packed an airline bag with a change of clothes and headed along Parramatta Road for fifteen minutes before being overwhelmed by the particulars of my next six decades and that night's dinner. So I turned back, the sudden prospect of a house to live in again, with all its mod cons and guarantees, like manna from heaven. It was a brief escape, but great to get it out of my system. Even better: no one suspected a thing!

What makes Munich vaguely newsworthy so far out is the small 'advance party' of likely Olympians leaving soon for a short European tour. And I'm on it, of course. My interviewer is Rex Mossop, an ex-footballer with a cistern-sized head, a voice that makes you wonder how many times his nose was smashed, and a decidedly manly manner. I step up to join the man famously called 'the Moose' at his panel desk, and find his welcome surprisingly disarming for a brutal ex-prop. Because there's a strict two-minute interview limit, he wastes no time getting to the nitty-gritty: 'So, Brad — are you going to bring back a gold medal for us?' I don't want to hold the show up, but this is such a brain-dead question that I can't dignify it with a straight yes or no.

'I-it's pretty hard to say,' I stammer. 'It's not like I'll be the only one trying.'

To my surprise, the Moose is in agreement, chuckling, 'I'm totally with you on that.' Just when I think I'm off the hook, he adds, 'But I'm afraid you're going to have to put a far more positive spin on it. Just for this show.'

I'll put a positive spin on it alright, Rex, I think straight back. How about — *There are experts everywhere these days telling us we're losers even when we win; that the moment you're sucked into this whole identity-through-winning farce, you're pretty well ruined for life. Either you'll be one of the hordes who never get within cooee of winning, or you'll be some twelve-year-old world-beater who trips at the last hurdle into a life of pissy platitudes like the supposed 'lessons of losing'. Unless, of course, you're one of the lucky ones like me who fall through those cracks onto a treadmill of ballooning expectations. Is that positive enough for you, Rex?*

But out in the world of real voices — by the time mine turns up — it's my more measured tone I'm hearing: 'So … of course I'll be giving it everything, but it doesn't pay to be overconfident.' Meanwhile the Moose continues with his bouncy, adenoid-choked chortle, as if he's saying, *Can you believe this kid?* And now I suddenly wonder with dread if he's been taking the piss all along. But no, I have to say he seems genuinely titillated. On cue, he thrusts out his hand so I can submit mine to a masculine mauling. 'It's been terrific chatting with you, Brad, and I know you're going to win for us,' he finishes, when I think, *Christ, he's still at it*, before shuffling out past the cameras, sets, and cables, oddly prouder and more confused than I've been for a while.

At last our team of Olympians is on the way to its barnstorming tour of European swim meets, no less than four capitals on its thirteen-day itinerary. Laurie Lawrence is the coach, and most teammates agree the atmosphere already seems much lighter than in previous tours with Talbot: Laurie's ribbing, footy-club bawdiness is the complete opposite of Talbot's Victorian uptightness. On the plane he spends hours flitting from swimmer to swimmer, getting to know our goals and hobbies, even taking short cuts over the tops of seats until the stewardess reprimands him (*'Scout's honour, I'll stop for you, sweety!'* he fires right back). When he gets around to me, I foolishly let on that I read the odd verse collection, and he immediately begins frothing about Wordsworth's 'Composed upon Westminster Bridge'. 'Imagine sitting on that bridge, Brad — *being Wordsworth* — jotting those lines as they come into your head, shuffling them into pentameters, peering across that vast scene of boats and mists.'

'I'm ... more into recent Americans like Berryman and Lowell,' I explain.

'Never mind, that's great too,' he pants, casting around for another victim.

Two days after touching down in Paris, we're sitting around in speedos and waiting to race in Marseilles when Laurie calls some of the male team members together. He barks at us to pay attention to his address, apparently one to decide fates far into the future. 'So listen up,' he snorts: 'There are absolutely to be no more groin tufts left after shaving down, because it makes me puke.' A few of us glance down to find we are indeed the proprietors of scourer-grade tussocks our razors have spared, amid childish cackles and good-natured taunts. Two girls within earshot stand and walk off self-consciously, though Laurie had made it clear this pep talk wasn't for them.

Soon the togs-tuft syndrome is a poolside phenomenon, some of us even competing to *out* unsuspecting international offenders. 'Scrotum mo in the Yanks,' I mutter when the Americans shed their tracksuits, echoed soon by, 'Sack scrub in the Krauts,' and, 'Ball walrus in the Swedes.' Fifteen minutes later, when our attention's drawn to the hush of teammates crouched tightly on the blocks for the first final, one of the younger girls lets go with, 'Bag shag in the Brits,' her teammates' delighted squeals drawing frowns from officials.

In a team walkabout two days later in London, Laurie spots two skinheads pacing the opposite footpath in their braces and hobnail boots. 'What if those punks attacked us, boys?' he suddenly pivots, eyes popping, eyebrows up. 'Just imagine it. They come in swinging. *Our* backs against the wall. *We* come back swinging like crazy. Isn't that what you live for? *Backs against the wall, fighting for your life?*'

A few of us size each other up. 'You go first, Laurie,' I tell him. 'We'll back you up — with the police in ten minutes.'

At our next competition, in the Crystal Palace swim centre, Laurie's annoying me with his usual frenzied pre-race pumping. 'Do you really think your jumping up and down makes a difference to swimmers who spend their lives training for these few minutes?' I ask sharply. Enjoying the thrill of my new hectoring tone, I continue: 'Like, we train five hours a day and still need someone to tell us we're desperate to win?'

But Laurie's unflappable. 'Too friggin' right I do!'

I shake my head in annoyance and soon join teammates at a poolside bench.

The following day is our last free time in London, and we all spend a few hours shopping — which for me is strictly the pretend version because I blew almost everything I had in duty-free. London has an oddly haphazard layout and is always kind of disappointing. I went through New York in the back of a cab last year just to change airports, and that one ride seemed to put London in the shade.

In Belgrade the day before we leave, four of us boys veer off the cobblestone into a tiny cafe, almost as if by multiple thought-osmosis. We sit at a cramped and stained pine table and open a menu, but only for the liquids. I'm down to my last few travellers' cheques, so I know these will be my last beers on this tour. The ones the waiter brings out are a disappointingly small version of a stubby, but they're packing a ten per cent alcohol content. The labels say Bip. *Who would have thought to name a beer Bip?* I wonder. We sit there and don't move for forty-five minutes while we chat and sink four of these mini time bombs. When I stand up, I go from making sense to fully drunk in two seconds flat. Two of us sit straight back down and say, 'Bip Bip Bip,' before jumping straight back up, and it's all laughs until we're out on the street. I've never been drunk at midday before, and the coming afternoon along these black medieval lanes promises to be magnificent.

On the plane back home, we talk about girls. When Laurie overhears us, he tells us a story of a 'great girl' he flirted with briefly in his young rugby-union days, the sort of girl he thought he could end up with. This was overseas somewhere, maybe America. An adventure addict, she was always heading off to hike forest trails, sail coastlines, and paddle rapids. And this clearly is Laurie's idea of ideal womanhood, judging by the way he growls and braces when he mentions these activities. When Laurie gets around to mentioning her dad, he makes a fierce face to indicate some hard-bitten patriarch, suddenly wearing the eye patch Laurie's right hand has slapped onto his own eye. The dad was a crazy outdoors-person like his daughter, a former marine too, and I'm wondering why Laurie would be telling us about her dad when he goes uncharacteristically coy with this odd defeated expression you never see with Laurie, and you put two and two together and know it was the dad that came between them. He cranes his neck around the seats to check how everyone's travelling, before sighing, 'Oh well,' and rising to bounce up the aisle. It was an interesting insight, and generous of Laurie to share this snippet from his ancient star-crossed-lover days.

A week after the tour, I'm in a car with Talbot, unsure how much longer I can take these toxic fumes. We're headed for the airport in his wife's Beamer; it's a little blue one, and a far more boxy and austere affair than his own sleek saloon. But halfway there he discovered the brakes were completely gone, and for the past ten minutes it's been handbrake on the hills, handbrake through every corner, and handbrake at every red light. The smell is like a tyre franchise on fire, no doubt from the friction of a handbrake jerked more times in a minute than in a normal month.

We're in a hurry because he decided to put me on a plane back to Brisbane at only a moment's notice this afternoon after getting fed up with me lagging in training again. (That's what he says, but maybe he'd booked the flight days ago, and today was a pretext.) Ever since my return he's been saying my swimming's so bad I'd be better off quitting. Maybe he's right: I normally take a day or two to come down from the sensory and social overload of a tour, but even after a week this time I'm struggling to stay motivated. (Now I understand why I'm always hearing of swimmers taking a month to get back in the swing of things, and of others quitting for good.) Neither of us has been talking in the car, if you don't count him repeating, 'You've got some serious thinking to do up in Brisbane,' each time in slightly different tones, like he's just practising. This time he adds that he doesn't want to see me in his lanes for at least a month; and even then, it's still a big 'if' he'll have me back.

At last I get the courage to ask if I can wind the window down. 'I'm choking on these fumes.'

'Me too,' he chimes, and it's the first thing he's said that hasn't sounded hostile, maybe because he's enjoying this driving by the seat of his pants.

Back in Brisbane with my father, we ponder what to do with me when my month exile's up. That's if I get the okay to return. Ashley's moved to Zillmere to be near work; I'm in the top bunk, he's below (this is a concern because farts rise, and old people's farts are the worst, and he's now almost two years older than his *old* old). More bad news the next day is when Ashley tells me he's in no doubt Talbot will take me back, subject to my thinking things through, of course. When I ask if I should enrol in school in the meantime, we decide I'll start back at Brisbane State High on the off-chance I don't go back to Sydney. On Monday I'm back in uniform and reunited with my old classmates Roland, Dale, and Bruce.

With still no word from Talbot on the horizon a fortnight later, Ashley shocks me with the news that Forbes Carlile has written with an offer to take me on, and that the Goulds would put me up until permanent accommodation can be found. Since a return to Sydney now seems inevitable, one way or another, I pull out of school to concentrate on regaining some swimming fitness. A few nights later, Ashley's chuckling at the sink over a telegram he's just received from Talbot, screeching in caps, 'MUST HAVE BRAD HERE,' no ifs and buts about it, and not a single mention of thinking things through. I suddenly wonder if Talbot got wind of the Carlile offer, maybe from Ashley himself; I wouldn't be surprised. Now he places Carlile's letter pointedly beside Talbot's telegram for me to read. Carlile begins by stressing his policy of never accepting elite swimmers from other squads. 'Keep reading,' Ashley urges. The very next line says he's made an exception for me, but only because Talbot recently breached coaching etiquette by instructing the Carlile champion Karen Moras on her pacing at a recent championship. It seems there's been a turf war going on between the coaching titans, and Ashley's enjoying this contestation-from-afar for his son's services. The next morning when I tell him I'll go back to Talbot, he quips, 'The devil you know, eh?'

My immediate future settled, I'm energised to step up my training from once-a-day maintenance to twice, hopping in alone at the Valley Pool after Gordon's squad finishes. It's great to see Gordon again, though we don't chat (and to be truthful, I feel like a bit of a traitor, and get around his pool with a pronounced slink).

I've been working on my backstroke kick lately, which has always had an odd crossover beat — where a foot crosses over the opposing one — though only on one side. Common in freestyle, crossover kicks are almost unheard of in backstroke because there's less counterbalancing for the legs to do. (Wearing a pool on your back doesn't allow for the kind of body roll that makes freestyle legs want to counterbalance.) I'd never tried to address my backstroke crossover because I suspected the extra body roll it permitted freed my arms to mimic the lateral sweeps of a freestyle pull. (*Though why just one side? I've always wondered.*) So today I'm experimenting with a both-sides backstroke crossover — an upside-down edition of my freestyle kick — but soon feel my arms severely straight-jacketed. This is when I finally settle for an orthodox backstroke six-beat, meaning just straight up and down kicking with no time for crossing. For the next week while Ashley settles things with Talbot, I become more and more comfortable with the discipline of my new kick, an initial timing awkwardness now a thing of the past; and my times show none of the short-term fall-off associated with stroke tweaking. I'm really onto something, I tell myself.

DIRTY WATER

A few days later, I'm on an Ansett flight south. Not to Sydney just yet, but on the way to my new mate Bobo's place further along the coast. This gives me nearly a week at his family spread, where waves spill across the rock shelf at the foot of their block on high tide (and where Bobo collects the oysters he's promised we'll be gorging ourselves on). There's a stairwell winding up from rocks to their breakfast room, where the shimmering sea light transforms the walls into Edward Hopper's breathtaking painting *Rooms by the Sea*.

Early on my second day, Bobo and I walk a narrow bitumen path to a nearby ocean pool for some token training. On the pool deck, fifty-year-old surf-club stalwarts, some with spectacularly marbled walrus guts, greet us with strange expressions like, 'Yerz keepin' that dirty water off yer chests, boys.' When I ask Bobo what they meant about the dirty water on our chests, he says it's an old surf-club way of asking if we've had any luck with girls. 'Right,' I reply, none the wiser.

When Bobo notices a swell running after training, he lends me one of his surfboards. I could swim thirty kilometres in the ocean if needed, but I'm a little taken aback to find our point of entry is the lighthouse rocks. I've never surfed on a board before, let alone entered the ocean with such risk. I watch nervously as Bobo mimics how to time the lazily heaving swells to leap onto your board the moment the spill rakes your ankles, then to paddle like crazy. If you hesitate a moment, according to Bobo, the water's sudden retreat can leave you 'paddling with two broken arms on oysters below'.

(He's right, I concede seconds later, as those oysters are exposed when the swell sucks back.) A few surges after Bobo's entry, I pick my time and paddle out to the dozen or so surfers lolling about in steamers for their next wave. But I sit out conspicuously beyond them, as if these small sets aren't worth the bother where I come from. After twenty minutes playing community shark bait, I paddle discreetly to shore and walk back to Bobo's alone.

In the afternoon, we wander up to The Oxford in town for a beer and a game of snooker. Again we're greeted by cheerful surf-club characters, whom Bobo introduces in quick succession along a line of stools as 'Wags', 'Fats', 'Ant', and 'Dog'. The pub's a font of salacious gossip for Bobo. 'Those two suits at the bar,' he leans into me and whispers, 'they're crooked Ds' (he never says *detectives*). 'Over there, that's the mayor who lanced a few of my old schoolmates, but he's never been charged. That dealer at the end of the bar could have us killed, just like that.'

Bobo plays a great trick on my third day. When I wander into his lounge room, he yells 'Catch' from behind the door as I spy him from the corner of my eye shaping to pass a football. Only it's not a footy, but their Persian cat, and when I lift my arms to brace that blur of fur and claw hitting my chest, it rakes its rear legs in panic, mincing my abdomen. This happens a few more times over the next two days, until I discover how to prevent a shredding entirely by accident: it's when I'm late with my arms and the cat happily bounces off my chest on lightly drumming paws, claws retracted. Once Bobo sees I've cottoned on, moggy-tossing's a thing of the past.

Doomed to return to Sydney to rejoin Talbot within a few days, I'm wondering how I can repay Bobo's hospitality when I remember Ashley's sister Edna lives in a unit in Dee Why. This fits in perfectly with Bobo's Sunday surf carnival at nearby Collaroy, so I suggest we stay Sunday night there, because the following morning we have to meet up with Ming. 'Is it cool with her?' Bobo asks.

'Isn't she my aunt?' I shrug. But she's also an aunt I've never met, if you don't count one or two reported visits when I could barely walk or talk. (I suspect her being sole beneficiary of their widowed mother's estate might have long ago estranged Ashley and her.) On Sunday afternoon, I ring Edna from a Collaroy phone box to ask if it's okay for us to crash at her place — 'The lounge would be fine.' By her hesitating approval, she's clearly uncomfortable with the idea, and she sounds even older than I'd anticipated.

When her front door opens two hours later, the impression's confirmed, but then I remember she's Ashley's older sister, and Ashley's a young-looking sixty-three. A clenched 'Hello' barely escapes her lips through Ashley's crowded upper teeth on a prim falsetto, before a gothic, 'Do come in.' It's soon obvious that a pushing-seventy divorcee and two knockabout teenagers have nothing to talk about except family. I'm rattled, though, to find her opinion of Ashley has none of the restraint of her demeanour, reminding me of my mother's story of Edna becoming my father's first management 'project' when, at barely twenty, he'd supposedly bullied her into a modelling career she'd only been lukewarm on. When her final word on him is, 'A very bad man, your father,' without a crease of irony in sight, I'm tempted to share an awkward glance with Bobo, but lock my gaze on the carpet in case we both lurch into guffaws. I can see it's been unsettling for her to dredge these impressions of her rascal brother — in fact, the visit has been a terrible mistake — so I offer to make us all a cup of tea, which she declines before standing to sigh, 'Help yourselves, I'm off to bed.' When Bobo and I buy milk and cereal from the local grocer the next morning, we bring back a small bunch of flowers and leave them on the kitchen table before heading off.

HEARTS

On Monday I discover Talbot's found a new training billet for Bobo and me to stay with — together this time — and barely a minute's stroll to Hurstville pool. We're guests of the Halls in St Georges Parade. The squad returns from Auburn next week for winter, so the timing couldn't be better with Munich just four months off and Queensland training camp in three months. At long last, we're in the home straight!

Because her only child, Kevin, once trained under Talbot, Mrs Hall says she knows *all about swimmers, and Talbot*, hinting nothing could surprise her. Bobo and I are given parallel adjacent beds in Kevin's old front room, now that he's baching with mates around the corner. I'd heard the word *matriarch* but, until I met this Mrs Hall, could never picture one. Tall and brassy, she'd have ordered the family car in a floral print if they were available. She's jolly, rules the roost, and ploughs along with a slight tilt because downhill's her preferred speed. The control tower for all that order and sprightliness is a tightly braided bun perched on top of her head. Her husband's fine-boned and barely half of her, but their three halves seem one big pin-up for marital contentment.

In my third training session back, Talbot accuses me of having 'done something to my backstroke' while away. I don't let on about my new six-beat kick, which has me feeling stronger and more balanced with each swim, and reply cannily, 'Haven't changed a thing — just tried not to do anything wrong.'

'I'm not saying there's something wrong,' he insists. '*In fact, whatever you've done looks far more even, more powerful.'* And on that upbeat note, I'm sorely tempted to admit I really did tamper with my backstroke kick, but can smell an old rat and stick to my guns because he set me up like this once before and I paid for it, big time! (He was timing 25-metre walk-back sprints in our warm-up for this year's Nationals when he angrily demanded to know if I was going my fastest. Of course, only an imbecile goes flat out in a warm-up, even in short sprints, because you want to save it for your race. But just to get him off my back, I said I *was* going my absolute hardest. Then he completely lost it in front of everyone and barked I should never, *ever* go flat out in a warm-up.) And this is why I'm not letting on about my backstroke kick today, especially if he can't even tell the difference between a six-beat and a unilateral crossover.

Within a week, Bobo's warmed to Mrs Hall's earthiness. Out comes his working-class rhyming slang (despite a middle-class childhood) and his jerky, sneering over-familiarity, his 'sweets', 'spewins', and 'filthies'. Kevin and his girlfriend sometimes drop in to watch TV, as they have again tonight, when we're all settled in to watch *Number 96*; after Mrs Hall kills the lights, only popcorn could make it more like a cinema. In the first ad break, she demands to know which character Bobo and I prefer, out of the ludicrously pouting Bev and a tamer yet no less alluring brunette neighbour. 'Abigail, of course,' Bobo scoffs as if slurred by the question. When I plump for the other lady, Bobo and Kevin break out in cackles before Mrs Hall leaps to my defence: 'I can see Brad likes the mature, subtle ones.' And with her endorsement, the snorting tops the Richter scale, with even Mr Hall joining in.

At a loose end on our second Saturday at the Halls', and with no training on Sundays, Bobo and I take the train to his parents' place for the rest of the weekend. Near the Hurstville ticket office, a feisty old guy in a battered pinstripe suit steps into our path. Ruddy, short, likely with a nickname of Nugget from his footy days, he seems a booze 'n' snooze regular from the local park. He's got a slight stoop today, but when a growl hits the air with a shocking resonance, it hints he's not much past fifty. 'Let's have a good fucken squiz at youse two young turks,' he cranks, with a big show of studying our eyes for character, starting with me. 'Yeah, well *you* ...' he begins, a metho reek almost flensing my face. 'Sorry to have to fucken say this, but straight-up I see you're weak as piss.' Turning to Bobo and tapping the point of his shoulder so hard he almost spins — 'But this cunt over here, *now you've got something inside. You've got it!*'

We snigger nervously and step around him. 'Dumb prick,' Bobo hisses as our assessor calls after us. When our train banks on a breathtaking escarpment thirty minutes later, I'm still thinking about the old tosser, astonished someone smelling of moss and cat piss can't see he's forfeited all right to judgement. Ticked off, too, that he'd found Bobo the more worthy.

When we start at Blakehurst High on Monday, I feel as much on the outer as at Hardwick and Homebush; all I can do to stick it out is number the days to the Olympics. Neither of us is sure which class to attend, so we check at the principal's office. When the secretary finally notices us and hauls a hefty timetable to the reception desk, Bobo seems to recognise the young woman teacher hurrying from the staffroom. 'I'm pretty sure we're with *that piece*,' he calls to no one in particular, as we dive off in pursuit before the secretary can verify Bobo's intel.

At dinner a fortnight later, Mrs Hall asks how I'm doing at our new school. To fob her off, I quip that my maths is still hopeless, and I'm glad when she leaves it at that. But the following Monday night, I find a maths tutor sitting at a desk beside me, a tall redheaded uni student in a jaffa V-neck jumper and fetching ink-blue corduroy slacks. But whenever the equations I'm meant to be following tumble from her mouth, they're lost in the soft sounds and breath carrying them, and I can't tell a number from a noun. I'm numerate enough, however, by our next weekly rendezvous, not to be mistaken about the scores of red biro hearts she's suddenly cramming the margins with. Of course, hearts are a sign of *amore*. Or am I drawing an impossibly long cupid's bow when she's only doodling in boredom? (Could she really be keen on such a maths clod?) Let's see if she's still drawing these hearts next week, I tell myself, seeing her to the door.

Sundays are normally our sleep-in, but Bobo's picked up a five a.m. penalty session to face Talbot alone. By the time our room's in full sunlight, I'm stirring through crazy dreams of faces and eyes catching fire. When my hand breaches a dream and explores my real eyes to find them damp and slimy, I leap up to discover Dencorub smeared on my face and pillow, eyes suddenly searing with pain: Bobo must have unloaded an entire tube on my pillow when he left, because of the ribbing I gave him last night about losing his sleep-in. Virtually blinded, I lurch through the house to wash my eyes in the bathroom, but collect a chair on my way and hit the floorboards. Mrs Hall, who's been camped with her usual early cuppa in the kitchen, scurries in and helps me to the nearest tap. Soon we're seeing a doctor, or at least she is, and he writes me a prescription for a rinse and an ointment. It takes all morning for 20/20 vision to return.

The next day Talbot announces he's separating Bobo and me. But I'm only moving next door to the Powers', who, according to Talbot, also had kids who trained with him. When Mrs Hall finds out, she's crestfallen. Yet oddly her loudest complaint is that I won't be able to continue my maths tutoring. (It's a concern of mine too, but not for her reasons. *Or is it?*) When she unexpectedly lets on that she'd been paying the tutor from her own pocket, I'm struck both by her generosity and by her tactlessness in letting on. I'm also curious about my own blindness to the issue of fees. Had I thought the girl was doing it for nothing? *I don't know.* Or that Talbot was forking out? Not on your life. It's a pretty safe guess my tutor won't be following me to the Powers'.

After the Dencorub incident, Bobo's on his last caution from Talbot. (He was kicked off last year's state team for squirting Dencorub through a girl's swim bag.) I suspect he's also been warned off me, because he keeps a low neighbourhood profile for a week; I now see him 'only' at school and training. But his love of cartoon-grade pranks soon kicks back in with a vengeance when he makes a foray into Powers territory. I'm on my new hosts' outside toilet when the door's pushed open and the last thing I see as Bobo's head pulls away is a bucket of water sloshing over me. I can't get up to close the door because I'm tailing, and can hear his cackle trail into the safe distance anyway. But a minute later when I'm wiping, there's another bucketful. This time I hear his retreating hyena hysterics accompanied by creaks of the old paling fence being scaled, so I'm certain there'll be no third drenching.

I usually don't mind playing hapless Wile E. Coyote to Bobo's Road Runner; I'd be a hypocrite to be too precious. I went too far myself at last year's Nationals in Hobart, totally blind to any outcome but the fun of the prank itself. Five interstate swimmers were setting up for another game of Flushin' Roulette, where someone relieves himself into one of their half-dozen or so stubbies for blindfolded players to take their chances. But the moment the blindfolds went on in Hobart, they were called to an urgent team meeting and shot through, telling me over their shoulders to put the stubbies in the fridge. 'We won't be long,' was the garbled call. As I stood at the fridge door admiring my circular revolver-homage arrangement, I pondered the male urge to play risky games. I'd heard it was common for Flushin' Roulette players to swallow with a poker face if they received the loaded stubby, intent on taking at least one other player with them and knowing they'd be washing the taste down with the next stubby. Likewise the next player, and the next, meaning a game might end with everyone swallowing a bit more than their pride — but with no losers. By the time I'd left, the chance of washing the taste down with an unadulterated beer was zero, and I wondered how all those poker faces would look by the third turn.

Earlier that day during my nap, someone had turned my electric blanket up to max. Waking in that hot prickly swamp, I leaped across the room in fear of electrocution. I'd also been getting to know a tall, pale, highborn Carlile girl whose angelic half-smile had nothing to do with you. As we two smooched on her bed that evening, I overheard a familiar voice lecturing on kissing technique from another bed. It was Talkback, *stuck with another dud kisser!* But her tone was more sympathetic this time, because recent nasal surgery had evidently given her shock-haired Carlile boyfriend trouble synchronising smooching and snorting. And if all this wasn't enough, I was on red alert the whole time in Hobart, avoiding a loudmouth Laurie Lawrence girl who could silence a room by bellowing, 'Get real!' at anyone in need of rescuing from anonymity, pretence, or poor fashion taste.

When the Blakehurst first-period bell sounds on Monday, I can't find my bag. I know where I left it, so someone's mistakenly picked it up or Bobo's playing a joke. As I scan the corridor, Bobo erupts in euphoric gasps the moment we make eye contact. 'Where is it?' I ask hotly, the passageway deserted and classroom doors closing. 'We're already meant to be in class,' I bark at him, 'so *fucken tell me!*' But my exasperation's fuel to the fire, his guffaws increasingly tipped with mockery as he writhes against the rail, barely hanging on. I take three rigid steps and hook him in the jaw. In the movies he'd either crumple to the floor or go tumbling backwards, but neither happens. Instead, he rocks with a hideous wobble before dropping on one knee to spit shards of tooth enamel and amalgam crumbs into a cupped hand before looking up in disbelief. I brace for retaliation, expecting him to fly at me, but he straightens up and storms along the balcony to gesture furiously to a garden one floor below, where my bag sits in a crater of bark chip.

After school when I phone his dad and offer to pay for dental work, he laughs it off, his shit-happens laugh. I'm relieved Bobo's dad's not angry with me, but for the rest of the day I feel terrible about doing my cruet with Bobo: there's no pride winning a fight with someone who won't hit back. And it wasn't cowardice — he was just too shocked. I could see in his eyes that he hadn't a clue I'd be so upset. The angrier I'd become, the funnier it was for him. I get it now, because it *was* hilarious to see me fretting like a five-year-old about being late for class. And now I'm sure I could never hit anyone again.

After dinner, I can't help remembering the first story I'd ever heard about Bobo, from Hal, the occasional Ming boarder who'd grown up with him. They were wrestling on the beach at a surf carnival in their early teens when Hal lost it and took a swipe at Bobo, glancing his cheek. Hal wasn't even sure he'd connected, but when Bobo went limp and couldn't be shaken or shouted back to consciousness, he ran off for help in panic. Barely a minute later when Hal returned with a first-aid officer, the body was gone. Bobo, no doubt sniggering maniacally from a hidden vantage point, had made a complete fool of his friend. In another beach grapple, Bobo managed to remove Hal's tracksuit top before running the entire beach length waving the trophy triumphantly above his head. For all his crazy antics, Bobo's a card-carrying pacifist.

SHOWER POWER

The Powers and Halls don't speak to each other, from ill feeling dating back to their kids' competition days. But this is only according to Bobo, who prides himself as a gossip magnet.

Yet my new hosts are proving every bit as likeable as their allegedly estranged neighbours, and similarly at ease with life's intimate, messy intrusions. Mrs Powers teasingly calls her husband 'my old, grey monster', and both lay about in bed Sunday mornings in a ramshackle breakfast-and-papers ritual. Their satisfied, complacent existence leaves me wondering why people like me train all hours to feel special. Mrs Powers shows only passing interest in my swimming, and then only to tease about a girl whose parents gave me a lift to my last carnival, or the one she calls my 'squeeze', Esther, who occasionally phones.

Returning from school today, I'm pondering the Powers' impressive insouciance when, on impulse, I take the afternoon off training in homage. But soon I'm nervously checking my watch and at 3.35 wonder if it's too late to change my mind; I could still run down to the pool, towel on shoulder, to pant convincingly that the bus was late. By 3.45 I know there's no turning back. Anyway, at least once a week I struggle to drag myself to the pool, and this is the first time I've acted on it in months. In fact, I sometimes wish I'd taken up wrestling instead of swimming; it'd be a handy lifelong skill if I found myself in a tight situation — once a swimming career's over, it's useless to you. I'm sure I'd have been as good a wrestler as swimmer: in all my play-wrestling bouts, not once has anyone, even Bobo, been able to get me off my feet. And another thing: I loathe getting wet. I never had this problem before training with Talbot, so maybe I'm stuck in some weird Pavlovian aversion to those freezing September outdoor starts, turning any sudden immersion into a shudder of misery until I shake it off in the warm-up, when I'm fine with water again. In fact, after ten minutes it's not even wet anymore; whatever we're grappling through could just as easily be confetti or cotton balls. It's only that moment jumping in. And then there's swimming after dark, which makes me feel like I've fallen off a wharf at midnight, regardless of how many floodlights are glaring over us.

I know I'm stretching things with Talbot by taking the afternoon off. I did exactly the same six months back and had to go riffling through the Yellow Pages for the name of a cemetery where I might have attended a distant cousin's funeral in case Talbot doubted me, though this seemed unlikely with such a morbid alibi. When he asked for that cemetery's name the next morning in a token interrogation, I answered with authentic hesitation: 'It was some really weird name, like … *Field* of something. Is it Field of Mars?'

'Yeah, that's it,' he snapped, saying to jump in with the others.

I must say, I'm thoroughly enjoying my impromptu afternoon off. The guilt's a bonus. With the Powers still at work and the house to myself, I make a sweet, creamy coffee, and settle on my bed with a paperback Karen Moras lent me, *The Carpetbaggers*. At one point I come across a line where some smuggler is described as *a lone wolf*, and wonder if I could fit that description, at least for this afternoon. After a few chapters typically plucked at random — beginnings always seem a waste of time — I hear a heavy rap on the front door. Handily there's a square of frosted glass in the door to show the rough outline of callers, and this frosty visitor definitely has the rough mohair outline and buzz cut of Talbot. When his persistent knocking goes unanswered he'll probably storm back to the pool and finish coaching, but as a double precaution I scurry into the bathroom to hide behind the shower curtain. My red parka against the curtain's jade-green plastic is hardly best-practice camouflage, but I'm working with probability here, which is next to zero. *Hang on, is that the back door I can hear being unlatched?* Its tell-tale opening creak confirms it is; Talbot's got a hide to enter my host's home! But probability also tells me he's unlikely to enter the bathroom, let alone pull the shower curtain back. *Christ! He is in the bathroom.* Can he smell me? Has he followed the fear twig-snaps of a domestic escape trail? I'm flush against the shower wall, tap handles hard against the small of my back, the odd nozzle-drip wetting my crown. I can see his smudged form through the mildew and fish motifs, so surely he sees my giveaway red-on-green. Why doesn't he end this stupid game by ripping the curtain back and shouting *aha*? (Does he think I'm armed?) But no; he turns away, the back door soon creaks, the latch catches. I give him a few more minutes in case he's waiting to spring a surprise once he hears me stir.

In the morning, Mrs Powers makes a point of accompanying me to the pool, where she's obviously telling Talbot some lie she knows he knows is a lie, and which can only make life worse for me with Talbot. I didn't ask her to do this, and now I'm a seventeen-year-old feeling like a seven-year-old hiding behind mother's skirts. But I'm amazed when Talbot says absolutely nothing of our shower non-incident, a silence he maintains all week for the loudest possible contempt.

PART TWO

~~~~

TIMES

(THE 1972 OLYMPICS)

RACE TIMES

The 20th Olympic Games, Munich, West Germany.

1 September 1972.

I am eighteen.

At one end of the pool, behind the medallists' podiums, stands a large black display covered in yellow digital letters and a white analog clock face. Along the top, it reads:

400 M FREISTIL HERREN
ENDLAUF

WR   4:00,7
OR   4:04,5

The world record had been set last month by the American Kurt Krumpholz at a meet in Chicago, but he hadn't made the US Olympic team. I had set the new Olympic record in winning my heat to qualify for this race.

The finalists are Werner Lampe (West Germany); Bengt Gingsjo (Sweden); Brian Brinkley (Great Britain); Rick DeMont, Steve Genter, and Tom McBreen (United States); and Graham Windeatt and me.

McBreen had set the world record in August 1971, to be beaten by me six months later at the Australian Olympic Trials in Brisbane, to be beaten by Krumpholz six months after that.

We race.

Names and numbers appear on the display:

1. DEMONT, RICK   USA   4:00,26 OR
2. COOPER, BRADFOR   AUS   4:00,27
3. GENTER, STEVEN   USA   4:01,94

'BRADFOR' is me. DeMont is in lane three. I'm in lane four. I reach across and clap him on the back in congratulations.

We stand on the podiums, from left to right: silver, gold, bronze. The flags are raised, from left to right: Australia, America, America. I shake Rick's and Steve's hands. Steve shakes Rick's hand.

Three days later, the 1500-metre freestyle men's final.

I won my heat by 15.26 seconds. DeMont, who had set a world record only last month, should be in the final too, but has just been disqualified.

I and the other seven finalists take our blocks. We race.

Mike Burton wins with a time of 15 minutes 52.58 seconds, setting a new world record. Windeatt takes silver, 5.9 seconds behind Burton. I manage not to come last, placing seventh with 16 minutes 30.49 seconds.

END TIMES

The morning after my 1500-metre implosion, my one unspent emotion is relief — at the completion of the Olympic swimming program. And now I have four days of free time to savour it. I'm even comforted by the likelihood I'll never attend another Games, because I've had enough of monastic routine, tiredness, boarding, and dereliction of school life; I'd once loved exams but had lately not bothered turning up. Olympic dorm life has been hilarious, but the inevitable prickly banter and relentless swagger probably didn't help anyone's racing. (*How are dorm allocations made?* I wonder. I'm the youngest in mine, but my age peers, Grub, Bubblehead, and Bobo, are together in a four-man dorm in some other building.)

Even had I actually wanted to go to another Olympics, the recent acceleration in global improvement might have other ideas: the nine-second drop in 400-metre times between Mexico and Munich will probably be repeated in Montreal. And I've already been so lucky for my career to peak in perfect synch with the quadrennial Olympic cycle. The Games are a graveyard for short but otherwise stellar careers labelled 'counter-cyclical', the great Karen Moras a prime example. In the three years after winning her Mexico Olympic 400-metre freestyle bronze as a rapidly rising fourteen-year-old, she broke the 400- and 800-metre freestyle world records, only to have become a spent force here in Munich.

In midafternoon the fallout from DeMont's disqualification takes the worst possible turn (from my point of view) with news the IOC will declare the 400-metre gold medal void, leaving me with silver. But I'm hoping Australian officials are on the ball enough to at least protest, since it's standard practice to advance all placegetters behind a disqualification. Further speculation seems pointless, so I brace myself and look forward to the plane home.

Within minutes of our rising the next day, all personal concerns go on hold when our usually laconic (though now plain tired) general manager, Roger Pegram, arrives unannounced to confine us indoors with the news, 'There's been a shooting in the Village' — and that's all he'll say. None of us has a clue what this might mean, though the consensus is that some crazy Yank had a gun in his dorm and got into a fight over a girl. That's my bet too, because I've seen how easily tempers can flare with even a mild dose of cabin fever from everyone being cooped up for so long. When Spiderman (one of the steadiest people you could meet) was putting in a bit of work with his new American girlfriend, 'The Prairie Prowler', he lost it momentarily when teammates kept opening his bedroom door to see how he was getting on. After a bit of shouting, with Spiderman and everyone jumping up and down in his doorway, it all soon settled, but I wonder what might have happened if there were a gun lying around. The closest we have to guns are the beautifully decorated knives everyone came back from town with yesterday — along with Bavarian kitsch like cuckoo clocks and fake watches. I watched those bedside blades nervously as arms waved and curses ripped, until everyone left Spiderman and The Prairie Prowler alone again.

At noon we're let out none the wiser, though in a nearby billiards hall a Hong Kong swimmer is soon gushing about his team's terrified pre-dawn corridor dash below an echoing volley of shots, and now I suspect the whole thing was just someone letting off steam by firing some ammo into the sky. I listen half-heartedly to his breathy yarn, noting only the phrase 'We didn't look back', and by the time he and his teammates have been narrated to a safe-house, I've sunk the pink and blue, and am lining up the black.

A few hours later, now overhearing vague discussions of a still-unfolding drama behind that gunfire, I'm flabbergasted to learn the gold's officially mine. But I find in the evening that not everyone is in a mood to smile on my good fortune. In a standing-room-only Olympic Village nightspot, the Canadian Ralph Hutton takes it a step further when he seems to challenge my moral custodianship of the medal. Six years my elder, twenty kilograms heavier, and several shouts drunker, he's really wound up about something. *'Yeah, sure, you'll go home with your gold and not even mention DeMont,'* he steams. The rawness of his slur stuns me to silence, though I'm getting edgy: I've just watched his chin buck accusingly through a riot of horns and cymbals from the Who's 'Pictures of Lily'. But into this brew steps an Australian approximating Hutton's heft, the ever-genial Neil Rogers, who calls, 'Hey Ralph, Brad's nothing like that!' (*Really?* I ponder) before Hutton baulks at this uninvited feedback to pivot back to his lively circle like nothing's happened. And Rogers is as incredulous as I am. 'Did that really just fucken happen?' he groans, both of us suddenly sputtering hysterically into our Lowenbraus.

Forgetting the face-off's a cinch in such spirited surroundings, and I soon learn that the bee in Hutton's bonnet likely came from his own past Olympic misfortune. He'd dived into his *Mexico* Olympic 400-metre final the latest world record smasher and hot favourite, only to be beaten by a winning time an entire three seconds slower than his mark — probably a victim of Mexico's altitude challenges. The one consolation I can take from his diatribe is to better prepare myself for future conversations about the 400-metre.

When our dorm lift sways to an unexpectedly nauseating stop at the end of this high-flying night, I heave generously towards a gleaming semicircle of shoes before apologising profusely to the nimble-footed wearers. All three are in the blazers of stratospheric officialdom, and smile wryly at my condition.

Only the following morning do press photos of masked, Kalashnikov-toting terrorists glaring from balconies suggest the gravity of an apparent hostage crisis. Few of us have sufficient German to take much from the various radio updates, but officials reassure us by late morning that all danger has passed, the *Black September* terrorists having been captured or killed in an overnight airport fire-fight.

In the evening, still hungover and suddenly numbed by reports of the slaughter of eleven Israeli athletes in the Village itself, I'm receiving my gold medal on stage at a team celebration when I recognise my presenter's blazer and Florsheims from the dorm lift the night before. And now I know his name and title: Australia's chef de mission, Julius Patching.

As he loops the chain over my head, I'm not sure what to feel. It isn't as if I expected the weight of an *actual* gold medal on my neck to instantly purge its recent symbolic burden, though it comes close. I'm also grateful that new gold medals can be struck so quickly, on news DeMont flew home with his. And now I remember those poor Israelis dying for *their* Olympic dreams.

FINE TIME

Only in the forty-eight hours before flying home do I find time and any inclination for reflection. Fully relaxed for the first time in a month, I range perspectives so trivialised by recent events.

First, there were the uncanny medical parallels between all 400-metre placegetters: DeMont with his well-known wheezing; me with my breathing arrhythmia; the bronze medallist, Steve Genter, with his collapsed lung on arrival in Munich (though some say it was Genter himself collapsing with a lung infection). Diving in for our final, none of we three could have been confident of even finishing, let alone monopolising the spoils. And after DeMont lost his medal, the former world record holder and legally blind American law student Tom McBreen was drafted to the bronze, having come in fourth behind Genter. *Had such a musical chairs of Olympic swimming infirmity ever occurred before?*

Another big oddity was the absence of the 400-metre world record holder. Barely a month ago, Kurt Krumpholz swept all before him in the heats of his American Trials with a new world mark of 4 minutes 0.11 seconds, erasing my 4 minutes 1.7 from *our* Trials. But his nation's Darwinian selection rigour didn't care about world records set in heats; it took only swimmers who could deliver medals in finals. Krumpholz's inconceivable sixth in his Trial final fell three places short of selection. Rubbing salt into the wound, his world record was still intact after the Olympic final, though barely: DeMont had swum 4.00.26; and I, 4.00.27.

And another likely-but-absent finalist was the West German

former world record holder Hans Fassnacht. His own three-year-old contribution to the fastest falling record in the books was a still-respectable 4.04.0. That time would have qualified him among the first few into the final, but he'd gone nowhere near it in the heats and would barely have made a B final, had there been one. It wasn't Fassnacht's swimming that had kept me shaking in my boots these past few years, however, but his kicking prowess: he also held the unofficial world record of 4 minutes 40 seconds for 400-metre freestyle *kicking*. So freakish was that kickboard dexterity that his fabled mark was only a few seconds slower than my routine freestyle training 400s. I'd long harboured a real fear that he, or some obviously comatose aspect of his physiology, would one day suddenly twig that swimming should be a couple of minutes faster than mere kicking. But then, maybe he'd simply made a bizarre fetish of his kicking prowess at the expense of swimming.

Touching after McBreen was my teammate Windeatt. In last place was the 200-metre bronze medallist Werner Lampe, whose bold pre-Games statement of shaving his head bald was unheard of before Munich. But apparent remorse saw him sporting a luxuriant toupee around the Village, taken off only at the last moment and with pathetic surreptitiousness before mounting the blocks. When its last removal for our final brought rowdy valedictory hoots from a section of the stands, that globe burned with the wattage of his surname. Lampe's sensitivity was in stark contrast to fellow finalist Genter, the collapsed-lung swimmer who'd quickly followed the 'chrome dome' example of the German, but preceded him in the battle to the wall for the 200-metre silver behind Mark Spitz. On the presentation dais, the unapologetically wigless Genter had routinely flouted new Olympic sponsorship covenants by wearing Adidas on one foot and Puma on the other.

There's also my memory of the 400-metre itself. *What memory?*

comes the shocking reply. I'm no longer sure which lane I was in, though it must have been one of the centre ones, always kept for the fastest qualifiers — DeMont to my right as we dived in. My first vague hint of how things were going was at halfway when I felt DeMont and I had inched ahead, the rest evidently hitting their pain thresholds and falling away. Not that you see the field with chessboard clarity, since, without goggles, any sudden play of light on an outside wall could be a swimmer you'd overlooked. You just don't have the reserves of concentration at this pitch of effort to check — watching is for spectators — and you trust there are no barnstorming finishes because everyone's had years to find their best pace. So it was all doubt, trust, and desperation. Then more doubt, the same shaky species of rational scepticism that kept you on your toes over the seasons as you watched true believers quit in bitterness at failed locker-room credos. In our last lap it was blur vs blur to the wall, with me hoping against hope I wouldn't arrive and see lane eight — *that play of light* — already propped on lane ropes with arm raised. What I saw was worse. Two identical times on the display board; a moment of confusion — now a hundredth-of-a-second difference but thinking it'd gone my way, when, with the shock of acceptance and the reflexive sportsmanship of a pat on the back for the winner, I knew it'd gone DeMont's way forever.

Then there was the race to leave my regrets about the new electronic timing in the shade. *My* fingertips had touched the wall one-hundredth-of-a-second soft, but the system was skinned to a thousandth. Just two thousandths separated American Tim McKee from the 400-metre medley winner, Sweden's Gunnar Larsson (yet another former 400-metre freestyle record holder). McKee was inconsolable after seeing the results board, rocking in a kind of foetal position beside the pool afterwards.

Shane's effort of three gold medals, one bronze, and one silver has been called everything from disappointing to heroic. I guess if you were naive enough to expect her to win every Olympic event for which she held the current world record, she'd have taken the four freestyles — the 100, 200, 400, and 800 — but this may or may not have excluded the surprise 200-metre medley win. There were too many American girls close to Shane's level coming into the Games, and all it needed was for one of them to have the swim of her life to cause the upset. And the job of preparing Shane for such a range of distances, each requiring its own bias of endurance and speed, would have been challenging. But this is where Talbot's at his best, because he's quite good at judging the right mix of speed and endurance. ('Tapering' for race day is likened to a plane dumping fuel for an emergency landing. Ditch too much and you won't get there; keep too much and you'll hit the runway in a ball of flames. In the final stages of preparation, a swimmer's workload is severely cut to reclaim speed and vitality compromised by months of grind. Crash landings are not uncommon.) In the end, he probably tried to focus on Shane's middle events, the 200 to 400 range, in which Shane had most of her races, while hoping she would retain just enough speed for the 100, or just enough endurance for the 800. It's one thing to set records for every freestyle distance at different points of the calendar when all your ducks are lined up in a row — *but all in the same meet?* As it turned out, the 100-metre and 800-metre were bridges too far, even for Talbot to conjure. Had he gone for a distance-only preparation, Shane may have won 'only' the 400-metre and 800-metre freestyle. Had he gone in hard for the sprint, she may have won only the 100-metre and 200-metre freestyle. For her part, Shane didn't falter. You couldn't possibly fault her nerve. And this was after some American team members had been going around in T-shirts with 'All that glitters is not Gould' emblazoned across the front. Of her losses, the least surprising in hindsight was to Keena Rothhammer in the 800-metre, because Keena broke Shane's world record by five seconds.

When not pondering all these Olympic vagaries, I'm taking an interest in the modern Olympic movement itself, its template hatched by public-minded European aristocrats around the same time as that other global cause for youthful betterment, Boy Scouts (my brothers dumped swimming for Scouts the week our parents separated). Scouting teaches duty and hygiene, but even the elitist Games has its own propaganda wing of *Olympism*. I discovered this by accident after a squiz at some flashy brochures in the room I share with the Mexico Olympic sprint-freestyle double gold medallist Mike Wenden, a seven-year veteran of national teams. Ever since the swimming program ended, he's been out and about networking with Olympism's youngest and brightest from around the world.

From what I've read, Olympism's charter strives for a better world by making sport an integral part of everyone's lives. *Fair enough*, I think, though I'm hardly the best judge, because I have no idea of the alternative: life without sport. How could you even begin to do a study on that sort of stuff? Maybe all those sedentary types are similarly chuffed with their *No-Sportism*, but are too considerate to rub our noses in it. Maybe that's where hippies come into things. Go figure.

Not that Wenden's the only one pushing the Olympic spirit here. I'm not entirely sure how this happened, but our entire dorm seems to have channelled the ancient Greeks almost overnight, because we all decided — by apparent telepathy — to go starkers around the dorm for the rest of the Games. We got back from the pool one day and it was suddenly birthday suits all round, *how do you do*. It's obvious our manager's not impressed, because you only ever see him last thing at night when he just rocks in and crashes.

You wake next morning to see him pulling on his trousers and he's out the door. But that's fine, because having intergenerational nudity mightn't have been good for anyone's morale. Anyway, there's loads more laughter around the dorm now that the duds are off. Or maybe its just that the competition is over and the pressure's off — along with the clothes.

Chatting with Wenden can be like some charming Old World benediction, with his kindly musical voice and eyes constantly twinkling as if piloting a punchline down for a landing. He's a natural storyteller, but you won't hear the really good ones from his own lips (like the time he won his race in Mexico before momentarily blacking out with the altitude problems) because he doesn't like to blow his own trumpet; you have to hear those stories from someone else. The yarn I have to settle for today is from his old uni marketing degree days, where some tutor said that just by colouring a humble potato peeler blue instead of brown, sales instantly doubled. Which is pretty cool, but also a tad alarming when you think about it, because it means we're all just bower birds making decisions based on some deep reptilian chromatic response rather than informed judgements.

Wenden hasn't been able to repeat his Mexico success here, though he still made the finals of the 100-metre and 200-metre freestyle, even bettering his Mexico time for the 200-metre by almost a second. Except that the rest of the world — namely Mark Spitz — has moved on by three seconds. He's been doing it uphill all year anyway, after getting married and starting work in a bank. I don't know how he's managed to do as well as he has in Munich. But at least the pedants are finally happy. They couldn't stand it when he won in Mexico with his fierce overreaching freestyle and uneven kick. When he goes helter-skelter up the pool like that, he reminds me of fast-forward footage of a climber going up a precipice with picks. *What a hoot!* The pedants were so righteously pissed off with him beating the classical stylist Don Schollander in Mexico that if an official had joked that he had the power to disqualify Wenden for incorrect technique, they might have fallen for it.

TIME OUT

Wenden's the official swim-team captain, but there are our hands-on captains too, now that he's all around the Village networking with fellow junior Olympic delegates. These can be captains of almost anything: of fun, of swearing, and, most importantly, of big trouble if you break the rules of who you are — in other words, never get above yourself in the company of veterans. And these personnel can change from day to day, depending on who you hang with and who can give you big trouble. You tend not to finish a sentence in the dorm without swearing, or at the very least some sort of rhyming slang. If you ask someone why they plaster themselves in toiletries from dawn to dusk, you'll get, 'Because it shows you were brought up, not kicked in the fucken guts and told to get up.' Or you'll see someone tear his shirt while dressing for town, and he'll curse that fucken Don and Bert because it was his last clean one, and then he'll be in his Reg Grundies and trying to insert one of his Ginger Meggs into his fucken jeans and he'll fall over laughing, and very soon everyone's guffawing their head off. Everyone, that is, except Wenden and the manager, because they're out hobnobbing it in the trousered world. When I ask Spiderman why his particular crew tended to crow about everything they buy in town, even when it's a total dud, he looks me in the eye to quip, 'And there are people who don't?', and suddenly I'm in the know.

I don't go into town as often as the others. It's embarrassing anyway — not being able to buy anything because I spent almost all my dough on a puny JVC recorder before I even arrived. Every day, someone comes back from town trying to outdo the others with the biggest suitcase-style double tape deck, or Nikon or Canon camera. Or they'll spend up on a whole bunch of minor stuff like sex toys, albums by the Stones, and silly Bavarian knick-knacks like clocks and traditional dolls. Now we have *Sticky Fingers* playing all day, along with this weird but interesting album by an African group called Osibisa. *Who ever heard of African pop music?* That's Jim Findlay's album. Anyway, at least all the new music gets your mind off the fresh-set cement stink still hanging around the building.

People say Leonard Cohen is depressing, but they must only listen to the words, because the music's as uplifting as any I've heard. It'll always remind me of Munich, I'm sure. And everyone knows song lyrics are second-rate anyway, because they have to rhyme and fit in with the music. But every now and then if you do actually listen to Cohen's words, you hear a couple of gems, like a German Shepherd's 'collar of leather and nails', and 'when we were almost young'. The only reason I know Cohen's music from a bar of soap is because my old Valley Pool squad mate Arthur Shean left his album at the Ming Hotel when Talbot told him to leave for having the odd night out and otherwise daring to have a life. That's what Jon says anyway.

This afternoon, I'm on my bed with my favourite Cohen chorus from 'So Long, Marianne' blasting away in my ear when there's a knock on the door. Thinking it's just a dorm crew returning from town keyless, I walk over drowsily naked and swing the door wide open, but it's definitely not them. Instead, there's this whole multinational posse of bright-eyed budding chefs de mission looking for Wenden. As I cover myself and say Wenden's out looking for them somewhere, one of the less humour-strapped girls pledges, 'We won't tell, I promise,' and I slink back to my bed and imagine people I'd meet in Cohen's songs: unscrupulous bluedbloods of breeding, beauty, or taste, in Hydra cafes or mysterious retreats, now sipping ouzo and now swaying on a building chorus, their torments eased by Cohen's priestly tones. I've heard some of them are people you might want to meet, like Marianne and Suzanne, though not necessarily the 'Sisters of Mercy'. Cohen's songs have the same powerful effect on me as Peter Sarstedt's old number, 'Where Do You Go To My Lovely', whose rags-to-riches heroine receives a racehorse for Christmas from the Aga Khan, steals a painting from Picasso, and wears a topless swimsuit for an even suntan on her back and legs. (*Really?*)

I know there's a contradiction between being a rooter for flower power and a sucker for high-strung, jetsetting libertines, but if I had to choose right now, it's flawed glamour and the Olympics. Where else would you want to be this month than under all those translucent stadium covers, stretched across the sky on poles like giant webs?

What are the modern Olympics, anyway? I wonder. They're definitely some kind of fabulous pop-up micro-state, a roving Vatican whose month-long gig pimps tired capitals into flesh-friendly festivals.

Today it's the official swim-team photos. First the full team pose; then the medallists, like me, holding our hardware to the camera before the usual biting to test if they're real, though in my case there is far more gold in the teeth doing the biting. The photos are a day earlier than scheduled because Talbot's off to Canada tonight — it's no longer a rumour. He's the only one not in uniform, as if to say, '*It's all on my terms now.*' Instead, he's come encircled in this uber-bland slab of Bavarian suede falling right to his thighs. It's the garb of a man with no fashion pretensions, bought for him by someone without inclination, from a store full of clocks and lederhosen. Soon we've all moved to the food hall, and Talbot's actually looking happy and excited in his new Alpine burgher blazer. You never use the adjective *expansive* about Talbot, but that's how he's behaving right now. He's even telling anecdotes from early in his career. This particular one's a story you read about in the papers sometimes, and now he and the manager Roger Pegram are kind of giggling their way through it, because Roger was there on the night in question. 'So I saw this scrawny ten-year-old Wenden kid absolutely killing everyone in his first state title races,' Talbot says. 'And right then I knew I had to get him into my squad, except he's being coached by this former SAS brute, Vic Arniel.'

Pegram can't wait for Talbot to finish. 'And then you ...'

'Well then I go up to this sopping-wet kid and tell him he should join my squad, but he says right back, "I'm with Mr Arniel, thank you"' — and the whole table erupts in laughter.

Sometimes I think we should all try to be more like Wenden, who says all his running about with those junior delegate types is to put something back into sport. But knowing me, I'd just think I was trying to put myself back into it.

Neither could I ever be sure the Olympics is the force for good that all those Olympism boosters around the Village seem to claim. Surely the choice of the Village itself for the latest instalment of Middle Eastern terror is designed to grotesquely mock its lofty political pretensions. I'm for the greater good too, but doubt the existence of any measure beyond an avoidance of totalitarianism. Anyway, humans have bumbled along for tens of thousands of years in various forms of rural grind, urban pomp, and ruin, the inventors of wheel, speech, chair, cheese, trousers, and a thousand other useful things passing totally unacknowledged. (But, tellingly, the mythical sixth-century-BC inventor of the modern practice of progressive-overload training techniques, Milo of Croton, is still celebrated in sport folklore. He'd supposedly lifted a newborn calf above his head and then repeated the feat daily until it had famously grown into a lot of bull.)

Am I better off for having achieved some scratchy Olympic glory? I don't know, but there's definitely no living to be made, because amateurism looks set to outlive another ice age. I've also wilfully abandoned my schooling, and will go home with a degree of sporting fame but not of education, not even my leaving certificate. And there's no way I'll be repeating my final year at any of my recent schools as its celebrated-but-obsolete student-jock — a living curio.

Far from becoming more like Wenden, in our final night in Munich I graduate as a clone cum laude of my fellow *Lord of the Flies* dorm survivors, revelling in degrees of drunkenness with athletes from around the globe and girls from all over Munich — girls who simply scaled the Village fences like the terrorists. In waiting lounges and on connecting flights home — between my occasional but urgent micro-scrutiny of rest-room basins — I'm reminded by teammates of what good form we were all in, yet am unable to recall some of those alleged antics. When I'm bestowed with titles like 'Master of Mayhem' and 'Captain Carnage', I know they're taking the piss.

PART THREE

~~~~~~

WARM-DOWN

(LOOKING BACK)

FOR WHAT IT'S WORTH

After swimming I float spread-eagled on my back to watch the sky as my pulse falls. There's a pleasant sensation of wheeling today — minuscule — but convincing enough to prompt a sideways check of the lane ropes, to find I'm still parallel. Laying my head back again, I see some high-up bird peel off its line to circle, as if eyeing this belly-up floater for a feed. At sixty-three, I'm just back into my laps after a winter break, but hadn't quite considered myself carrion.

Neither had I intended ageing forty-five years within a page turn of Munich, the cracking onset due entirely to my editor suggesting I write the remainder of this memoir from the eyrie of late middle age.

With retirement pending, I'm looking forward to maintaining my swimming and mountain-bike exercise routines. I have retired friends who taunt me with videos of their current cycling trek in the Victorian high country or along spectacular New Zealand coastal trails; at the moment, I haven't the time to join them.

I've been coaching for much of my life, and one of my swimmers is working towards the Tokyo Olympic Trials in 2020.

I feel lucky to still be involved with swimming. One of my biggest thrills came recently when my Tokyo hopeful climbed the stands after an impressive performance, to where her parents and I sat, and beamed, 'That was fantastic.' She wasn't referring to her time or whom she'd beaten, but the sensation of mastery she'd relished throughout her performance — one of those rare occasions when you seem to have a lever for every contingency.

And I couldn't recall ever having climbed from a pool to use the adjective 'fantastic'.

If this swimmer decides the trek to the Tokyo Trials is worthwhile — constant review is expected at this level — she and her cohorts may eventually join the push for significant assistance. As valuable as this assistance is, I find it a mystery that Australia's very best swimmers — the Hortons, McEvoys, and Campbells — receive only around $60,000 a year. This may vary somewhat from year to year, but it is a tiny fraction of the $450,000 their national head coach takes home. Such a modest return for their efforts seems an anomaly in world sport, where elite athletes typically fare better than coaches. There is an argument sometimes made that Olympic athletes shouldn't receive government money, as if they were still meant to be amateurs, or as if the public purse should revert to ancient policy staples. (I still think there should be room to reconsider public sports funding. The mounting assault on fair play by the unstoppable march of doping technology might one day require it. If refusing to dope eventually means you've no hope, even government funding won't make a difference.) Yet it seems odd that these same — often anonymous — voices rarely protest that the coach is paid so generously while their charges who actually fight for the medals still have to face the prospect of national opprobrium in cyber-hate-land if they fail.

The swimming budget for the so-called 'Pathway to Rio' was reportedly $33 million (some estimates have it as high as $38 million). But it has been estimated that less than ten per cent of that went directly into swimmers' pockets over the four years of the funding program. When our Rio performance of three gold medals and seven 'minor' medals brought profound disappointment in the media, I wondered how we might have performed had all that money — even half of it — gone straight to swimmers in medal incentives. If our swimmers suspected they were being denied their true worth, I wondered, would they be capable of competing like winners?

I also wonder if they know how much power they have in this situation. Currently, much of the Sports Commission funding is spent on so-called developmental programs. A thirty-strong Australian team sent to the world junior championships in Hungary in 2017, for instance, took no fewer than twenty-two official support staff. I'm sure it was a high-water mark for such appointments. In the not-too-distant past, that number might have been fewer than eight. In Munich it was five. It's these accelerating numbers I think of when I recall AOC boss John Coates returning from the Rio Olympics and accusing certain sports of financial 'bloat'.

Swimming Australia says it sends away more and more junior teams with these extra coaches, physios, race analysts, medicos, masseurs, sports scientists, and psychologists to 'prepare for the future'. There may be legitimate duty-of-care aspects to this apparent 'minder-mania', but there's also a growing list of mid-teen tour veterans quitting before they benefit from that supposed experience and care. At least three Games medal-winning sixteen-year-olds have retired within two years of those peaks in the past several years. Tours force adolescents into a sudden cascade of social pressures. Whatever uniqueness and prestige they feel about representing their country can give way to the worst of garden-variety peer dramas within that tour hothouse.

Sport has also entered a high health-risk phase. There is an epidemic of arrhythmias, for instance; every other month, a soccer player seems to drop dead on a pitch. That sports scientists are now retained by most elite institutional programs might suggest an epidemic of nefarious intentions, but much of their input is in routine athlete education and procedural oversight. Their ethical conscience has been demonstrated to range from one of extreme caution to 'whatever it takes'. Although Swimming Australia Limited's own supplement policy document offers a generally sound mix of ethics and sanctions-based advice, athletes (in point #3) are curiously advised to be sure their chosen supplement works. *'Does it work?'* the policy asks in bold typeface — seemingly contradicting its preamble insisting supplements are no substitute for hard training and dietary rigour. Such is the official ambiguity swimmers must typically wade through.

And few would pretend to know what internal levels of moral tolerance such governing bodies apply across the supplements spectrum. For example, there are always legal-but-dubious substances displayed on WADA's 'Monitored' list. The list has become a euphemism for drugs soon to be banned. Taking all of ten seconds to google, it's a handy guide for the intending first time 'user'. (Presumably, WADA sees the logistics of actual acquisition as sufficient caution against such misuse.) Yet there is no accessible information to indicate how often Australians use Monitored drugs, even though WADA routinely furnishes SAL with such names. Does SAL counsel such 'tagged' athletes? With this seemingly legalist approach, it might be seen as okay to dope with substances which could be banned before the year is out (as happened with the now-illegal heart drug Meldonium) and whose ultimate health consequences may or may not prove as catastrophic as those suffered by former DDR athletes. If SAL announced that it at least cautioned swimmers using Monitored substances, its accountability would be applauded.

Similar filtering of information is seemingly found in statutory panels (ASDMAC) charged with approving Therapeutic Use Exemptions, or TUEs. TUEs license athletes to dope with medical consent. The academic researcher Bradley Partridge complained a few years ago (in *The Conversation*) after his request for statistics from such a panel was denied. His main concern was being unable to assess the appropriate use of therapeutic drugs after ASDMAC refused to disclose the number of TUEs granted for each of the thirty-seven different substances approved. He was not seeking names. The sports with most TUEs were AFL, swimming, cycling, and athletics.

Even something portrayed as innocuously as altitude training can be dangerous, but swimmers are generally expected to participate in such funded regimens. The literature on altitude training says it either 'stimulates' or 'provokes' the kidneys into secreting EPO into the blood to adapt to the oxygen deprivation; this is the same EPO that the cheats inject to increase the number of red blood cells to deliver super-oxygenated blood into their muscles. Among the health risks of altitude training are suspicions that it can accelerate the growth of otherwise slow-growing tumours anywhere in the body. The IOC says altitude training is 'not in the Olympic spirit', but doesn't ban it. Such concerns come on top of the 'default' occupational hazard for sportspeople — and other 'performing' vocations — of significantly reduced life spans. (This phenomenon is easily googleable, though the exact causes of the discrepancy between these unfortunate occupational cohorts and their counterparts in, say, the professions, office work, or the military is not easily explained. Or perhaps this is an error caused by sporting vocations beginning earlier than sedentary counterparts, thereby skewing mortality figures by including younger age groups more prone to misadventure.)

Meanwhile, elite athletes are currently required to submit their intended daily whereabouts for up to a year in advance for randomised WADA drug testing, adding yet more stress to their pressure-cooker existence. When they miss three WADA testing appointments in a row, they receive lengthy suspensions, as three swimmers did in 2017. Not only this, but also such athletes can feel tainted because of speculation associated with a rising public cynicism about the reasons for the missed tests.

Swimmers are increasingly questioning if they receive a deserving share of the funding pie. For a while there, in the '90s, and in the so-called 'noughties', this might not have mattered, because swimmers barely out of their teens were reputed to be accumulating a net worth in the seven figures. There seemed to be no Olympic gold medallists or world record breakers incapable of tapping into this blue-sky endorsement manna. They kept popping up in lifestyle and reality television shows, in ads, and even on radio. Then, suddenly, the money began to dry up with the post-retirement difficulties of Ian Thorpe and Grant Hackett.

The pendulum has swung a long way since Don Talbot complained that coaches of his generation struggled for legitimacy in the eyes of amateur officials — 'blazers' as they are pejoratively called now. But few coaches complain now because a surfeit of funding means teams are no longer restricted to employing just one coach, or a pair (as Talbot and Ursula Carlile operated in Munich). In fact, the majority of swimmers on national teams have their own coaches along, at the taxpayer's expense. The number of coaches with a national tracksuit these days is legion, likewise the physios, medicos, and masseurs — all forming a widening network of sport-'serving' professionals prepared to buttress the new coach-led status quo.

Even when coaches were complaining about their powerlessness all those years ago, they were still able to command the attention of the press. But no journalists asked them if they thought their top charges were showing signs of social and educational distress, which they were. Neither did they ask swimmers anything more probing than how they felt after a winning — or losing — performance. It was the prerogative of their coaches to pontificate on the various social indicators of their charges. Many of my generation got off to shaky starts in their post-swimming lives because of this benign dereliction. The coaches who led that accelerated Nietzschean ('*what does not kill me makes me stronger*') push for ever greater training mileage in the early '70s — Talbot and Carlile — seemed to feel insulated from that responsibility, as if swimmers' life transitions were the exclusive domain of parents. But those parents seemed to have been just as dazzled by the footlights of their offsprings' exploits as the swimmers and public.

The more I consider this subject, the more I'm certain that today's elite swimmers are being taken for a ride. My Olympic funding model (because all suggestions must be called 'models' these days) would award every swimming Olympian $300,000 for hopping on the plane. This might at least buy them a cheap retirement cottage in regional Australia for their trouble. Then there would be $400,000 for an individual medal of any colour, with a personal limit of $2 million. The 'bill' for such success wouldn't even account for half the budget for Tokyo — and if it did, would at least mean we'd have done far better than in our last two diminished Olympic efforts. Their media appeal could only be boosted by financial enrichment burnishing their overall 'success quotient'.

Changes to the disbursement bias would threaten the so-called 'high performance' coaching infrastructure. The various 'Podium Centres', where elite athletes must train or lose their funding, would be first to suffer. Critics of these fixtures say they constitute a semi-government cartel serving to choke off emerging maverick coaching talent in favour of an old-guard bureaucracy who rose to prominence under the once-decentralised system they now renounce. The Podium system's protected status supposes that it is the exclusive repository of essential technological advances. In fact, the pace of world-record improvement is at an all-time low, and no Australian currently holds an individual world record. What actually causes all improvement is the constantly increasing population of swimmers. Even when general populations are static or in decline, net historical populations still increase. It is this constant expansion of numbers doing a particular activity that creates new standards. (No doubt this expansion is also delivering records for the worst swimming ever seen, except nobody bothers noting these.) If Australian swimmers received a much bigger slice of the funding pie through success incentives, they would hire the coach of their choice at the going rate, or retain one on a success fee. Podium Centres would no longer be needed. Such an individualist approach would put instant fire in the bellies of swimmers and swimming families around Australia.

I suspect changes are inevitable because training for elite international sport is now almost a full-time job. Why shouldn't Olympic swimmers aspire to be compensated at the rates of their AFL and NRL counterparts, whose average annual salary is $350,000? The usual counter to this query is, 'Duh — because football can pay its own way with telecast rights.' And the counter to this is, 'Because it's been quite a while since governments began monetising the value of the Olympic Games via sports funding.' (To match footballers' salaries, a swimmer currently needs several hefty sponsorships, in turn condemning them to wear a virtual image detention anklet for the media to track any departure from an impossibly sanitised lifestyle. Even then, endorsements must be vetted by SAL to honour its own sponsorship covenants.)

Any full discussion of the Olympics acknowledges their exploitation by participating nations for the projection of 'soft power', aka 'war by other means' via medal-table success. (The

Olympic movement never intended this — its ideal was for athletes to compete as individuals.) Given the geopolitical stakes, athletes unable to grasp their primacy in delivering such theatre may not know their true worth. It seems odd that other foreign-service professionals (diplomats, defence forces, etc.) should be well compensated, while the front line of our nationalist sporting forays are on virtual rations.

As president of one of Australia's hundreds of suburban swimming clubs, I am well placed to note the recent urgency with which schemes and exhortations to arrest declining memberships arrive from the various strata of Australian swimming governance. One year there might come a call to relax membership restrictions, the following year a rush of incentives for clubs to plaster their Facebook pages with images of kids hamming it up in their allegedly hard-grind training lanes. No doubt professional services are retained to promote these earnest initiatives, but when I ask parents of swimmers why their kids are choosing an extra night of karate or dance over chasing the next tier of swimming competition, the answer is loud and clear: 'There's nothing for swimmers at the end.' (You can almost hear the footnote, *And there should be.*)

Such parents are charmed by the lively post-race sisterly interview banter of Cate and Bronte Campbell, but they almost immediately find themselves wondering if these two great ambassadors for Swimming Australia Inc. are fairly compensated for that role.

It is no longer a sustainable ambition to aim for sporting glory on its own. The public will only respect athletes who are adequately paid. To retire with Olympic medals and little more is, in the eyes of today's jaundiced commentariat, not an act of patriotism, but an entry into the ranks of the misguided and mismanaged.

Even if it were enough, the prospect of achieving such goals is under increasing attack through what is called a 'doping arms race', whose latest front is undetectable gene tweaking via the injection of viral bodies. Neither can athletes count on moral support from the most informed members of the community. It is not uncommon among academics, for instance, to take the stance that doping is small fry compared to the gulf of genetic and socio-economic difference that has always dictated who takes the sporting laurels. (When I read such opinions, I wonder which of these academics would have risked their tenures against former disadvantaged peers allowed to bridge their talent and demographic gaps with brain-doping drugs or affirmative exam coaching.)

Fair sport is also under assault from the increasing manipulation of the TUE (therapeutic-use exemption) scheme. The worst examples were from the American baseball league, where players were schooled on how to answer a GP's questions on their claimed ADHD problems, in order to walk out with a Ritalin prescription to pep up their pitching speed.

For these reasons and more, it is surprising that swimmers are not agitating more loudly for a better deal.

CATCHING UP

It now feels odd to recall that my father was exactly my age (sixty-three) when his eighteen-year-old chosen son hopped off the plane from Munich with a gold medal in his pocket. Cities were spots on the map or how they felt around you, and nothing better skinned you in Brisbane after a marathon of re-gifted cabin breath than those first spring zephyrs on the staircase. I bounced down the steps appropriately: not just with the usual relief of having been spared an instant mile-high cremation, but because the month-long bother of Munich was also half a world behind. This last thought made my prize sound petty, which it wasn't: I couldn't have been prouder. In fact, I was militantly proud — for having climbed triumphant from those two years under my overlord Ming. Now *that* was over too. *Praise de lode!*

Ironically, it wasn't my pugnacious Sydney overseer but a lettered American coach who'd handed over the keys of my transformation into an Olympic freestyle contender. Had Jon Talbot and I not goofed off from our usual Sunday drudgery cobbling Ming's line of exercise equipment to check his mail, I'd have gone to Munich a backstroker. (Thank you, 'Doc' Counsilman.) And this stars-and-stripes irony extended to the 400-metre freestyle final itself when the American DeMont and I were followed into the wall by his countrymen Genter and McBreen.

And I was militantly proud *again* — because after the disqualification, I'd had to put up with the odd press sniping for winning under rules which generously permitted opponents the use of a stimulant. And even after the margin of DeMont's positive guaranteed the dismissal of an immediate American protest, his plight was still lamented by the odd outspoken medico whose typical condescension to sport was that it privilege inclusiveness over rigour. *Strange*, I'd thought, when sport seemed the intended opposite of inclusiveness. (When you *sported* a new hat, it wasn't with the intention of sharing it. And wasn't this very *ex*clusivity the difference between sport and recreation, sport and exercise, sport and role-playing?)

On the plane, I'd also been mulling over the flawed notion that taking a stimulant-based medicine constituted a moral and physical leveller. In my view, that chemical complication turned a swimmer's biochemistry into an omelette that could never be unscrambled into equivalency. Yes, there was always a *natural* brew of unpredictable biochemistry bubbling in an athlete's system that could alter a sporting outcome in a blink, but this relativism hardly licensed additional outside interference. Doping by doctors — *droping*, as I'd heard it called — even with noble intentions and within sanctioned limits, seemed an entirely separate class of racing, and entitled to its own category. And from that moment I resigned myself to having become some kind of doping fundamentalist, hoping that one day there would be zero tolerance for any pharmaceutical in an athlete's bloodstream.

But I didn't envy DeMont's dilemma. He'd been a victim in the purest sense of the word, having taken an assortment of drugs for wheezing and chronic competition anxiety from his earliest racing. (I'd also heard reports that in the period of administrative mayhem between his 400-metre positive and scheduled 1500-metre appearance, he'd been summoned to appear before a panel of sceptical Olympic medical experts and ordered to graphically simulate a 'typical' asthma attack. The apparent purpose of this degrading ordeal was to test his medical bona fides.) His dependence on drugs by now was probably both physical and psychological; his father, a dentist, would have been an informed steward for his son's long pharmaceutical journey. It was reportedly DeMont's wheezing before the Munich 400-metre final that led to him exceeding the therapeutic prescription standard to which the ephedrine threshold was pegged.

Pondering this, I'd never felt more gratified to have rejected the quinidine prescribed for my own breathing ailment, even though it had never appeared on any banned list. I also carried a little residual bile at the glibness of Talbot's referral to the Lewisham Sports Medicine Clinic, and its doctor's complacency in prescribing quinidine, which I later learned could cause its own problems. (The clinic would go on to a chequered history when its research director Tony Millar, a Commonwealth Games team doctor, publicly admitted he'd administered 'thousands of steroid injections' to Australian athletes during the 1970s, justifying it by claiming they'd have otherwise sourced them on the black market, and thereby slurring an entire generation of Australian sportspeople.)

At last I've done it, I thought — *all this*, as I strode the tarmac, *for Ashley and me. All this ... shit! These last five zig-zag years with their nineteen addresses!* Not that a sense of resolution hadn't dawned on me in-flight; maybe it took a tarmac to slam it home.

And how far I've come, I pondered wryly, almost smugly, *from Ashley's supposed conjugal prescience at my cruise-ship conception.* I felt magnanimous enough to allow him his myth, and myself the creepy complicity of its manifestation. And even that old cruise-ship story was eerily twinned by Ashley's insistence on his grandfather having been *grand champion* of the British fleet in the days when the few Englishmen who could swim to save themselves were mariners.

And at this point I had that passing yet always confusing sense that none of this existed, as if I'd imagined it all; not the facts, of course, because facts could be corroborated — but that I'd imaginatively anticipated, step by tiny step, an entire sequence of interactions and their calculated risks to contrive a thoroughly conventional outcome that people liked to call exceptional. Whenever I struggled with this impression, there was also a slight sense of having been compromised, or having taken a wrong turn of identity or ontology, Faustian by increments.

But it couldn't have been all contrivance. There was also a good dose of luck, the kind of serendipity people believe had made them once choose to enter one door over another. *But of course we'd be saying this*, I thought, *even had we chosen the other*. And in this sense, we *had* chosen the other, but seemed compelled to retrace the past as a linear providence, because how else would we have arrived intact at this exact point of reflection?

I looked up at the terminal with its modernist lines, and knew I'd been thinking nonsense again, except when I tapped that gold disc in my pocket and visceral sense came flooding back. Then, to an ant, none of this changed a thing, and the ant conclusion was usually the sign to concentrate on placing one foot before the other, the cadence itself a celebration.

We three — Ashley, medal, me — and maybe the odd stowaway ant, soon stopped off for beers at an RSL, where Ashley again requested his 'Solitary Man' anthem to beam around expansively into the faces of discomfited patrons. And suddenly I was looking forward to leaving; the beer, jet lag, and Neil Diamond had begun not playing well together. But right then, Ashley rose again to stalk the stage, even with requests over. When the players put their instruments down mid-song and a decidedly managerial figure appeared with a mic to air my name, Ashley's mystery trip to the back of stage was a mystery no more. What followed was an awkward interview that went something like, 'Well, Brad, welcome home, and congratulations on your Olympic success. *How was it?*'

'What would you like to know?' I replied unhelpfully: I was now incredibly tired, and angry with Ashley for thrusting me in front of people I felt I had nothing in common with.

'Well, for starters, it must have been exciting over there.'

'Yes, you could say that. There were so many … striking … well … you might say … of course … *sorry, I'll start that again.*' After another few minutes of similar wretchedness, I was allowed back to my seat, and with a cymbal smash the band rejoined the severed song.

I was soon in dismay again to learn Ashley had moved into a new flat in old, flat Redcliffe. I had nothing against Redcliffe, site of my Olympic training camp. Level land was sensible land — cheaper to build on and easier to get about. But getting about that featureless peninsula, particularly after the topsy-turvy of Munich, now made me feel oddly claustrophobic. *Maybe it reminds me of sea-locked Singapore*, I thought, as Ashley guided his new mustard Valiant Charger down the home stretch, his thumbs still doing their ritual rubbing on the wheel. Yet for once I appreciated the mottled groves, stilts, and slopes of nearby Brisbane; I'd warmed to Brisbane while away.

Within a week I'd set a firm deadline to be gone: one month, thank you very much, unless Ashley beat me to the punch by upping stumps after noting a new freckle while shaving, or whatever voodoo his life now jerked to. Against a creeping but not unpleasant funk during which I routinely slept late and swam not once, I grafted a new routine of long morning walks and even longer lunches while replying to congratulatory cards still trickling in. Then I would dawdle to the post office, by which time the sun was well on its downhill run: I had the circadian intimacy of a pensioner. And once again, songs provided the tenor. Had there ever been two more saccharine, maudlin ballads than 'It Never Rains in Southern California' and 'Down by the River'? (I wondered how many songs I'd remember from here, having calculated in my Ashley drifting days that I retained two favourites for each month of a stay; a log as accurate as knots slipping through a sailor's fingers over the stern.)

Then I spent what seemed an entire morning irritably lifting cushions and garbage lids in search of a misplaced card from a surprising source — my old Maroubra Bay co–class captain Melinda. We two had thrived on being a pre-teen team in Mr Egan's steely, nicotine-fingered, trench-coated presence, and it was the first time I'd noticed girls could be fun in an eager, almost-too-bossy way. Yet our friendship wasn't anything but that: I'd had my eye on the smoke-skinned, pigtailed Florence, whom I'd liked since watching her mother huffishly minister to the state of those plaits at a parents' day. But Melinda's card was on our kitchen table one day and gone forever the next, and Ashley claimed never to have seen it in the first place.

The next day, Esther turned up from Sydney, dismissing any bother by claiming she was visiting a girlfriend (Tupperware was a monastic vow against her networking). Much of that first day was spent atop one of Redcliffe's middling peaks — a strip of lawn, swings, and seesaws — taking in the bay, elevation six metres. We then dined at Breakfast Creek before watching a dark and jerky movie where a blue-collar dad shot dead his feckless daughter's drug-dealer beau before visiting the same edification on an entire hippie commune for taking her in; we left in muffled bursts of laughter at the contrived peppering of misery, glad the real body count was only photons deep.

It was only when I saw Esther off at the airport that I knew our relationship was incipiently doomed. Even before Munich, we'd occasionally both behaved as if we were in the last throes of splitting up, and I was slow to contact her in my first days back. I kept thinking, *Must ... ring ... Esther*, but struggled for time when I was buried in time. And yet for those few days in Redcliffe, rather than resolve anything, we had nothing but fun. She was still her clownishly self-effacing self — still had the appealing giddy-up in every syllable — though I was now ready to admit that some of what I liked in her seemed what I thought I *should* like. I would sometimes try to blame Esther's olds for this indeterminate state. Not only did she think they deserved the Nobel Prize for parenting, but their trust in *her* seemed so complacent as to anticipate transgressions: when she'd once insisted on my turn of the family automatic she drove to training, then urged me to plant my foot for the thrill of auto kick-down acceleration, I'd felt both privileged and compromised. Compared to the average family, hers was almost *disturbingly* generous and welcoming, its oddly emasculating embrace denying me of any sense of being the interloper — and this seemed important. Maybe we could just be great friends, I half resolved. Still, I had her to thank for snapping me out of whatever torpor I'd been languishing in.

The day after she left, when I was treated to a kind of mini Olympic homecoming near my old Kenmore home, I was shocked to spot Nickname and his dad in the crowd, waving and cheering like nobodies in particular. Their suddenly touching and awkward presence as mere fans made me wish I'd been able to visit them in their home instead. For nearly two years, not a word had passed between Nickname and me. (I never got around to posting the long letter I wrote to him in my first Ming months. *Typical!*)

Their gesture brought back a moment's nostalgia for all my former lane mates under Gordon. All rich kids who turned up for training in their private-school uniforms (boys in boaters from BBC, Grammar, Gregory Terrace, and Churchie; girls under banded panamas from Grammar, Clayfield College, and Somerville House), none had ever given me, or seemingly one another, a hard time. Mostly from professional homes, it was as if they'd inherited a lawyer's aversion to errant ways. Their parents had run the club with a cheery and unsung efficiency, and I'd been welcomed to their homes in dress-circle suburbs like Chelmer, Indooroopilly, and Ascot. Sydney, on the other hand, had been a shock. Many of Talbot's squad lived an hour apart, and no two members arrived at training in the same uniform. In all that time, Esther's was the only one of their homes I visited, apart from my Ming Hilton stint.

I don't know how Ashley talked me into a tonsillectomy in my third week back, because I hadn't required a doctor for four years if you didn't count Talbot's directive to see one about my breathing problem. (How, I wondered, had Ashley arranged surgery without a consultation? Or at least one with *me* in it.) And then, perhaps I *hadn't* needed much convincing: I might have lapsed into a familiar deference which had blessed me with the occasional hyper-economy of volunteering my utmost to a cause — filial or otherwise — while copping the critiques of superiors likely bereft of their own utmost. And when Ashley waxed with the authority of Hippocrates about 'rotten tonsils' and their seeming plot to 'poison the whole body', I might have forgotten the obvious counter to surgery: that I was far healthier than the average punter, and had stayed that way through years of torrid exertion to become a world-class athlete.

I blinked from the anaesthetic convinced I hadn't been saved from a life of chronic illness, but outraged by some backwater of medical befuddlement that still credited 'humours' and bloodletting: my gullet was on fire. In his ward visit, the first thing Ashley told me was that my surgeon was another top sportsman, in a kind of hallowed hush to suggest this confluence would be today's headline in the Akashic record. That's when I wondered for a second if the whole exercise had been some bizarre, clubby plot of Ashley's to ingratiate himself with another champion, just because he could! And maybe he'd used my recent fame to bypass the normal referrals that licensed fellow humans to take a knife to your throat.

I'd never been angry with Ashley before; resentful or fearful, yes, but now I was just angry. With myself too — for being so compliant. From my first club nights, Ashley had conditioned me to be humble, to always understate my success. And I was so precocious at this that I was sometimes taken to task for not showing pride in my achievements; I'd have presumed flattery but for the sometimes pitying, other times scolding, tone. (Even post-career I was still apparently exhaling ketones of apology. I bumped into my Uncle Martyn at the Mosman Rowing Club one night in an unsettled week; he wasn't one to lecture but obliquely chided me by tut-tutting that we lived in 'the age of the antihero'. I assumed he knew what he was talking about, being by now a lecturer in sociology.)

Yet I also knew Ashley's brainwashing had helped me weather the rough and tumble of sport, to lose without losing heart, since losing was what kids mostly did. I'd actually loved the rituals of sportsmanship, especially shaking hands. This time-honoured custom, win or lose, at least guaranteed first place in civility, and never failed to warm me (so much that at ten I experimented with shaking hands *before* races, to prove I wasn't later merely glorying in being a great loser. But reaching out for idle hands before the gun didn't last long, and I gave it up after an intended beneficiary turned his shoulder to scowl, 'My dad says you're a pest').

But how, after that decade of righteous indoctrination from Ashley, could I tally it with his recent grandiosity: his exultant RSL

'Solitary Man' theatrics, fastidious scrapbook entries, and reported bragging to my mother to contrast my glories with the suburban failures of *'your boys'*. Likewise his oddly proprietorial attitude to my life: I would never forgive the tonsillectomy, but there were also other breaches. At a major championship, he'd told a girl I'd been friendly with to 'keep away from my son'. I knew this because she confronted me with the complaint within minutes. Another thought: was he responsible for Melinda's card going missing? But I was also in too much pain to grind out answers. That evening I was given morphine, and all night it seemed to play with me. One minute my bed was the size of an ocean liner; the next, a pebble; then back to the ship. I was desperate for dawn to dock.

At the end of my life's first post-tonsil week, I decided to resume my swimming career. *But under which coach?* I wondered. Talbot was now in Canada, of course — his drastic post-Munich relocation as much to escape widely known personal tumult as any reported frustration with the Australian swimming establishment. He'd left his family behind, and, as he would later document, his assistant in that new university tenure was Bobo's former coach, whom he had married en route. And he would have been acutely aware that there was no squad worth coming back for — at least none that would hold a candle to those pre-Munich days. Of the six male Munich-bound swimmers in his top lane, three had been considering retirement and two had already signed up for American university scholarships. That left only me to come back for — his headache. His Auburn lanes had since gone into a decline as sorry as any dammed spawning ground denied *its* thrashing bodies.

And it wasn't as if his junior lanes had promised obvious replacements. For years, Windeatt's cachet as a Konrads-in-waiting (instanced by the magical pedantry of his style) had almost single-handedly sustained the Ming legend with its ability to draw talent from elsewhere. But, finally, there had been no 'Windeatts-in-waiting'. In any case, the catchment required to replenish such a stellar lane wasn't a pool full of outstanding juniors, but a hundred such pools. This was made plain by the fact that even Talbot, over an entire decade, had managed to incubate just one graduate for his own alpha lane — Windeatt; Australia supplied the rest. This rank-and-file poverty was even more marked among the girls. His Munich gold medallists, Gail Neall and Bev Whitfield, and the distance swimmer Karen Moras, were imports like me.

Yet when Talbot eventually put pen to paper about his big move, he wondered if his boyhood reveries about 'the Canadian prairies' had as much to do with it as anything else.

The only swimmer to follow Talbot to his new base at Thunder Bay on Lake Superior was Gail Neall, whose unforgettable 400-metre medley triumph I'd observed in digital form in the Munich call-up room. The new domestic reality was that the decade-long Talbot–Carlile duopoly had left a generation of coaches with stunted resumes, and sorting them would be like looking for Michelin chefs in a tuck shop. Carlile should have seemed the natural option for Talbot's swimmers, but the two coaches were so distant in sensibility that no one took it.

Within a week, I'd moved to Sydney — this was as close to Ashley as I wanted to be for the time being. I felt the only way to judge which squad would be suitable was to sample them for myself. I owed coaches nothing and felt some 'squad tourism' would be fun. In my first few weeks in Sydney, I tried out several venues — some for just a few sessions. As long as I told the particular coach I was just visiting, there would be no complications. And of course they were more than happy with this situation because the chance — even a slight chance — of snaring an Olympic champion in their lanes would likely do wonders for business.

Out of the blue, Bobo contacted me about a new squad in his home town, which he seemed to be enjoying as much for its more casual approach as for any fitness benefits. So I moved down and stayed at his place, even starting school again, though the main thing I learned was that teachers could be wild men too, when our Rasputinish English teacher crashed his motor scooter into the kerb in the main street of town one night where Bobo and I just happened to be searching for a nightclub. His ramshackle form finished sprawled on the footpath right at our feet, and he was too drunk to know if he'd hurt himself or even say it. After we righted and parked his scooter, we helped him onto a bench seat, where he was still snoring when we left the nightclub. Mr Rasputin was back at school on Monday with a few bumps and scrapes and a stiff back, but only Bobo and I knew the secret of how he'd got that way. Bobo took a new interest in English after that and began thanking him on the way out from every class, but neither of us ever let on about the crash.

After being a free agent for so long, I could no longer take school seriously, even as our charmingly flawed English teacher awarded me top marks for an essay on Patrick White's *Voss*, and despite my growing infatuation with the serious rosy-cheeked daughter of a firebrand anti-corruption MP.

The next coach I took a punt on was Talbot's exact social opposite: a single, self-described bon vivant on the North Shore. I'd always envisaged a bon vivant as a sprightly figure in a bow tie and eccentric glasses, but this one came in seal-grade flab, polonecks, a Rolex, and gold chains. One of his funnier nicknames was *Pitts*, the acronym for a crude directive he barked at older girls hopping out for a quick pee. '*Pull it to the side*,' he called, to save them peeling down a clinging wet swimsuit; at least I assumed it was for a pee.

Pitts never hammered a motivational staple like Talbot's self-belief, though he was known to carry on about *motivators*. To hear this plural, as if there were shelf lines of the stuff, came as a surprise. And one of the biggest, according to Pitts, was *love*, an aural marshmallow of a syllable so far from Talbot's prickly poolside lexicon as to seem laughable: *why would a sportsperson try harder because he or she loved, or even admired, someone?*

One day under Pitts, I was cheered to find Talbot's former assistant Ruth had hired lanes in the same pool.

Yet another happenstance was to glance casually down from the balcony of the Mosman unit of the ironman coach Lonny I'd cadged a room from, to see a Brisbane friend passing on the footpath. This was Cyrus, the karate champion and part-time lifeguard from my Brisbane days. The odds of this coincidence were surely a million to one, but when I called down excitedly, his response was so low key that I had to wonder if he was clairvoyant or simply disoriented. Cyrus was the most unlikely martial-arts expert imaginable. An inch shorter than me with a wavy, golden pageboy haircut, he was a waif-like seventy kilograms. After I rushed down, he explained that he was in Sydney to visit his grandmother in Collaroy, a disappointingly banal circumstance for a figure of such mystique: his family was from East Africa, his dad a magistrate. Cyrus himself was a second-year uni student who had played the classics on the piano since age seven, routinely shoplifted, and regularly visited his personal karate sensei, a noted collector of rare books, in Tokyo. When Cyrus spoke, it was in a terse monotone via a clenched jaw and a smile that was little more than a devious grimace. I saw this inscrutability as a Zen-like affectation from his Japanese contacts, and forgivable in someone so gifted. I'd never met anyone as simultaneously demure and judgemental as Cyrus. When I gushed once about liking a particular song, he scoffed at pop music's unsophisticated structure before dragging a stick from the gutter and tapping it on a plastic bottle while humming a simple melody, to show how bog-easy it was to conjure a pop tune. On the other hand, I was oddly thrilled with his assessment of a car magazine I'd been reading in Lonny's unit, as 'not bad journalism at all'. He kept chuckling at a reviewer's derision of a new coupe's gearbox as 'agricultural', and a reference to 'shockies in need of a feed'.

Over coffee in Cremorne, he told me that the last time security guards caught him pilfering in Brisbane and tried to walk him back into the store, each firmly attached to an elbow, he'd dropped them both with a short outward blow to the ribs. Instead of running off, he'd waited for them to recover and resume their task, an etiquette evidently consistent with his view of theft as a noble subversive duty. I didn't ask, but assumed his magistrate dad was expected to airbrush such untidy details from his CV. (It only now struck me that Cyrus might have been interstate not to spend quality time with his granny, but to escape some heat. This would also explain his guarded response to my balcony call.)

Yet I wasn't at all tempted to emulate his light fingers; neither did I understand his contempt for capitalism, or whatever he was railing against. I saw it as a fashionable political gesture, a conceit, and wondered if it was a deep bitterness or superior insight that could turn such clever people into public pests. Cyrus and his brother enjoyed a lively uni social life back in Brisbane, though neither ever seemed to have had a romantic interest; the one time I saw the brother's room, it was a virtual poster shrine to the anthropologist Margaret Mead. And the last time I saw *him*, at a party at the brothers' Toowong share house, he'd sat mutely in a semicircle of plastic chairs with other heavily scarfed and stoned students in a freezing backyard, eventually breaking the silence with the supposedly sage observation, 'Today is yesterday's tomorrow.' And he too was aberrantly engaged with consumerism, shelling out several thousand dollars at a time on the odd shopping spree. (Was this a brotherly gesture to compensate the retail trade for Cyrus' plundering?) When Cyrus confided over our next coffee that his brother had a compulsive spending problem, I was hardly surprised. But to me, the issue wasn't whether his brother had the odd mood swing or couldn't resist a bargain, but how a student could quickly get his hands on a few grand at a time.

The day before his alleged holiday was up, Cyrus tried to teach me how to break roof tiles with a technique he called a palm thrust. But I either lacked the explosive power for success, or was too worried about breaking my wrist. He also shared some arcane chi-enhancing rituals passed on by his sensei, such as a daily quaff of your own urine and fifty bracing testicle squeezes on rising, and I found myself experiencing both the next day. Fearing I might not have squeezed hard enough, I consulted with Cyrus on our final meeting, when he seemed a little circumspect (had he been pulling my leg?). 'Of course there should be discomfort,' he volleyed with an unusual tonality, even a reprimand, 'but nothing like the bellyache of a kick in the nuts.'

'Right,' I replied gingerly, but abandoned the practice midway through the next squeeze-fest, lest my host walk in and misconstrue the mid-sheet rustling. I quit the piss nightcap too. There must be a reason your kidneys don't dispense it in five flavours.

Catching up with Ruth and Cyrus within days of each other, and so fortuitously, gave me the fillip I needed to consider staying in Sydney; I'd been so bored I was ready to head back to Brisbane. Then, the very day after Cyrus left, while 'Daniel' played on the radio and I found myself thinking Taupin's lyrics were so ordinary that Elton John could turn a soil analysis into a work of melancholy genius, Bobo turned up with Anne, a friendly girl from our Ming days. He needed a bed to bed her. I suggested mine, but he'd already spied the king-size in the other bedroom. When I told him my host kept odd hours and I hadn't a clue when he'd turn up, Bobo heard permission.

'Don't get under the sheets,' I carped. 'And put a towel over the spread. *Open a window!*' I was nervous for the next ten minutes, twitchy for the following ten, and sweating every additional second in case we were busted. And then in walked Lonny. There's something extrasensory about guilt. In the cock of his head and his stiff eidetic scan of the lounge room, he knew something was afoot the moment he was inside. I chirped 'Hi' much more loudly than my normal greeting, hoping Bobo heard it, not that there was anything to be done in there except appear presentable. Lonny now headed inexorably for his bedroom, his arm extended for the doorknob. But he paused and, instead of turning the knob, put an ear to the door. Whatever shushing or laboured breathing Lonny heard, it was enough to deter him, and he retreated to the lounge to wait for his quarry to emerge. Still there fifteen minutes later, he checked the time, snatched his keys, and was soon heard driving off. Were I not so distraught I could have dwelled on the sportsmanship of this gesture as I lurched for the bedroom door. But it seemed Bobo had been following the situation closely, and before I was even close he and Anne rushed out fully dressed. She flashed me a clownish, sympathetic smile as she was badgered to the front door by Bobo, who called back, 'Sorry, mate, catch up later.'

Even though I'd been craving familiar company as recently as a fortnight earlier, I also had limits — I preferred it regulated. Just when I thought I'd exceeded that quota, Esther phoned one evening and came over. I made two coffees but struggled for things to say; there seemed so little we had in common now. How different it was from the bright simple Saturdays after our Ming laps when she sometimes drove me to her parents' place in bustling Bronte to feast on Coco Pops with real milk (Ming Hilton breakfasts were drab Weeties with a homeopathic taunt of skim milk). It stayed a slightly awkward evening and she remained one of the funniest and most likeable people I knew.

Soon after my evening with Esther, I began hearing of the Lazarus-like surfacing of a storied coach from the past, promising to make Brisbane — of all places — the new swimming Mecca. Nicknamed 'The Fox' for reasons unknown to me, Dawn Fraser's old mentor Harry Gallagher had descended on the northern capital with a fresh-faced team from Adelaide — after a decade of near ignominy in the long shadow of his '50s and '60s glory days. More than this, he'd managed to attract the only swimmer in Australia still capable of leading a world-class distance lane, Graham White.

Whitey was an entire Olympiad my senior, and the reigning Commonwealth Games 400-metre freestyle champion. His jovial presence had been an understated but crucial link in steadying the Ming juggernaut as it lurched towards Munich under an increasingly stressed Talbot. Whitey's torso, with its powerful barrel-like tapering fore and aft, answered to a checklist of successful mammalian adaptations to marine environments, but not to the pool cliche of stringy athleticism. His swimming style seemed the male equivalent of Shane Gould's super-buoyant, natural cadence. He always appeared to thrive in training camps, in dorms, and on tour, but seemed to have gone to ground immediately after Munich; the chance to team up with him again was a siren call to head north.

Within days of my return, I'd bought a cheap motorbike for the twice daily return trip between my mother's place at Ashgrove (she'd recently remarried) and The Fox's new coaching lair at the Art Deco–inspired Centenary Pool in Spring Hill. Gallagher's relocation seemed a career masterstroke. With that one big move, it looked like he would sweep up the dregs of the Ming era to fill —

along with Carlile — the duopoly vacancy Talbot had opened. Even more: he had garnished his lanes with the most promising distance talent to appear for a decade, Brisbane's own fourteen-year-old Stephen Holland, previously nurtured in his father's Carina lanes via a tutorial correspondence with Talbot's former assistant Ruth. There were even some of Gordon's old swimmers; the most talented was Jon Van Opdenbosch, whose phonically weaponised surname alone had kept me looking over my shoulder during my last days under Gordon.

The lane chemistry was chipper, and Harry's sessions were challenging enough, though without Ming's crushing extremes, and often with the whiff of bygone technical eccentricity — sets could feature quirky innovations like towing a rubber strap around your ankles with a lead weight attached (I wondered what effect several kilograms of raw lead washing up and down the lane would have on acidic pool chemistry). Harry himself struck me as an inscrutable figure, a bookish James Bond with an Edwardian air, and a far less visceral coaching presence than Talbot. But behind that urbane charm was something that bothered me — or would have bothered me had I been looking for a permanent base. The fact that so many in his top lanes were students from Adelaide, all of whom would surely soon need to choose whether to stay or return south, gave his squad the temporary sense of a summer camp. But because I wasn't committed to staying, I had no grounds for complaint.

Even though I'd made this clear to Harry, he invited me to his nearby bedsit one evening to discuss a proposal. 'The door's open,' he called when I knocked a few hours later. It seemed I'd caught him already ensconced for the evening in his lounge room: he was in surprisingly formal attire, I thought — long slacks and business shirt. He gestured towards a chair from his own richly embossed club chair, where he'd just sat his Dewar's on the armrest. The proposal proved to be an offer of a scholarship at one of Brisbane's top private high schools, organised through some old swimming alumni whose own children had been Harry's latest recruits. I was annoyed that he seemed to have disregarded my previous declaration that I intended to remain a free agent, and was sufficiently resolved to require only a minute or two more in his presence. Walking out, I knew this would be a blow to his plans to establish a permanent foothold in Brisbane, but that was his problem, not mine.

A month later, I was back in Sydney, training alongside another distance-loving Stephen — a giraffe of an athlete whose style was a fabulous discombobulation of limbs, yet whose recent progress had rivalled that of his Brisbane namesake. His coach, Tony Fraser, had been a national butterfly finalist in the late Konrads days. For the next several months, I buckled down in Steve's not insubstantial wake, from which I emerged only in races, except for the 1500-metre at the Nationals in Adelaide in March the following year, which he won. Steve was great training company. For someone who bookended each day immersed in a sterile box, he was extraordinarily perceptive and generous. Nor were his *land-based* passions entirely typical for a swimmer: JRR Tolkien, and the English first-division soccer premiership.

Unlike Talbot, Tony was always open to discussion and didn't depend on coaching for income, though beyond casual mentions of a high-end sandwich bar and importing kitchenware for retail chains, he seemed not to do actual work. When he eventually offered me the management of that sandwich bar on the condition that I commit to staying, we soon agreed that it sounded a bit too hectic for someone of my limited energy reserves. Like his protege, Tony had attended an eastern-suburbs private school, and seemed to constantly bump into 'old boy' contacts from the professional world around town. He persuaded one of those friends to sponsor a scholarship for me at a Catholic college, where I then boarded until I quickly grew resentful of having to leave my door open until nine p.m. for a patrolling cassocked figure to check that we 'roomies' were still at our desks. I despised all shows of religiosity at the time, whether garb, beads, beards, headwear, prayers, or special days. I'd always liked Ashley's description of the perfect faith as one 'that shunned all means of transmission'. When I met Tony's mother in her upmarket home one day, I was moved by his apparent reverence. It was nothing outward, just my sudden awareness of his captivated patience and a peculiar stillness. I sensed him trying to read her, his posture solicitous, amused — even as she searched purposefully for the vacuum nozzle. I don't know why this ordinary domestic scene left such an impression on me; it was as if I'd been surprised to find coaches had mothers. (His was certainly the first I'd actually seen.)

A few years later, I caught up with Tony in Sydney and again fortuitously bumped into Ruth Everuss, who shared coaching rights with him. But now Ruth was in the men's change rooms, trying to cajole out a work-shy teenager who'd mistakenly presumed safe refuge. I was shocked to see Ruth with a nosebleed. It seemed either the boy had been overly aggressive in his resistance, or Ruth had ruptured a vessel with the effort of hustling his six-foot frame towards the door. She aimed me a coyly defiant smile as I passed. When I turned to ask if everything was okay, the pair turned and headed back to the pool, the boy leading the way.

After a lengthy winter break which encroached on early summer, I returned to the Valley Pool in Brisbane, to train under not Gordon, but the former Commonwealth and Olympic freestyler John Rigby, whom I sensed would be my last coach. This was unfortunate, in a way, because John had insights into swimming most other coaches lacked. He knew to avoid silly exhortations and platitudes, and at last I felt I was on a sound footing.

MAKING NOTHING
HAPPEN

In 1974, at age nineteen, I achieved three things in one day, or thought so. I quit swimming, started as a junior writer in a Brisbane ad agency, and decided to become a poet.

I'd just read a book claiming poets were the brightest and most creative of any vocation; and if they didn't catch TB, drink themselves to death, or drown (like Shelley while sailing, or Hart Crane jumping off a ship), mostly stayed above ground long enough for me. There was also attraction in the seeming economy of effort: a few lines here, a few there, the odd page — making it the exact antidote to all those interminable kilometres of my swimming career, except that neither paid.

Not that I was totally ignorant of poetry's technical challenges. In fact, the old rules of rhyme, rhythm, and metre seemed to have been abandoned for various schools of free verse, some based on obscure theories of breath, others on colloquial speech patterns; they could seem more pathology than art form. These new styles had names: some comically pejorative, such as 'Martian' and 'chopped prose'; others accommodating, like the transatlantic 'New Poetry'; yet another had the stiffly romantic label 'Black Mountain Projectivism'. Poetry was shedding centuries of aural strictures towards an ideal of artless purity of diction. And 'artless' seemed to mean not an absence of art, but technical prowess of such an order as to be apparent to only the most forensically gifted reader. Yet release from formalism had also made verse not simpler to write but trickier, its readership not wider but reduced, its critiquing contentious.

I'd read poetry in and out of school hours right through my Ming days, even when I wagged. *Particularly* when I wagged. For escapism, it rivalled my relief when I daydreamed of towns Ashley and I had once passed through and liked. Even when I was so bamboozled by modern poetry's lack of punctuation, tricks of syntax, and general spareness that my mind drifted off, I still held the page in front of me like a cerebral tanning machine whose rays I'd prepaid to keep shining. I bought books and books of it — the brighter the cover, the more promising the contents; Picador had the best jacket-design department.

I also liked to read *about* poets — what they got up to above the ink, though the purists frowned on this bio-voyeurism and I agreed. (It was refreshing to be frowned on by smart, earnest people. Under Talbot I'd often felt myself frowned on by an opportunist despot.) I was intrigued, for instance, to read that my favourite poet, Wallace Stevens, had a fistfight with Hemingway, though this was a mismatch in age and athleticism: portly insurance executive Stevens against action man Hemingway — it went how you'd expect. There was another story of James Wright and Theodore Roethke getting drunk watching Floyd Patterson fight for the World Heavyweight title in Seattle, which had made me suddenly realise that you never read about Australian authors liking sport. Or writing about it.

In fact, I was intrigued to find sport mostly written out of Australian life. At the time, it was common to hear about local fiction outgrowing the bush cliche for urban settings, but sport stayed safely on the shelf, not *in* the shelves. Yet sometimes I too had thought this omission justified because sport could seem a kind of distraction from life's 'real' challenges. Then again, if you picked up an *American* novel, you might very soon be reading about a pro woman golfer and a former gridiron player in *The Great Gatsby*, or wrestlers and basketballers in Updike, and I suspected sport was at least an inevitable suburban speed-bump in the journey of so many western lives, and therefore deserving of the odd fictional guernsey.

But poetry seemed immune from such criticism; it could thumb its nose not only at sport, but also at many other concerns of the worldly self, a dereliction recalling W.H. Auden's famous line, 'poetry makes nothing happen'. (In the really — *really* — long run, however, it was obvious that everything else made nothing happen too. And maybe this was Auden's point: that poetry didn't pretend, while anthems and speeches did.) And whatever had or hadn't been made to happen to Auden himself, you could see by the epic folds and sags of his face that the process had been long and momentous.

While staying at Bobo's parents' place briefly the following year, I opened the volume *Shabbytown Calendar* by the Australian poet Thomas Shapcott, and was shocked to find his piece 'Epitaph for the Eldest Son' citing a family tragedy suffered by our former 'housekeeper' (aka Ashley's then girlfriend Mrs O'Rogan). Shapcott and Mrs O'Rogan were from the same town, and the poem's subject was a just-married (though unnamed) stock-car racer who'd died from a twisted bowel after a crash: this was Mrs O'Rogan's new son-in-law, because I'd recalled Ashley confiding these exact same circumstances in me, six years prior in Brisbane, and I'd never seen her since. Shapcott's portrait of him wasn't flattering: a sulky, pampered shocker of a young man. And at that moment I'd also felt a personal flush of accusation, as if Shapcott was rebuking all sportspeople — yet another sport-hating Australian writer! But although I was disappointed to hear such a negative rendering of someone so close to a woman I'd liked, it piqued my weakness for biography; I felt a sharp visceral connection with this supposedly pale and muddling vocation. It was also a novel sensation of poem-as-reportage, though Shapcott's six-year copy deadline wouldn't have cut it in the tabloids.

I revisited this vicarious 'off page' experience as recently as 2017 when I spotted the major (though being poetry — *not famous*) contemporary poet Anthony Lawrence at my local beach; he was standing at the edge of revegetated dunes and jotting notes against a post, when I happened to be passing on my regular bike ride. (I'd seen his photo many times and knew he'd recently moved to my town from Tasmania.) When, after a few months, one of his recent works was shortlisted for a prize and published in a magazine I subscribe to, I wondered if he'd been working on this very poem as he stood there taking notes. Its subject matter certainly seemed rooted in those dunes. Once again, I felt privileged to have been witness to that creative process, even at such a whimsical tangent. Grateful too, that this thread of awe had stayed with me all these years.

When a film crew was commissioned to shoot pre-Munich backgrounders on the Olympic swimming team back in 1972, Bobo and I were asked what activity we'd like to be filmed doing, to show how we spent our free time — as if we had any. They liked it when Bobo nominated surfing, because it meant he and I donned board shorts and paddled out to a Northern Beaches reef on a dark and filthy day to catch waves — Bobo standing up and working the shoulder all the way in, me standing up and instantly coming off to swim the rest of the way, hands brushing the odd rock to make me buck and freak in the black water. Three times we had to repeat this before they were able to get footage — inch-age, really — of me staying up. The cameramen weren't quite as impressed when I then asked to be filmed browsing poetry shelves in an inner-city bookstore. But they were good about it, even giving me money to buy a volume by T.S. Eliot, though this turned out to be kids' verse about old possums and cats. Bobo stayed well outside the store and almost fell over laughing as the crew squeezed through the shelves with me.

Bobo died in a single-occupant car crash at thirty-eight. He was driving a small hatch fast and recklessly and under the influence and hit something big; nobody else was injured. People have since said that they saw all this coming, or that he was 'lucky to have lasted that long'. *I'd* never seen it coming, though his teen years and early adulthood had been full of what perceptive adults might have called 'red flags' — mainly it was his love of fun and not knowing when to stop.

Even when, a few months before that crash, a mutual friend pointed out to me a flattened chainmesh fence at a local T-junction as 'Bobo's handiwork', I still thought, *That's Bobo for you*, and imagined this sort of behaviour continuing into old age.

Bobo.

I had little contact with him for his last decade or so, but we lived in the same town and bumped into each other socially. Unlike me, he'd kept competing, as an ironman. Even at the national level, he was still beating most of the field, some of his opponents up to fifteen years his junior. He'd had substance-abuse issues in the past, well documented in the papers, but I assumed that to stay so fit he was keeping them under control. He dropped in at my workplace unexpectedly six years before he died and asked for a loan of ten dollars. Stuffing my bluey into his jeans pocket, he quipped cheekily that he would use it to buy a bottle of cough mixture, and I wondered if he was kidding. Once again, I thought, *That's Bobo.*

When I bumped into him outside a pool a year or two after that, he excused himself and said he was in a hurry because he'd left himself only an hour to train. Asking what kind of set he hoped to get done in that short time, I was flabbergasted when he quipped, 'Ten fours on five,' before slipping through the turnstiles. Of course, *ten fours on five* was old Ming shorthand for 'ten 400-metre freestyle swims, leaving every five minutes'. I was shocked he could still do such a set, because it differed so little from something Ming might have barked at us on the afternoon of our farcical film shoot. And such a compact set! — executed without warm-up, drills, or warm-down. It made perfect sense for the time-strapped: you could easily be in and out of the pool in under an hour. 'Ten fours on five,' I marvelled — a four-syllable fitness plan you just added water to. I left in such awe and envy of his having kept alive this visceral link with our Ming days that I started back training myself. It took me most of that summer of almost daily effort, but I eventually did my *ten fours on five*. It — along with similar variants — was still my exercise staple a decade later.

Sometimes I wondered if Bobo kept his sporting career alive to extend the endorphin roller-coaster of his youth in the binges of the competition arena and the penance of training; other times I thought it was to redeem himself the only way he knew — heroically. It seemed he'd never been allowed to quit the desperation treadmill that took him to the top in our teens, never able to suck the post-career sigh of relief I did when I felt myself devolve awkwardly back to mundane life — happy enough to be spat out a has-been, never to be a never-was.

A year or two before his car crash, Bobo tried to talk me into buying into a property speculation. He'd already done well enough with the help of his father and a colourful realty mentor whose famous mantra was 'Never sell'; he just needed a bit more for this new one. As usual when Bobo was gunning for trust, he frowned, blinked, and pouted as he stammered his way through the details of his project. This was sincerity in extremis, his staccato blink-blink-pout-pout-frown-stutter pitch, and not too far from the palpable apprehension that could throw cold water on my attempts at a sales pitch.

Barely a month later, he asked me to write his story, and once again I refused. His was an interesting one, but fatiguing, because there was something almost inevitable in his circumstances. At his worst, Bobo could seem an aggregation of unstoppable drives, some of which were rarely denied due to his athleticism and pop-star looks. In the morning, he might resemble Rod Stewart; by lunch, James Reyne; and later, Jon English minus the raw bonhomie — and sometimes all three in one. (Bobo once insisted he was descended from Napoleon's favourite general, who'd risen from a humble family of barrel makers (*my* surname actually *meant* barrel maker!). But when we went searching an encyclopaedia, I soon wondered if Bobo was down from Napoleon himself, because in the painting *Napoleon on the Bridge at Arcole*, on the page facing us, there was Bobo waving that standard.) I finally suggested he try someone with experience ghosting biographies. Although I was sympathetic, I wasn't ready for the old roller-coaster that frequent contact could bring.

I didn't stay long in the Brisbane ad agency. At nineteen, I was more than a decade younger than my workmates. They were a mix of cheerful and staid ex-sportsmen who didn't write ads but had impressive titles like 'account executive' and wives and houses and waistlines, and I couldn't wait to get out. Then there was the humiliation of being hauled across the coals by the owner after I absentmindedly let a film crew in without seeking permission for them to film a brief 'update' on my new post-swimming career. So when Bobo wrote one of his 'Dear Mate' letters to tell me his local pool was looking for coaches, I went down there, but not before Laurie Lawrence tried to talk me into a comeback. I'd trained briefly under Laurie before my final tour — this time as team captain, where one of my more thankless tasks was to confiscate the Vespa a drunk teammate had been drag-racing along a medieval Parisian alley.

When I bumped into Laurie in one of my ad-agency lunch hours, he said, 'Why don't you come to the swimming carnival at Redcliffe this weekend as a spectator — *it might be interesting just to watch for once.*' I should have known what he was up to because Stephen Holland had been complaining about a lack of decent training partners under Laurie and was considering a move to the US. When it was time for Laurie to make his pitch at the carnival, he panted, 'Doesn't all this make you want to get back into it, Brad?' Then, stretching his arms wide and high, he gushed that I'd only used half my potential. Apparently the unused half was as big as the world beyond those outstretched arms, but all I saw was Redcliffe, which reminded me of training camps. The effect was to make me feel like jumping the turnstile and running all the way home. I felt sorry that Laurie had to reduce himself to such chicanery to hang on to Holland, but that was his problem. Soon after, Holland left for America, and, on the news that week, Laurie announced he would take an indefinite break from coaching.

I stopped writing poetry when I realised I was out of my depth. I'd had the odd poem published, but those magazines were so small you wondered if you'd had competition. Besides, I'd read enough to know how scholarly and uncompromising career poets were. When you read them, you realised how much you *didn't* know, and this was with them actually trying to hide their erudition. While I'd been pinballing between pool ends through my teens, they'd been reading Catullus and Ovid and gaining arts degrees.

When I went and stayed with Bobo after my encounter with Laurie, I was in the last throes of my supposed poetry career. We were now twenty. I had to hide everything I wrote because Bobo thought poetry ridiculous and kept trying to find my latest efforts; when he did, he'd read them aloud and laugh maniacally. His other friends didn't make fools of themselves trying to write verse, but we two still seemed to have enormous fun. The one book *he* owned was *How to Win Friends and Influence People*, and only because it was compulsory reading at the realty firm he'd part-timed at through his teens and where he was now rentals manager in his first full-time year; it sat on the rear seat of his Alfa 1750 GTV all summer long and its jacket looked to have fused with the leather. I suspected his contempt for books echoed his occasional contempt for his mother, a former alcoholic who now spent much of the day curled in a chair, reading potboilers under a salt-sprayed window through endless tea. Bobo associated all reading with dysfunction. If he caught me with a book, he called it *moping*, and wouldn't leave me in peace until we went to the beach. Sometimes I wondered what life would be like without books, because I found them so rewarding, if only to pace my day and make me feel clever. Without them, I suspected you might be compelled to go plunging from one activity to another, like Bobo, and I had nowhere near his energy. I counted reading as an activity.

His mother's mother was an alcoholic too, bad enough to be institutionalised, so you needn't have been a statistician to guess where Bobo's temptations lay, particularly if he'd told you his mum had chased him around the house with a carving knife when he was four, all the while screaming he was possessed; and that he'd watched his dad struggle to stop her climbing out a window to join her long-dead grandfather who'd swooped from the night sky in some spectral carriage to squire her who knows where. (Not that I believed addiction was any more heritable than staring at the sun. But it seemed likely that the poorly nurtured would nurture poorly, and thereby perpetuate a dynasty of self-medication until diluted with happier histories.) When he'd told me these things and more through our teens — always with the caveat, 'I don't know why I'm telling you this' — I wondered which other elite athletes could have overcome such formative challenges. *None, of course.* And I couldn't imagine his mum laying off the bottle while pregnant with her only child, adding a further, if unknown, degree of difficulty to his scorecard; on the other hand, I had never seen him physically injured or ill. He was in a league of his own for toughness, and one of my few swimming heroes along with Windeatt, Holland, and Max Tavasci — the swimmer who'd asked Ming for more. Karen Moras was my favourite female swimmer because her freestyle's ruthless abuse of the pool was a sight like no other.

Bobo cured me of poetry. Writing it, anyway. One day stands out. We were in the pedestrian mall of his home town when he retreated a few sharp steps and pulled out a crumpled page evidently torn from one of my notebooks, before stiffening himself into a formal oratory pose to bray, 'Hear Ye, Hear Ye.' When he began reciting some excruciatingly familiar doggerel, I snatched unsuccessfully at the page before escaping down the nearest laneway. After a safe distance, I glanced back to see him still on the corner, gesturing after me in paroxysms of laughter for the benefit of a puzzled few. By this point in my life, I was aware my pretensions could make me look an idiot, and soon saw his excoriation as a kindness.

Bobo impressed me the first time I saw him compete. This was at the 1971 NSW championships where he sensationally won the boys' fifteen-years 200-metre freestyle. *Sensationally* because he was a surf swimmer and surf swimmers were only meant to be pool part-timers, typically lacking the discipline to put up with diligent training and bombastic coaches. But on that day, Bobo was the heroic exception. I almost laughed out loud at the way he got around. While everyone else wore nothing but their best synthetic-fibre tracksuits (with a big 'NSW' across the back if they were really good), Bobo just wore baggy stretch-cotton bottoms and a white sloppy joe, its crewneck full of holes he'd burned in with acid or chlorine. His walk was fabulous and ridiculous. A tight string could have been connecting nose and toes: when his right foot shuffled forwards — it did shuffle — his head snapped down that way, and then likewise to the left, with enough supplementary throws and jerks to need a licence. That strut defined disdain better than any dictionary, and his eyes never left the ground to check where he was headed. But after the famous boil-over win, it was obvious to everyone that he couldn't contain his new pride, because that head dropped even lower and swung like an axe.

About the time I signed off writing poetry, Bobo was signing *on* to something new in his life. We were twenty-one. Within the space of a few weeks, he doubled his normal number of nights on the town: from two to four, sometimes five. The one time I accompanied him for the entire night, I could see there was no stopping him: after a venue closed, if he saw an open car door he'd jump in, but only if it was headed for another nightclub or party.

I wasn't working much around this time. Coaching in Bobo's town was casual, and then only if an ocean swell hadn't dumped sand on the lanes overnight. And the pool was far too cold to train in winter. Any other work I took was at the bottom of the skill rung: jobs where having a pulse was resume gold. And because that wouldn't do for someone who'd recently retired a global leader in his field, it was important not to appear to be trying; my daily self-assessment roved a continuum from mild to acute embarrassment. But sometimes my defences failed me when I felt encouraged in my job searches to be judged a cut above the ordinary. While applying for a position at the steelworks, I peered through the grille of a dark booth where a swarthy, middle-aged interviewer recorded my details. On the *comments* side of his ledger, he scrawled 'Good type', and I walked home with a spring in my step.

Fortuitously, the local TAFE college had just opened its art school to students who lacked a leaving certificate. It was only a one-year painting course, but completion qualified you to attend the Alexander Mackie College in Sydney. *I'll give it a year*, I thought, because I liked Bobo's home town and the hardy, cheerful people in it, and had always wanted to be a better painter, though with no great career aspirations, at least none with the intensity that had fired my swimming dreams. (I was convinced swimming had exhausted some finite level of striving in my system.) I enrolled, moved into a bedsit across the street from the TAFE, and mostly enjoyed myself, eventually making several new friends who, like me, just wanted to paint better pictures.

I did my best to avoid Bobo. I'd recently come across him at a party where he sat at a kitchen table with two other young sportsmen, the trio chopping into gritty grey lumps with razor blades, stopping sometimes to funnel the residuals into a plastic envelope. When Bobo looked up and saw me, he crowed, 'We've just been down to the ships,' as pleased with himself as a preschooler modelling playdough. If we crossed paths on the street, he never greeted me any way but exuberantly.

When Ashley phoned me not long before I moved out of Bobo's, I mentioned my friend's plight. After a brief gesture of sympathy for Bobo, and without missing a beat, he told me something I hadn't known: that he'd taken the hallucinogen mescaline in New Guinea during the war. *'And I wouldn't wish it on my worst enemy,'* he added. I was still so deferential to him that I didn't pursue the matter — not to mention the potential embarrassment. Here I was in the process of writing off a friend because of his habits, and now I had to imagine my sixty-five-year-old father as some wartime jungle acid-head. Later I wondered why he'd kept it a secret for so many years. Later still, I would learn that thirty years — the elapsed time between his war service and mescaline confession — was also the official embargo period for classified war secrets. The final phase of the Second World War was a hotbed of research into hallucinogens like mescaline as the great powers competed for 'truth drugs' towards more effective prisoner interrogation.

Mystery and obfuscation had always surrounded Ashley's honourable discharge late in the war. It seemed every time we children asked, there was a slightly different answer, his most repeated evasion the comical 'wounded in the privates'. My mother later dismissed this, but neither, it seemed, had she ever been told of the mescaline. Her insistence that Ashley had suffered a breakdown towards the end of the war, I felt, might be linked to the mescaline experience ('*wouldn't wish it on my worst enemy*'). Yet she herself had always put it down to the shock of his first wife divorcing him. Maybe Ashley told her this as a red herring, or for sympathy; and maybe it flattered her. I'd long heard (though only from my mother) that Ashley had tried various ruses to get sent home from the war, and if an early honourable discharge was on offer for allowing yourself to become a living biochemistry experiment, he might have volunteered; he wasn't to know the war would be over within months.

Was his military psychiatrist, Huxel Stuart, his assigned psychotropic guide, and the gift of Elbert Hubbard epigrams a kind of healing desiderata? Mescaline would have been hard to come by in the war beyond a military setting, not least in New Guinea. Both German and US military seem to have been well abreast of mescaline trials on humans since the 1920s. Ashley's subsequent occasional references to his 'TPI' (totally and permanently incapacitated) war pension meant that something serious had been inflicted on him, though clearly not physically. Still, this was all speculation based on my father's one mention of a wartime experience, and I had no way of finding out the truth; he would stay an enigma.

A few months later, my mother contacted me, which was a rare occurrence. One of the things she had to say was that Ashley had initiated an unexpected rapprochement with my older brother; the pair hadn't exchanged a word in the decade since the divorce. *Bully for them*, I thought disingenuously, wondering if my rebuffing of Ashley's frequent invitations to return to Queensland had something to do with it. More hints than invitations, these mostly took the form of postcards on which he scrawled enticing cliche holiday slogans, from the mostly beach locations he now favoured. In fact, I was relieved that he would now have someone else to practise his impresario urges on. When my mother then added that he'd also found employment for my brother via old cinema-industry contacts, my sense of release seemed complete.

One Sunday morning a month later, after I'd given no more thought to Ashley's efforts with my brother, I was in a newsagent's reaching down for the weekend stack when my hand recoiled as if a snake had passed under it. There was Ashley's photo on the front page, with a story of how much money my swimming career had cost him. But I didn't hang around to read much. I was worried I'd be recognised, and bolted. '*Prick*,' I cursed when I got outside; any residual sympathy I had for him living alone now vanished.

It was only when I began to browse Ashley's scrapbooks for this memoir that I read the full article. (I was surprised he had the hide to paste it.) Several paragraphs below the whingeing about the money, he went on to say that it had been my older brother with all the talent and that I'd merely been a willing trainer. Of course, this claim was silly because my brothers hadn't qualified for competition above inter-club level from their first swimming lessons, the fate of the vast majority of swimmers. Ashley had clearly been on a mission to ingratiate himself; he would again be kingmaker, launching my brother into a facsimile of his own cinema career, and inventing virtual sporting triumphs for him. My brother had routinely heard similar praise from my mother through his teens, except that she'd placed my *younger* brother at the top of our sibling talent stakes. (Much later, both brothers would laugh at these trite, partisan anointments.)

A few months after hearing from Ashley, my brother quit the cinema trade and the pair pulled up the drawbridges to resume their previous long silence.

Despite the new friendships I was making in my painting course, I felt more and more uncomfortable staying in the same town as Bobo; he hadn't changed. I'd also begun to suffer from something I could only describe as a cloying hyper-empathy which was so far up itself it came out the other side as a free-floating guilt. My usual dread of conversational silences was now so bad that I'd dredge up any nonsense to restore flow, and this could lead to the airing of premium drivel.

New physical phenomena seemed to be moving in on my body too. Like the odd heart flutter. I thought these serious until several acquaintances said things like, 'Oh yeah, I get them all the time.' Or, 'Lay off the coffee.' *I* didn't get them all the time — maybe one every few weeks, and only for a second or two. Then there were the head explosions, when I'd be lying in bed, and bang! — one of those twopenny bungers from my childhood had just gone off inside my head. With that first detonation, I wondered if I'd had a stroke and waited for the paralysis to set in, but it never came. By the fifth or sixth, because there was no pain, I put them down to some harmless tension reflex, perhaps an auditory version of the so-called 'primal drop' many people experience when nodding off; I later learned this was pretty much the case.

Those spectacular blasts were sometimes the highlight of my week. But one day when I was in the middle of a flu and had cut my thumb on a rusty saw, I thought I'd better get off to the doc for a tetanus shot. And while I was in the waiting room, I decided I should unload about the flutters, explosions, and occasional anxiety. But then I vetoed all of them because now I was on the *inside* of his surgery and any one of those symptoms might have suggested further investigation, and I suddenly needed proof this wouldn't be happening.

Then he asked if there was anything else wrong, because I seemed a little edgy for a mild case of the flu and a cut. Once again, I gave him no rope but got around to some spiel about a famous hippie handbook I'd just read and thought he might be interested in, by the famous Harvard 'flower-power' professor Dr Timothy Leary. I might also have briefly mentioned the spiritualist Gurdjieff, since I'd been attending self-realisation courses in his name in an unlikely suburban bungalow a ten-minute drive north of me. My teacher had supposedly once sat at the feet of Gurdjieff's assistant Ouspensky, though most of *my* evenings were taken up with mastering the steps of so-called 'sacred dances' with the frocked matrons who were my fellow initiates. That's pretty much when the doc sucked on his pen for a few seconds and started to jot notes, looking up after a while to suggest I try a special weekend retreat he sometimes recommended for 'uptight people' like me, and gave me a number to ring.

I decided not to go, then to go, and not to go again, until those vacillations orbited wide enough to manifest me there, where all I learned about myself was that I could donate good money to people who disdained it infinitely less than I did. But at least I gained new tools to see why my past was what it was always going to have been, and why my future was best ignored, at least according to one fellow patron coming off an abusive relationship with a well-known action actor. She also had a toddler and read palms for pocket money. She read everyone's: the dentist who walked out on his practice with a waiting room full of toothaches, the 'director of luxury car sales' who booked in routinely to clear his head of hyperbole, and garden-variety wrecks too.

Getting around to *my* palm, she suddenly squealed like she'd won the lottery, because it had a special little cross between the head and heart lines. Then she double squealed to find I had it on both hands: the *double* cross, supposedly foretelling high achievement. 'I wish I'd known,' I told her, 'I could have saved myself a lot of effort.' Then she said *if it was any consolation*, my life line showed I would suffer a major trauma late in life but make a strong recovery to live a near-vegetable existence for another decade or so. Strong recovery? *Vegetable?* I pondered.

LIVING IN THE PASSED

In my brief time at the ad agency, I enjoyed swotting up on famous campaign slogans. The most impressive went, 'At sixty miles an hour, the loudest noise in this new Rolls-Royce comes from the electric clock.' Being at the wheel of your twenties could also be like hearing a clock ticking, a persistent drone from your future saying it's on its way to meet you on a corner. You can try to justify ignoring it by insisting that the young have a birthright to live like there's no tomorrow, but the clock keeps going, and the preordained corner floats up from your imagined future to cloud your forward vision. You've lived long enough to notice that measurable outcomes proceed by tiny increments — particularly for sportspeople — and that if you miss too many, they can't be redeemed. *And then you will have been left behind.*

I didn't finish the art course. It was enjoyable, but I was there for more than that. Its teaching seemed at the forefront of recent fashions favouring creativity over rigour. Our classes encouraged composition, not representation; spitting non-toxic pigments onto the canvas, not brushing or scraping; enculturation, not concentration; car-pooling up to Sydney for brunch with our teachers' artist friends, not rote drawing — and so on. I left because I'd enrolled to paint well, not apprehend well. I might have needed a Ming to stand over me for hours on end to make me sketch the perfect still life, but nobody at the TAFE worked that way.

I returned to Brisbane, where my younger brother and I rented half a sturdy old Queenslander owned by Alf, an ageing but spritely former England first-division soccer player. He and his wife lived in the other half. My brother and I used that long, enclosed verandah for handball matches while drinking with friends on Sunday afternoons. When I asked Alf if our games were too noisy, he said he and his wife liked having 'young bucks' next door occasionally to deter potential intruders, but I would ask this same question almost every time I saw him. 'We just pretend it's distant afternoon thunder,' he chuckled across the non-existent time that made one of us old and the other young under the clothesline one morning, and I knew he was being too kind. *Maybe I'll end up like Alf too*, I thought: an ex–sporting champion and his wife making believe the occasional racket next door was a benign protection racket.

The following year, at twenty-five, I completed my high-school matriculation year at a Gold Coast TAFE college. A month or so later, I began a cadetship with the *Tweed Daily News*, wondering if there was something portentous in my first day also being the first day of the 1980s. My first hour of my first day was spent accompanying a photographer and a curmudgeonly journo just a few years my senior in search of post–New Year's Eve celebration 'yarns' amid the rough sleepers and litter. As the journo kicked out in disgust at the contents of an upturned refuse bin outside his favourite cafe, I wondered if reporters should be so partial.

I stayed at the paper for three years, graduating as a fully graded journalist and working from my own Gold Coast branch office. Brian Styman was the editor, and the chance he took helped restore the traction I'd lost since Munich. I couldn't have known when I left the *News* to run my first public pool that this would be my vocation for the next three-and-a-half decades. Until that point, even with the journalism behind me, I'd sensed my opportunities slipping. I remembered my old primary-school teacher Mr Grange knocking repeatedly on the blackboard while exulting that opportunity only knocked once; and Mrs Talbot reminding me of 'the incredible opportunity' I'd been given with my swimming after I'd publicly blabbed how hard it was for swimmers to cope — and how I'd resented her for that. Yet I suspected soon after I began running pools that this was the very corner on which my ticking future had been waiting. It *had* to be. I was twenty-eight, and within five years I would be married with children. I'd left Bobo back in his home town, but within three years he'd be up in my part of the world and running pools too. This had been his father's vocation, and he helped set up Bobo with his first.

Life's early achievers are easily accused of resting on their laurels or living in the past, especially when the years typically bring no further honours. I would wonder if my Bobo-inspired enjoyment of a return to daily training in my mid-thirties was a nostalgic regression to my Ming days, or at least a satisfying purging. Even if those new solo laps *were* a form of living in the past, I assured myself, they were done not twice daily but just once, and were merely the bare bones of a session: Bobo's enigmatic *ten fours on five*. Neither did I obsess over performance milestones, my one goal to climb out with the glow of having completed my daily 'constitutional'. And its fifty-minute staple was pretty much what prudent health authorities advocated for people of my age anyway.

A decade after that regime had worked its way through my system — I now enjoyed pushing weights and walking the dogs — I was taken aback when a patron at my own swim centre abruptly quipped that I now lived in the past because I *no longer* trained. Since she was a paying customer whose penchant for wry taunts I accepted as my mercantile lot, I resisted telling her how perverse this one had sounded. Being used to robust barbs from other passionate sports-lovers, I easily deciphered her logic. Its premise was that former champions should maintain their profile with such public commemorations as leading their local fitness group, and that this was not living in the past but an extended conversation. It then stood to reason (at least for some) that if you rejected this organic link, you were probably living in the past. *Who was I to argue?*

Other patrons over the years had judged more than my personal temporal alignment: the father of a boy I briefly trained even felt he'd identified a dynastic failing. He'd been dragging his son from coach to coach and found them all wanting because the boy had not yet met his expectations. (There had been a much older son — now estranged from both parents — who'd ultimately retired without ever measuring up; so here were parents desperate not to repeat the mistake.) The day they moved on, the father quipped that I couldn't have been much of a coach because I'd been unable to turn my own girls into champions.

There were too many silly assumptions in this to bother replying; among them that my own success had been a fait accompli of genetics and that my 'progeny' needed merely a top-up of tutorial stardust. It was at this point that I wondered if he himself was consumed by a kind of dynastic curse — reflexive disappointment; and this could seem an inherent family hazard in sport. It occurred, I felt, because it was far too easy to imagine that you or your offspring could invest a unique energy in the skills and fitness required for success. And this belief was in a sense justified, but only within the absolute limits of personal excellence — because where was the proof that you were the most gifted of your peers, or that you weren't fooling yourself with your self-assessments? Otherwise sensible parents, gripped by the promise of a child's early triumphs, risked forgetting the sheer number of bidders their children would face in just one age group within a chosen sport, let alone those many age groups above and below them, each with its own champions, all eventually spewing out onto the Serengeti of open competition. Similarly, it could sometimes be taken for granted that the enormous effort their child put into daily training wouldn't run out, that the child trained purely from an ethos of daily satisfaction. Yet it often did run out. On the upside, however, there were always those whose only ambition was to be the best they could, to bask in the attainment of great competence, and to make new friends, and whose families sport would keep rewarding. I have heard Cate Campbell patiently explain to reporters that she and her siblings attended childhood swimming carnivals not in a chase for precocious glory, but 'mostly for Mum to get us out of the house' — showing that great outcomes can have unremarkable beginnings.

It didn't concern me in the slightest if my accuser, or anyone else, disparaged my coaching: I had no greater anticipation of becoming national coach than of being prime minister. Both might have involved a skill set or aptitude I lacked, and coaching was just one of the things I did to make my swim centre viable. In fact, I'd long ago been cautioned never to coach, because the expectations were exponentially higher for those assumed to have 'cracked the winning formula'. When well-meaning parents asked me if there were any secrets I could tell their kids to help them achieve what I did, I told them this was like asking a winning lotto ball how it had managed to bounce out first. Advice could certainly work, but it would never control the fates of the other lotto balls.

Yet there have been coaching successes along the way. Olympic relay gold medallists Mark Kerry and Chris Fydler had their first significant successes under me as teenagers. Multiple Olympian Adam Pine and Commonwealth Games backstroker Leigh McBean also swam in my lanes on different occasions. (When I had to shoot an email off to Swimming Australia a few years ago, the surprising reply began, 'Hi Coach.' This was from Adam Pine, in one of the positions he has held there.) In each case, I moved on to another pool before these impressive young individuals fully matured, always chasing a more lucrative contract rather than staying put in the hope of taking a champion to the top. (I was still 'once bitten, twice shy' about the costs of chasing glory in my own career, let alone hitching my star to the contingencies of another. By the time a pool lease came up for renewal, I'd already lined up another, ready to move on if my price was rejected.)

My twelve years leasing council pools were an excellent primer for my own centre, though that entire period could seem a blur of unbroken summer grind with only Christmas Days off, my daily obsession to never have a drowning; industry stalwarts had forewarned me that such blighted managers were sometimes 'never the same again'. Then there were those patrons who hadn't minded at all if they expired under my care, like the veteran lapper who refused to leave the water in a thunderstorm, insisting he'd swum through far worse under four prior managers happy for him to plod at his peril. I humoured him by suggesting his welfare was the least of my concerns; it was the hours of forms and interviews I'd later be subjected to that I dreaded.

For a time, I fancied I might even become a pool-management magnate, during a fluky phase of acquisitions that briefly saw my name on three contracts. But I quickly realised that the more pools that came under my control, the less I could exercise control … over public risk, staff behaviour, and revenue. The pools were spread across 1200 kilometres of eastern Australia. No sooner would I be notified that a casual lifeguard at one centre was making a community pest of himself by chatting up young mums at the toddlers' pool, than another centre would have problems balancing the books. Then there was the coach who threatened to quit on his first day after being confronted by a poolside delegation of aggrieved mothers demanding to know how he intended keeping their children on the ever-upward path the previous coach had touted. In short time, I succeeded in letting one pool revert to council management, and fully sub-contracting another.

Among the remarkable things I witnessed while running country pools was something that happened in 1987 in my then Northern Rivers centre, with a regional school championship underway. Three teenagers I coached were returning from their freestyle final clutching slips of paper. I knew these mementos had little to do with success because the boys' training habits were not up to this level of competition. The trio ambled across with wry smiles to show me their certificates, awarded to all their fellow finalists in recognition of the winner having broken a regional record. Emblazoned in lush cursive above the centre line was, surely enough, 'Share-a-Record Certificate'. The boys then shared a cackle before sharing their certificates with the contents of the nearest bin, and I suddenly wondered why educators had so little faith in students as to presume them incapable of allowing hardworking victors their moment in the sun.

And it also happened that neither was I too concerned what sort of swimmers my own girls became, since they were also involved in tennis, equestrian, and surf-lifesaving activities — each requiring its own practice time. There was never any question they would do sport; I'd heard of parents intent on averting future Christmas-dinner rancour by raising 'free range' children, only for those supposed free spirits to ultimately round on them with the interrogation, 'Why didn't you ever push me?' In other words, it seemed parents couldn't win. Sport was the community I'd grown up in — and trusted. I wouldn't have minded my girls swimming more, had they wanted to, but I also loved seeing them rise early on weekends to eagerly materialise in mustard jumper, tie, and jodhpurs for pony club — and hoped they would always cherish the memory of this ritual.

Horseriding didn't appeal to me — it was one of my wife's family traditions. I saw horses as not much more than unshackled trees with enhanced volition and nice but duplicitous eyes, though I occasionally sought ways to be involved. One free Sunday when my older daughter, then twelve, practised slaloms in our paddock, I strolled over to watch. Soon I had stopwatch in hand, timing her through swerve after powerful swerve when the horse stumbled, and in a flash of eternal regret I foresaw a mass of buckled horse and daughter on the ground, before the steed just as unexpectedly regained its footing. The stopwatch went away forever then: 'This is not swimming,' I chastened myself.

I was thrilled my daughters played tennis too. We had a big smooth wall in my swim-centre car park where they practised — and I practised — for twenty minutes, several mornings a week. We would stand some fifteen metres from the wall and whack hard and accurately enough at an imagined net height for the ball to keep returning with pace. And once a week we went to the local courts for a longer hit-up, with the girls in regional fixtures (we still play occasionally as a family). Then at thirteen, my older daughter began ballet classes at the invitation of one of our hard-working swim-club mothers, and six years later was performing with the Bayerisches Staatsballett, coincidentally based in Munich. She later returned to Australia to complete a podiatry degree. My younger daughter also danced, and now, like her paternal grandmother, models full-time, proudly booking all her own assignments.

There were other swim-centre clients over the years who asked if I kept up with old swimming friends, when the answer was no. Though not by design, I always hastened to add. It was just that 'keeping up' was something my Facebook-less generation of swimmers tended not to do, though if you bumped into any one of them it was surprising how much information there was to exchange. One former teammate, for instance, might have been thriving with five children and happily married to a tradie in a country town; another had gone to finishing school in Switzerland; yet another was now a professional tennis coach, of all things; and a few had teamed with well-situated siblings or parents to make millions. Or you'd be driving to work when the ABC news told you that NSW Fisheries scientist Marcus Lincoln Smith (an old Sydney age-group tormentor) had published his findings into mercury levels in fish caught off North Head.

But one day several years ago, my childhood swim-club mate (and Munich teammate) Jim Findlay wandered into my Gold Coast swim centre. Jim had married one of Talbot's daughters, the one he was keen on at Auburn pool when Talbot threatened to break both his legs if he found him near his home. Jim was easy to recognise when he came in: his hairline, which had begun receding aggressively in his teens, was not much further along. Except that now he limped in, not from injuries inflicted by Ming, but from a bad motorcycle accident in his thirties. When I introduced Jim to the passing mother of a promising young swimmer as my former Olympic teammate, she paused, offered a brief, courteous smile, and kept going. Because this was a woman who seemed keen for her daughter to succeed, I felt slightly offended on Jim's behalf by her coolness. But then I guessed my mildly ravaged middle-aged friend may not have been the cliche of spectacular success conjured by rose-tinted parent-glasses. Apart from raising a family, Jim had immersed himself in the sport of taekwondo over the years, despite the limitations of his injuries, and had become a prominent figure in a Korea–Australia friendship organisation. Sadly, Jim died unexpectedly of a heart attack not long before this memoir was completed. Jim's younger brother Ian was one of our clients at this time, his son a regular in toddlers' classes. (A very successful coach himself, Ian had taken a starring role in the annals of swimming notoriety when he and Talbot scuffled at a major championship to end up grappling in the pool lanes. The incident made headlines at the time because Talbot was still national coach. When Talbot filed for assault, the ironic guffaws must have been heard from Perth to Brisbane, and the magistrate sensibly threw the case out.)

Also around the time of Jim's visit, on separate occasions, Talbot's children Trevor and Lee popped in unannounced, though I was away both times and enormously disappointed to have missed them.

When that legend of every 1960s Australian swimming childhood Graham Windeatt walked into a public pool I managed at age forty, I was so excited I called to my wife in the kiosk to come over, because she'd so often had to listen to me talk about him. I hadn't seen Graham enter; he'd just materialised beside me in his togs with towel on shoulder while I was taking a chlorine test at the side of the pool. He seemed to have aged taller than me; we'd always been the same height back in the day, though if my torso had been put on his legs, one of us would have been much taller, the other possibly too short to aim high. As always in the past, I was struck by his mildly patrician bearing; other people stood, but Graham *anchored*. He'd done a business major at the University of Tennessee in his final years of swimming, and before me at that moment might have stood the president of some transnational conglomerate. At forty you don't want to say things like, 'I spent my childhood in awe of you,' or, 'I don't know how you survived all that childhood fame when it was the instant kiss of death for other careers,' but these — and a regard for his general decency — are my enduring sentiments about Graham.

Writing a memoir is obviously another cohabitation with the past. I was never one for keeping a diary — couldn't see the point of recording a life spent recording a life, even if that daily eclipse was modest. And with this book, there has also been a sense of temporarily damming a river. Even my dreams have had their haunts gatecrashed by long-absent acquaintances; most in these pages have signed that visitor book. I had a recent dream, for instance, starring Don Talbot. I was swimming in an adult squad somewhere, and a little miffed that my training mates were not former greats but recreational lappers. Talbot then appeared before a large iron poolside shed from which flares also randomly spewed. He was in a boiler suit and seemingly disdainful of his swimmers as he scanned the horizon distractedly. When I briefly caught his attention to ask, 'Am I trying hard enough?' he didn't answer but hurried along the pool to a more pressing issue.

I'm not a believer in dreams as portents, though they can evidently revive latent emotions. Talbot's uncharacteristic distraction in his dream role left me pondering my obtuseness to his inner life in the days when he was trying to turn brats into champions in spite of themselves. My first inkling of him being anything but a reflexive tyrant came when I lived with Bobo in my early post-career years and began hearing about a special friend Talbot had often visited in that very town. She was reportedly quite an elderly woman, a close family friend, and I was gobsmacked to learn that Talbot sometimes 'poured his heart out' to this unlikely agony aunt. *Poured his heart* was surely an oxymoron: it didn't square with the Ming I'd known. I even found the news mildly cringe-worthy. I was further surprised when Bobo, never a respecter of authority — he had no qualms addressing his father as 'you silly old goat' — also held back. I'd expected at least one of his lacerating cackles, but the Talbot expose was clearly emotional kryptonite for him too.

So when Talbot published his memoir many years later, I was almost relieved when a reviewer opined, *'reads more like a catalogue of triumphs, and rarely anything from the inner man'*. Needless to say, there was no mention of his matriarch mentor.

The book was a birthday gift from one of my swimmers who'd been flabbergasted to read within its pages a revelation about his own coach — that the crusty cynic who stood at the end of his every lap was 'the most talented swimmer' Talbot ever coached. I was happy for a prominent figure to briefly boost my stocks in the eyes of one of my charges, but my candid impression was that Talbot had leaped far beyond his usual public punditry into omniscience. It seemed silly to rate my abilities above those of John Konrads, for instance, who set twenty-six world records to my two. Silly — because sportspeople competed to end debate, not invite it. You could have favourites, but once you ranked athletes on inferred ability, the speculation was endless. I wondered if Talbot had mistaken my daily struggle with training consistency for a stubborn latent giftedness, when it was simply an athletic deficiency. This was a classic case of 'drowning, not waving'. I lacked the impressive energy of my peers, and tried to make up for it by being observant.

When my wife and I noticed Talbot on a TV panel show at this time, he again nominated me his most gifted swimmer, adding I'd also been 'one of the toughest'. Then he quipped I'd been 'a total nightmare to train'. 'Is he allowed to say that?' my wife asked with a start. I laughed and said I was in excellent company: Talbot's book was a litany of the sport's greatest names variously condemned as 'fragile', 'angry', 'their own worst enemy', 'lacking confidence', and 'never coming near their potential'. 'To be coached by Talbot,' I told her, 'was to be judged against the straw men of your teenage inadequacy and his infallibility.' And if you weren't inadequate, you might be 'cocky', as he labelled the Laurie Lawrence–trained Stephen Holland, who rewrote the distance record books in the mid-1970s. (As captain of a team Holland toured with, I found him not cocky, but upbeat, comedically self-effacing, and an inspiration to teammates.)

Yet beyond all this, I could now appreciate Talbot's frustration at having his injunctions for resolute training undermined by a swimmer who appeared to daily prove him wrong.

These and other Talbot pronouncements through his later tenures made me suspect he was currying controversy arbitrarily: in one five-year period his position on doping, for instance, swung 180 degrees from a laissez-faire 'Let Them All Dope' (*Brisbane Times*) to a blanket ban of all pharmacology in sport (*Sydney Morning Herald*). (My position has consistently been the latter.) Such opinions seemed to thunder even more loudly after 2001 when he gave up the Australian national coaching job to finally share the fate of swimmers — to suffer the adjective 'former' before his laurels. From here on, he would work as a consultant.

And soon came the mother of all Talbot public sprays, when he took up a consultancy with Swimming New Zealand and promptly told a major newspaper (*Otago Daily Times*), 'New Zealanders don't believe in themselves.' This almost biblical 'belief only through me' franchise of psychological hegemony had always worked on teenagers, *but an entire nation?* In my scan of his 2003 book, I couldn't help noticing how many times variants of his core mantra, 'records will always be broken', came up, always preceded by '*I'm a great believer that …*' as if he might soon patent his hunch that the sun would keep rising.

Yet this humbug had always served him perfectly in the masculine world of coaching, where chest-to-chest bluster counted for far more than flawed platitudes. Talbot exuded so much of this corticosteroid bluff that it was as if his entire endocrine system had migrated outwards into a tough exoskeleton. When you saw him playing hardball with people and reputations, you could almost see protein receptors bouncing and binding across that armour plate.

It was a measure of the hormonal maelstrom that could seem to pass for communication in the Talbot national coaching hierarchy of the '90s (Grant Hackett's coach Denis Cotterell confided in me, 'If he comes on like that again, I won't mind blueing with him') that few bothered to challenge his more outlandish statements. As I continued to read his memoir (in case I was quizzed by my swimmer), I came across the most brazenly false proposition I'd heard a coach make. Talbot, as ever, playing the goading iconoclast, had tried to make a case that swimming still had much to learn from athletics on the basis of an unfavourable contrast in performance fall-off between swimming and running events. But the events he chose to compare were not remotely of the same duration. Had he chosen races of similar duration, he would have found that both running and swimming suffer exactly the same performance fall-off — in this case, by the margin of 4.6 seconds (between the swimming events of 50-metre and 100-metre freestyle, and the running events of 200-metre and 400-metre, as indicated by their then respective world records).

That Talbot put such jabberwocky into print within two years of having been Australia's head coach showed a chutzpah beyond belief by normal sporting standards, but not by his. It was also an example of the deferential effect he had on colleagues, since neither of his two reputable co-authors evidently bothered to scrutinise this blatant howler. Either that, or they hadn't the temerity to raise it with him.

But Talbot succeeded spectacularly in his long career not on the basis of egregiously flawed technical speculations; he was simply from the start outrageously smitten with swimming. Whether in the competitive or skill sense, swimming seemed a mythological presence in his imagination. After a stint as a reputedly impatient school teacher in his early twenties, the serendipitous appearance in his life of two of the most talented siblings ever to don a pair of cossies — the Konrads kids John and Ilsa — sparked the lifelong passion he appeared to place before all else. Whenever I walked onto a pool deck that Talbot strutted in my youth, I had no doubt that few coaches on earth at that moment held such command over a team of athletes.

Elite swimmers sometimes consider themselves 'truer' personifications or exemplars of their sport's history than coaches, but it is hard to argue that Talbot's almost six decades of continuous elite coaching and administration doesn't confer similar status. Talbot gave his entire life to the sport in a way that few swimmers are required to.

By his own admission (and regret), he did not become rich, despite his pre-eminence. Perhaps with this in mind, he controversially chastened those swimmers who found wealth through success yet refused to share it with their coaches — to which swimmers would sensibly reply that they had already financially advantaged their coaches by burnishing their reputation in continuing to train with them. Talbot struggled to see why modern swimmers would readily give a percentage cut of their incomes to a manager, yet not to a coach. Perhaps he saw managers as usurpers to the control coaches traditionally exercised over swimmers. But when double Olympic gold medallist Susie O'Neill went public with her sense of outrage after Talbot's poolside castigation of her own coach, I'm sure she knew the value of her manager. (Swimming Australia now has a 'member welfare' policy in place to deter such poolside confrontations.)

Other casualties associated with such a proud determination are not hard to find in the Talbot experience. While acknowledging this, he also claimed to have been baffled by a perceived reluctance of luminaries like Susie O'Neill, Hayley Lewis, and Lisa Curry to fully resolve past grievances with him.

I know few contemporaries entirely free of a conflicted view of Talbot, though many, like me — on balance — consider him a vanishingly unique individual.

Those without reservations are usually from his earliest coaching days. John Konrads, for instance, told me that he had warmly regarded Talbot as 'a kind of big brother'. Less than a decade separated the pair. Talbot had then yet to face the full stresses of raising a family and finding a way to support his poorly paying passion.

In another recent dream about Talbot, I was back with my old Ming squad mates at a carnival where I'd been placed in charge of supplying towels. This ridiculous dream and my ridiculous task also had me carting around some medieval wooden trolley, its cargo of towels folded and compressed into the smallest possible bricks, like fluffy licorice allsorts. But I'd apparently packed many times the required number, because when Talbot noticed this mistake he spent the rest of the carnival gratuitously haranguing me.

It was this exact same haranguing note that had filtered through Gold Coast supermarket shelves one day in my forties when I overheard from the next aisle, 'Why would we even buy that curry? You wouldn't know how to cook it.' I immediately quipped to my wife in a shelf-traversing pitch, 'That man sounds just like my old swimming coach, and he's still telling people they're not good enough.' When the adjacent aisle fell silent, I took my wife around and introduced her to Ming and his third wife, and if he was embarrassed he didn't show it, though the pair seemed keen to get on with not buying stuff. More-generous souls would have left the couple to their unremarkable shopping tiff. I thought I was being droll, but probably went too far. And I didn't enjoy it. I relished it. At the 1974 Commonwealth Games in Christchurch, two years after Talbot last coached me, we passed much closer to each other than in those supermarket aisles — I almost physically bumped into him on climbing from the pool elated after my 200-metre backstroke gold. He didn't offer a *congratulations* or even a simple hello, but couldn't resist accusing, 'You should be four seconds better by now.' In that instant, I saw how puny an amateur sportsperson's place was. We generated fortunes for media magnates, kept their journalists in work, and sustained careers like Talbot's — all for fleeting praise or gratuitous poolside slights. (An image of Emil Zatopek collecting Prague's garbage popped into my head.) I couldn't wait to quit. Our supermarket encounter didn't make up for that disappointment, but I had a 'personal best time' of it, if a guilty one.

My father died in 1996. Regrettably perhaps, it was a month before I opened my new swim centre, though this prospect held no great atavistic pomp. Yet he did manage to visit the site near its completion, and promptly stumbled on a patch of loam to go headlong towards a pool still full of air. I caught his arm in time to prevent that dive. After a decent innings like his, bereavement can be processed soon enough, but in that same year another of my Munich teammates died unexpectedly, aged forty-two. In her 200-metre Olympic breaststroke win, Bev Whitfield became one of Australia's two Munich 'bolters', along with Gail Neall. Both had found the perfect opening at the perfect moment of their careers, showing a special genius most sportspeople only dream of. Bev died in bed during what might have been expected to be an innocuous and brief — for someone so physically powerful — dose of the flu. Ever cheerful in company, Bev hailed from Bobo's part of the world, the Illawarra, and epitomised the best in its hearty populace.

The deceased appear in my dreams more than the living lately, though I wouldn't use the word *frequent*. Unlike Bobo's dramatic end, my father died in his sleep in the retirement village where he'd rested his head the previous five years. On his bedside table was a bottle of pills, half full or half empty, depending on whether I worried he'd ended his own life, or accepted that pills were inseparable bedfellows with the elderly. But he was nearly ninety, and old enough to decide when, and how, to go. My older brother and I were the ones called to view the body and make arrangements.

My father's tired euphemism for death was *the big swim*. He exercised it so much that I half-suspected he was conditioning me for eventual news reports requesting public help to identify an elderly man last seen stroking in the general direction of New Zealand. He didn't die a lonely old man, the fate my mother had often shrieked for him. His last five years had in fact been full of retirement-village activities, and he retained his car until the end. Which was all a bit odd because for the almost twenty years after I left him he stuck doggedly to a solitary version of the roving life we'd had together, clocking an average six months per dwelling. Mostly he stayed in bedsits or caravans, though occasionally 'shacking up' with rich widows in their waterfront mansions. I visited him through all of those moves, his one constant the wall of photos of famous actors: *his* glorious past. I was gazing at Elizabeth Taylor's eyelashes one day as he leaned forwards to change TV stations with a golf club, when he quipped out of the blue, 'They were hard times after the divorce, weren't they.' I answered, 'Yep,' and ribbed him about his nine-iron remote.

He loved talking about his neighbours, often fellow itinerants, and always made their life stories interesting except for that of the old amnesiac next door at one location, for obvious reasons. Once when he abruptly ended a relationship with one of his rich widow suitors, she rang me with a distressed request for clarification of his goodbye note: specifically, the counsel, *'Don't take any wooden nickels.'* I thought she was either really dumb or, more likely, simply wanted me to stew in my father's juices. The only blemish on Ashley's otherwise charmed last years at the village was his feud with a pesky fellow alpha male, a stiff-backed sergeant-major type, who'd begun to steal his thunder and dance partners. 'Do you think I should just deck him, Brad?' he asked once. I wasn't sure how to answer, but joked he'd probably knock his nemesis' head clean off and go to jail and only get paroled in a box. One day I caught sight of a nasty surgery scar zipping that old pest's neck vertebrae from his hairline into his collar and knew I'd cautioned Ashley wisely.

I often wondered how much — if any — money Ashley had squirrelled away in those frugal peripatetic years, and when the will came out it was a modest sum that bypassed his own offspring for the pockets of his eight grandchildren, with my girls able to buy half of their first second-hand car with their share.

Ashley's appearances in my dreams are quite banal. The most interesting was where we were chatting in the manner of our many 'interview'-style later meetings, though this time he was sitting not on a lounge cushion but atop the backrest. This was so uncharacteristic of him — of almost anyone — that I laughed heartily, even reciting a mock advertising slogan for the brand: 'Our lounges are so comfortable that people sit on the backrest,' which was so *you-had-to-be-there* hilarious that I laughed my way out of the dream and marvelled at how revitalised I'd woken.

Bobo knows this memoir's pretty much done and dusted, because he doesn't drop in anymore — to my dreams. When he did, we'd mostly chat about the weather. His only visit to seem in any way complex or poignant concerned his son, who was also a father of young children when he too died in a single-occupant car crash. This particular dream had Bobo and me chatting easily, though I was also distracted by overhearing his son's voice and being unable to source it. Then I suddenly noticed Bobo concealing something behind his back, an iPhone on which I glimpsed his son's Skype image calling for him. I left them alone to talk.

A year or so before Bobo's son died, I was driving to work when a familiar voice phoned into a local talkback show; listeners had been asked to call with examples of parental sage advice. I was surprised Bobo's son identified himself with his real Christian name — it was exotically rare. And when he was asked where he was from, I knew the coy lilt that announced his suburb. I was so touched by his impulse to casually memorialise his father that I hardly noticed the nature of that sage advice, though it was along the lines of, 'When life hands you lemons, you make lemonade.'

The one dream presence that puzzles me is actually an absence — of my Brisbane coach Gordon Petersen. Puzzling because training under Gordon was totally uncomplicated: no constant threat of physical abuse, no crushing fatigue to make you think about quitting every other month. And I was living at home, as basic as it might sometimes have been with my father. Ashley seemed to think Gordon lacked charm, but perhaps Gordon knew how to switch it off to such parents who were likely never satisfied with his results anyway. In fact, Gordon was one of the most humorous and entertaining of coaches, if a little dry and curt at times. And maybe it's because of this fully resolved sense of training with him that I don't need him in my dreams.

I don't recall any recent dreams about my mother either, let alone advice — *considered* advice, anyway. But when she took the trouble to provide a eulogy for her own funeral in 2014, I wondered for a brief moment if *this* wasn't a dream. I was unaware she'd penned a piece addressing her three sons until the funeral director asked me to decipher portions of her handwriting, moments before I took the stage. Now suddenly the deceased's *fellow* eulogist, I had no time to speculate on her motive for this eccentricity. When her piece aired, there were no surprises: just her usual recollection of concern for my idle early twenties, praise for my younger brother's qualities of loyalty and friendship, and, finally, her dogged insistence that my older brother's arrival in her own young adult body had been 'a complete mystery', a reference to his birth exactly eight months after her marriage. *Was this Catholic guilt carried past the grave?* I wondered. I also wondered why she'd felt the need for this kind of post-mortem showboating. If she'd been proud of her sons, surely the fact that we were all self-employed and had in fact been net employers for much of our working lives should have been sufficient.

At one point on her deathbed, my mother's legs kept kicking fiercely under the sheet, as if scrambling for a foothold, and I pondered that life's most challenging moment was so often kept for those least able to apprehend it. *Or were they?* But then, I guessed, we're all equally diminished in those very last moments. Earlier, according to my brothers, who'd spent the morning with her, a priest had chanced in presuming to perform last rites, when our mother had the presence of mind to see him off with a few petulant air chops. This was in her second visit to palliative care; her first had lasted just a day or so before she returned to her flat beneath my older brother's home. In those forty-eight hours before returning to hospital, dressed to the casual nines, she hosted several final visits from friends and family — dips and drinks supplied. Looking at her, you wouldn't have been surprised to learn you'd been summoned to hear she'd mistakenly received someone else's diagnosis. It was gallows theatre.

While chatting with her that evening I boldly decided to steer the conversation to her early days with Ashley. I wanted to know more about his supposed conjugal declaration that the baby being created on the cruise ship (me) would 'be something special'. (*Yes, my mother was dying*, I conceded, but I felt I deserved an explanation after all the social capital she'd made of this bizarre claim over the years.) This was a kind of journalism, and not the most comfortable one. When I worked as a graded journalist for those three years in my mid-twenties, I'd often dreaded asking the tough questions, but this was worse.

'Are you sure it wasn't a misunderstanding?' I finally asked. 'I mean, he might have muttered some terrible bedroom cliche like, "*making* this baby will be special," and maybe you misheard him or were unfamiliar with the line.'

Her eyes narrowed. 'I know what I heard.' And that was that.

So, yes, your father was a total lunatic, she might have added.

Still, I wondered.

TWINS

When my gold medal disappeared recently, I went into a kind of shock whose callous calm told me the thief had known exactly what he was doing and would surely find a safe home for it. And this response sounded suspiciously like Stockholm syndrome, at least a vicarious version on behalf of an inanimate object.

This was after my wife and I ruled out any chance of having mislaid it. It had rested in the same room at our swim school for twenty years, entombed like Lenin in its own acrylic see-through crypt within a box of old documents. The odd moment I glimpsed it in all that time, its condition spoke not an anthropomorphic murmur of decline or abandonment. The room also housed some paintings I'd collected as part of a superannuation portfolio — *the only part* — and apart from a regular airing when I ventured no more than a few metres from the door, it was always locked. This was within a dwelling that was always locked. My only regular 'looking in' on the medal was in fact during those airings, but only as a knowing nod to its buried proximity. Immutable physics did the rest. I knew it had to be theft when I found the chain, and the chain alone, at the bottom of that box when I'd gone fishing for an old contract.

The abhorrent peace that impaled me at that moment denied me the curiosity of even pretending to search further, a denial that was to justify two more months of not looking. What was the point? The room was full of boxes and I wasn't going to go through the lot. And if I began there, why not the pool area downstairs instead, or the car park? Or Sydney and Melbourne, within whose myriad suburban walls it might have already rested in fraudulent state for years? Besides, the chain was the giveaway. It was where the medal should have been, always had been; I imagined the culprit leaving it behind as a taunt. (*Was there someone I knew who would enjoy this?*) My wife was good at searching, but when even she didn't volunteer, I resigned myself — steeled myself — further. Instead, she rounded on me with a charge of carelessness, to which I responded with mild bluster: I told her to mind her own business, and that if I couldn't care less, neither should she. Because it was my medal, *not ours*. And how could confining an object to the same secure room for two decades be carelessness? Benign neglect perhaps, but not carelessness.

Whenever I dared ponder those who might have known the medal was up there, in a tentative stab at sleuthing, a mild nausea chided me: these were all decent people — patrons, relatives, close friends. *But perhaps their confidants were not so honourable*, was my inner Sherlock's rejoinder. *Where was the sign of forced entry?* came another line of inquiry. *Locks could be picked*, was the obvious answer. More queasiness. What about the dog? *Experts could distract dogs*. It wasn't as if I'd ever gone out of my way to tell people where the medal was kept, but if anyone had asked with innocent fascination or courteous condescension, I couldn't see myself misleading them.

When my wife and I eventually got around to discussing things calmly some time later, we agreed there might have been just one occasion in the past decade when the medal had left the room. We both had a vague memory of swimming-club parents begging me to let their children see it. It had to have been at least three years back — perhaps as many as five, for the memory to be so fuzzy — but this detail hardly mattered now. We had obviously been in the middle of something busy — likely our annual club championships. It must have been a hectic evening downstairs, full of racing, awards, speeches; and I'd have seemed mean-spirited not to inspire the kids (I at least remembered my keenness to dispel this impression, and then of relenting). I would have been anxious to rush the medal back upstairs once the kids had had a turn of holding it, yet the act of returning it now completely escaped me. *What if it had stayed downstairs?* I wondered. *And then what?* The doubt and regret of this incomplete recollection made it preferable to go with the theft.

In the meantime, I kept up my charade of indifference, reminding myself my name would forever be in the Olympic records, often near an image of the medal. And whatever savings and assets were to have sustained me in looming retirement, the medal was not among them — at least, not one I'd ever factored in. Unless, of course, I was forced to sell it, as I'd seen Olympians do over the years when they fell on hard times. Yet now even this option was closed forever.

With this thought in mind, I googled the subject and was astonished to find that my medal's sole historic bedfellow, the Munich 400-metre medley gold won by the Swede Gunnar Larsson, was at this very moment listed for auction with Feldman's of Switzerland, with an estimate of 40,000 euros. *Bedfellows* — because ours were the first two Olympic swimming gold medals to require the full specification of the then-new electronic timing; at all previous Games, first and second place in our respective events would have tied, requiring two golds apiece. So now Larsson and I might both be relieved of our medals forever, though he at least would be compensated. The irony could not have been more timely or mocking. It momentarily crossed my mind to put in a bid for his, adding a whacky provenance some future bidder might appreciate.

Not long before this manuscript was ready for publication I decided my former medal room looked tired, and surely some of those old papers were merely fire hazards waiting to be thrown out. With the quiet determination of someone rearranging a deceased person's room, I emptied 'the medal box' first, took fifteen minutes to separate disposable papers from keepers, and pocketed the orphaned chain, and that was that. Then I tackled an adjacent box containing a slurry of merchandising carry bags — relics from past club presentation nights.

Tipping the box upside down, I heard a clunk from within those spilling carry bags hit the floorboards. I didn't dare hope, but, in the third bag I inspected, there was the medal, still in its crypt. Holding it, I stared and stared: this was as much face time as we'd accumulated in years.

Obviously I'd dropped it in the wrong box in my rush to get back to the championships on that night several years ago — I would also have been the official starter. Or perhaps it'd missed its intended target by millimetres. And maybe I'd noticed this and intended to correct things later, only to forget after the inevitable round of post-club socialising. And what about the chain? I'd likely left it behind deliberately, worried that children would catch their fingers when the medal was passed around, and I hadn't wanted it dropped.

Having my recent capitulation so suddenly reversed was invigorating; invigorating is a scarce descriptor after sixty. I displayed the medal beside my desktop computer, where I worked on this book for the next few hours (the intention of tidying the room was put aside for later). The stoic resignation that had sustained me for those months was now replaced by a genuinely surreal experience: belief teased by near-disbelief, keened by an almost unhinged happiness. I now wondered how my medal's Swedish counterpart had fared in its Swiss auction, and discovered it had been passed in. *Wow — two medals in another tight finish*, was how I saw it.

But mine now loomed as a kind of mystery toy, almost a talisman, as I gazed and typed and gazed. The last time objects held this power over me — to toss me between the real and unreal — was in Rocky: and there were two. The first was fire. *Was fire an object?* When my toy wagon trains, fittingly made from matchboxes with pins for axles, were circled by toy Indians who shot flame-tipped arrows (my mother's cigarette lighters sufficed), it struck me one day that those toy flames now reducing the wagons to carbon could also burn a real house down, not that I entertained this prospect. Soon after, when I inadvertently expanded my fire-toy adventures to the confined space between our trucker-neighbours' 1000-gallon diesel tank and its diesel-smelling dirt beneath, I found myself spontaneously launched yards away: Mr Cox had furiously grabbed my collar to wrench us both from the threat of a life-sized doom.

The other intersection of symbol and reality had been my Rockhampton God medal. For most of my life, the episode had been a religious mystery I was happy to entertain, having been raised Catholic (though by a lapsed mother, daughter of a churchgoing one). For decades I agnostically entertained this suspension of disbelief because I had no other answer, and always so vividly recalled the medal in its flip box on our neighbours' lawn, along with their daughters' unhinged insistence on its divinity. It was oval and silver, likely a St Christopher. Only when I talked the incident over with my mother shortly before her death in 2013 would I fully rationalise it. 'Ah yes,' she recalled, 'those neighbours did have a reputation for throwing little white "God medal" boxes down for local kids; I think their own children fell for it too, but your father put you straight.'

When I couldn't bring myself to return my Olympic medal to its old storage room — I had the ridiculous sense I'd let it down — I took it back to our farm and placed it in a bathroom drawer, where it stayed for several days. Again I wondered about its safe keeping, though here we had *two* guard dogs, not one: large box-headed mutts that made their presence known at the gate when cars or strangers loitered. So I drove the medal to work and back for several days while it stayed under my seat. I locked the car if I pulled up even for a minute, but still experienced an anxious moment when I returned to reach down into that well. And now of course I saw the idiocy of all this and regained my trust in its old hiding place at the pool. And that's where it is now, back with its Newtonian minder. Finally, I knew all this concern had come not just from a shock of personal dispossession, but also from a sense of archival failure: I had misplaced a cornerstone of recent Olympic history.

The only other time I felt my gold medal might have been lost was in 1992 when I took a phone call from a man wanting to be its next owner. It was Rick DeMont, my disqualified Munich nemesis. Two decades on, he was calling to say he'd just successfully sued the US Olympic Committee for 'its part' in his disqualification, and would now take his long-simmering grievance to the IOC. His tone was cheerful, with its solicitously musical West Coast lilt. 'Well, hi, Brad,' he'd started. I'd been forewarned about the call by my old friend Peter Montgomery from the Australian Olympic Committee, so I wasn't surprised. In fact, DeMont had twice previously sought redress from the IOC, only to be knocked back, partly because his ephedrine positive had been deemed too high to cast even the most optimistic doubt on the original ruling. But his recently successful suit against the USOC did not rest on the margin of his positive. (A defence witness, former IOC vice-president and US Olympic delegate Anita DeFrantz, had testified that DeMont's ephedrine reading had been 'off the scale', only to be robustly accused of libel by his new legal team.) Instead, his USOC case centred on the claim that his team management in Munich had failed its duty of care by not declaring his use of an ephedrine-based medicine. It now seemed this same lawyered-up angle was DeMont's best chance yet of twisting the IOC's arm.

By the end of his phone call, DeMont had clarified that it wasn't *my* medal he was after, after all. '*You would keep yours*,' he forecast, while he himself would receive 'a twin' (a worryingly portentous choice of words, since the reverse side of Munich medals was a relief image of the mythological twins Castor and Pollux, famously sired by different fathers, one of them Zeus). This might have seemed a just outcome to some, but not to me. I was mean-spirited enough to still resent some of the press treatment I'd received after our race, though this of course was no fault of DeMont's. I didn't see him as a *twin* winner, but as the legitimate winner of a category that didn't yet exist, the problematic category of fit, elite sportsmen unwell enough to require dubious medicines. The reported one-million-dollar-plus payout from his USOC suit was compensation enough, surely, I thought, if that's what he felt he deserved. Sporting officialdom had made the rules allowing stimulants, so it seemed proper for the system to bear that cost too.

Our conversation couldn't have been more stilted if we'd suspected we were being taped. The frequent pauses made me wonder if DeMont's team was hoping I'd fill them in by endorsing his quest; maybe they felt my blessings would be a good closer when they fronted the IOC board. But then, my mind was in overdrive.

Oddly, it was another eight years before his case reached the IOC, when, as in the past, there proved no basis for review and it was rejected.

At this point in my life, my wife and I were experiencing that 'happy valley' time with our family — the decade or so when you are so busy with life and your young children's promise that the world seems eternally at your collective feet. DeMont's challenge didn't cost me any sleep; it was a time when I couldn't have been further from my medal, in figurative terms. When a reporter rang for my response to the IOC rebuff, I was so disengaged that I was shocked to hear myself commenting on something novel I'd noticed in DeMont's response ('Dang, I'm sure disappointed,' he'd told AAP): I'd found myself more interested in noting that Americans still actually used 'dang', which I'd last heard in my childhood *Huckleberry Finn*–cartoon days.

Shortly after my editor asked me to write this post-Munich section from my present circumstance, I wondered about my ability to do it. It seemed that soon after Munich, my retention of key conversations — the spark which had ignited so much prior material — began to fade. It took me a while to work out the reason, until I remembered how leisurely I'd suddenly felt back then. *Disengaged* might be another word; *sluggish* yet another — it was a process, perhaps of self-debriefing. Before Munich, life seemed an act of constant desperation. I hung on people's words, was desperate to please Ashley, my coaches, myself. Every conversation, every exchange, seemed for life-changing stakes. I hadn't been the most pious of athletes, but there wasn't a week when I didn't experience some fillip or crisis to remind me of the stakes I was training for. But after Munich I'd felt so relieved that I seemed no longer obliged to 'take notes', was no longer on the lookout. Even eventual employment, marriage, and raising children came with this new complacency, though none of it without consideration or effort. From that point on, even songs began to lose their spell, songs which had once been my measure of passing events. (*Could you be exposed to too much music?* I wondered.) New artists emerged ever more frequently — or seemed to — along with a seeming cascade of new genre variants like glam, progressive, new romantic, punk, rockabilly, and eventually a dozen others. I even lost whatever sentiment had made me support certain footy teams. There no longer seemed any clear geographical or demographic link between a club's 'playing staff' and parochial pride.

I told my editor that writing about my post-Munich life fatigued me more quickly than the earlier material. Would I have the temperament to write with the kind of adult reflection she wanted? The truth was also that I'd never been one for reflection, unless you counted nostalgia, and what I had learned was that I was a fairly impressionable, impulsive, and at times facile person. It had been relatively simple to write the voice of an adolescent — often the carping of teen recalcitrance. I told her that the story of my adult life would be essentially the same as every other Australian married with children, and readers could get enough of that at home: hardly fire-breathing stuff!

'That's okay,' she replied. 'But still, any reflection would be great,' came the laconic reassurance.

Something I felt might answer her request was to find what DeMont was up to these days. Surely this would be expected of me, though I had little personal motivation to do so. Knowing he was a coach, I googled away and was soon viewing a US university coaching website which provided brief bios on staff, with a page or so for DeMont. Therein was the expected reference to his Munich drama, yet it was only the last line that should have sent a slight chill up my spine: '*I will never stop trying to get my Gold medal back.*' But really, I didn't care, and I didn't blame him. (I was far more interested in whether the plastic farm animals I interred at a Gold Coast caravan park half a century ago were still there — the caravan park was — and I'd never done anything about that!)

I'd long since satisfied myself that under all the jingoistic media sabre-rattling associated with our Olympic history, DeMont could be extraordinarily gracious. Yes, he'd hung on to his Munich gold until its surrender was made a precondition for his attendance at the following year's inaugural world swimming championships in Yugoslavia, but this was also where I would find him a real sportsman. I'd been shocked in the days before those championships to discover the press writing up a storm for our anticipated clash, billing it as an Olympic rematch. American media had apparently never let up on the 'we wuz robbed' angle of DeMont's Munich experience, and Belgrade was to be justice served. Even DeMont's coach joined the fray, with the quotes, 'I've never seen anyone train as hard these past six months,' then, evidently for colour, 'It was the first time I'd seen a swimmer throw up in training and keep going.' DeMont had obviously dropped the ephedrine-based Marax he'd used in Munich for another medication based on 'caffeine metabolites'. I wasn't sure what they were, but the bottom line was that they forced the bronchi to stay wide open.

The 400-metre final itself was another close thing, but in the final lap DeMont had more in the tank and won by half a second; we'd both beaten our Munich times and gone comfortably under the then-fabled four-minute mark. On the victory dais when American photographers were falling over themselves to capture their redemption cliches, one kept barking at me to raise DeMont's arm. Instructions heeded, I fished for the victor's wrist but he wrenched it away, muttering, 'Don't do it, Brad, they just want a Munich revenge shot.'

And suddenly it seemed an honour to have come second.

Three years later, the swimmer who'd come off second-best in Munich's other electronic timing controversy, the American Tim McKee, would also have a redemption of sorts.

After he'd lost the Munich 400-metre medley final to Gunnar Larsson by two thousandths of a second, the IOC voted to alter the future minimum timing increment to one hundredth. In other words, McKee had lost the only Olympic swimming gold medal able to be decided by mere thousandths; surely an argument, if ever there was one, to revise an Olympic outcome, though to my knowledge this has never been mooted. (My mere one-hundredth-of-a-second margin, on the other hand, continues its pesky Olympic duties — the most recent notable example being Australian James Magnussen's one-hundredth-of-a-second loss to American Nathan Adrian for the 2012 London 100-metre freestyle gold.)

McKee's experience was sufficiently crushing for him to briefly retire after Munich, but he rallied and fought his way back into the US team for another crack at gold in Montreal. He finished second again, this time by the arguably less-problematic margin of almost an entire second, despite having bettered his Munich time by some six seconds.

ACKNOWLEDGEMENTS

I thank Jon Talbot for his generosity in reading, and commenting on, sections of the text; Peter Montgomery, AM, and Dr Ken Fitch for their advice on historical sources; and my family for their patience. Thank you also to Diana Burstall and the Byron Bay Writers Group for the fun of our manuscript readings.

Some names in this book have been changed and nicknames invented for the usual reasons. In certain chapters, time has been compressed and events merged for brevity.